EDDY JOKOVICH +
DAVID LEWIS

DIARY OF AN ELECTION VICTORY

NEW POLITICS

The Diary of an Election Victory
ISBN (paperback): 978-0-6456392-1-6
ISBN (hardback): 978-0-6456392-2-3
ISBN (Amazon): 979-8-3681569-7-2

©2022 Eddy Jokovich & David Lewis

All rights reserved. No part of this book may be reproduced in any form or by any electronic or mechanical means, including information storage and retrieval systems, without written permission from the authors, except for the use of brief quotations in book reviews and promotional material.

December 2022. Published by New Politics, an imprint of ARMEDIA Pty. Ltd.

New Politics
PO Box 1265, Darlinghurst NSW 1300
www.newpolitics.com.au
Email: info@newpolitics.com.au

Production: ARMEDIA

Published and produced on the land of the Wangal people.

Cover photograph: Anthony Albanese addresses supporters at the Canterbury–Hurlstone Park RSL in Sydney's inner west, after Labor's election victory on 21 May 2022. (Reuters/Jaimi Joy).

 A catalogue record for this work is available from the National Library of Australia

CONTENTS

INTRODUCTION: ELECTION NIGHT, 2022 6
1. A SUMMER OF DISCONTENT AND THE BEGINNING OF THE END FOR SCOTT MORRISON 17
2. LOSING YOUR RELIGION 37
3. CHASING THE APRIL SUN IN CUBA 55
4. MORRISON'S WAR AGAINST EVERYTHING 69
5. THE CONTINUING CRISIS IN UKRAINE 84
6. ON WATER MATTERS 101
7. WHO IS ANTHONY ALBANESE? 121
8. RUMBLINGS FROM SOUTH AUSTRALIA 137
9. THE LONG NIGHT OF THE BUDGET 151
10. TROUBLES WITHIN THE RANKS 164
11. WEEK 1: MEDIA BEHAVING BADLY 181
12. WEEK 2: THE FINE ART OF THE SCARE CAMPAIGN 194
13. WEEK 3: COVID ARRIVES AND DUTTON'S WAR ON CHINA 211
14. WEEK 4: ALBANESE AT THE KITCHEN TABLE 225
15. WEEK 5: DEBATE CLUB 237
16. WEEK 6: JUDGEMENT DAY 250
17. EVERYTHING MUST CHANGE 267
18. THE AFTERMATH 285
GOOGLE IT, MATE! 293
INDEX OF PEOPLE 298

ABOUT THE AUTHORS

EDDY JOKOVICH is editor of *New Politics*, and co-presenter of the New Politics Australia podcast. He has worked as a journalist, publisher, author, political analyst, campaigner, war correspondent, and lecturer in media studies at the University of Technology, Sydney and the University of Sydney; has a wide range of experience working in editorial and media production work and is Director of **ARMEDIA**, a publishing and communications company specialising in public interest media.

DAVID LEWIS is co-presenter of the New Politics Australia podcast, historian, musicologist, musician and political scientist based in Sydney. His lecturing and research interests include roots music, popular music, Australian, UK and US politics and crime fiction. He has published in *Music Forum Australia*, *Eureka Street*, *Quadrant*, *Crikey* and has edited several books.

NEW POLITICS AUSTRALIA is a weekly podcast, providing analysis and opinions on Australia politics. It can be found at Apple and Google podcasts, Amazon Audible, Spotify and SoundCloud.

ALSO BY EDDY JOKOVICH + DAVID LEWIS

DIVIDED OPINIONS

THE NEW POLITICS ANALYSIS OF THE 2019 YEAR IN AUSTRALIAN POLITICS

As the mainstream media struggles to retain audiences and survive under new business models and shrinking revenue streams, independents are filling in the gaps left behind by the older mastheads. New Politics is one of the more important voices appearing in this new landscape, and *Divided Opinions* presents some of the best work from the monthly podcast, and a selection of articles published during 2019. Guaranteed to make you think; aggravate, or inform and enlighten—and maybe all at once—this is a must-read analysis of one of the most dynamic years ever in Australian politics.

Available in paperback and ebook.

Divided Opinions: The New Politics analysis of the 2019 year in Australian politics
ISBN: 978-0-6481644-5-6
ISBN (Amazon): 978-1-6611355-7-7
338 pages

POLITICS, PROTEST, PANDEMIC

THE YEAR THAT CHANGED AUSTRALIA

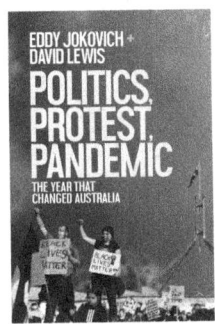

2020 was one of the most dramatic years in human history, shaped by the coronavirus pandemic that influenced society in so many different ways, combining health, politics, economics, business and education into the one sphere—and that proved to be difficult for many governments around the world to manage. *Politics, Protest, Pandemic: The year that changed Australia* is the story of the year in Australian federal politics, told through a collection of extended political essays from the New Politics Australia podcast series.
This is a must-read analysis of one of the most dynamic years ever in Australian political history.

Available in paperback and ebook.

Politics, Protest, Pandemic: The year that changed Australia
ISBN: 978-0-6481644-8-7
ISBN (Amazon): 979-8-7372030-8-5
414 pages

INTRODUCTION: ELECTION NIGHT, 2022

It's 7pm on election night, and a sense of unease had set in among those who were hopeful of a change in Australia's direction, after nine years of Liberal–National Coalition governments. It had been a hard-fought six-week election campaign and, before the polling booths closed on election day, it appeared the electorate had decided the Coalition was no longer fit for office.

The Morrison government was one of the more incompetent administrations to occupy the halls of power in Canberra: scandals plagued the government for most of this parliamentary term and many promises that were announced were either poorly delivered or not delivered at all. The prime minister, Scott Morrison, had poor approval ratings and his challenger, Anthony Albanese, had run a reasonable campaign, after some earlier mistakes and stumbles.

Yet, counting in the first hour after the polling booths closed in the eastern states suggested Morrison was tracking towards a second unlikely and narrow election victory, and for the Labor Party, the shades of the deep disappointments from the 2019 federal election loss started to seep in.

Results from the first dozen or so seats started to roll in from the Australian Electoral Commission and, momentarily, it appeared Morrison was going to claim another "miracle" victory. Rationality, fed by nervousness and despair, tried to take over. Surely, the polls were different this time; after getting it so wrong in 2019, pollsters had improved their methodologies, their algorithms, their demographic analysis. Surely, after all the poor performances and dereliction of duty over the past three years, the Australian electorate wasn't going to re-elect the Morrison government?

Morrison surreptitiously taking his family on holidays to Hawaii during the 2019/20 bushfires disaster, reluctantly returning to Australia, only to arrive on the south coast of New South Wales where he was abused by the public and few people wanted to shake his hand. The ignorance of women's issues; the debauchery of Australia's parliament house, where an alleged rape was committed in a minister's office; sex workers brought into the infamous prayer room for the pleasure of Coalition members of parliament. Corruption: land purchased in western Sydney from Liberal Party donors for $30 million, even though the land was valued at only $3 million. The poor vaccination delivery, the ongoing and meaningless culture wars. Surely, it was time for a change?

Election night was tense. The patchwork of results that streamed in showed confusing and contradicting trends and even the ABC's psephologist and election night analyst, Antony Green, struggled to deal with the meaning of these early numbers. Due to Australia's different time zones, polling booths in Western Australia didn't close until 8pm eastern standard time, and while a clearer picture was slowly emerging by that time, the booth results were still coming at a slow pace and questions were being raised about which key events had influenced the vote.

How were the vocal anti-government and Trump-style protests in Victoria going to affect the vote in that state, despite the popularity of premier Daniel Andrews? The Western Australia election in 2021 wiped out the Liberal Party, reducing it to two seats in a parliament of 59. Would there be any residual electoral feelings applied to the federal sphere, over twelve months later? The Morrison government teamed up with the mining magnate, Clive Palmer, in a futile attempt to end Western Australia's popular border closures between 2020–22. How would this affect the vote in Western Australia?

Despite the worrying trends that appeared in the first hour after polling booths closed, election night ended well for Labor and Albanese. As the night progressed, it became evident the Coalition would not be able to form government, and the trends throughout the evening suggested that it was only a question of whether Labor would win an outright majority—albeit a slim majority—or manage a minority government with the support of an enlarged crossbench.

But by 10pm, it was over. The early results from Western Australia showed a major swing against the Coalition government and a loss of many seats, confirming the patchwork of results from New South Wales and Victoria—as well as confirming an election victory for the Labor Party. Federal elections are usually decided by the time polling booths close in Western Australia—two hours behind the eastern states—but these results from the west validated Labor's decision to launch its campaign in Perth and, for the first time in many elections, Western Australia was the state which confirmed the result.

The Morrison years ended ignominiously. While there was some hope earlier in the evening, the result confirmed what opinion polls had been suggesting for some time: a narrow Labor victory, more independents in parliament, and a loss of many Liberal Party-held seats. The electorate voted for change and put their trust in Labor and Albanese as Australia's thirty-first prime minister, to resolve the many issues which had banked up over the past nine years. It was a rare election victory for Labor—only in office for around a third of the time since Australia's federation in 1901—and it was a win its supporters will savour for some time to come.

While many factors influence election results—there's no doubt that the poor performance of Morrison and his government was the leading factor—there are key factors that not only influenced this campaign but will change the dynamics of Australian politics for the foreseeable future.

A MOVE AWAY FROM THE MAJOR PARTIES

The Liberal Party had its worst result in decades. The Labor Party had its lowest primary vote since 1934. The National Party was relatively stable, not losing a seat. The Australian Greens gained four seats in the House of Representatives and now, there's the largest crossbench in Australia's electoral history. These are remarkable results and signal that there is change occurring within the electorate: while the primary vote for major parties has declined over many years—in 1949, major parties achieved 96 per cent of the primary vote; in 2022, it was 70 per cent—this election significantly translated the gain in primary votes by minor parties and independents, into seats won.

The teal independents, funded primarily through Climate 200 and the grassroots 'Voices Of' campaigns, were the main beneficiaries of the move away from major parties. Well-funded, articulate and very capable candidates ran successful campaigns in safe Liberal heartland seats in Kooyong, Goldstein, North Sydney, Wentworth, Mackellar and Curtin. Zali Steggall had already won Warringah in 2019 and further cemented her position in the seat, as did other independents loosely associated with the teal movement: Helen Haines, Rebekha Sharkie and Andrew Wilkie.

A DECLINING MAINSTREAM MEDIA

The Australian media industry is one of the least diverse in the world, with the vast majority of media outlets owned or managed by four entities: News Corporation; Seven West Media; Nine Media—and the Australian government, through outlets such as the Australian Broadcasting Corporation and the Special Broadcasting Service. News Corporation is owned by the Murdoch family; Seven West Media is owned by Kerry Stokes, a mining magnate from Western Australia; Nine Media is a publicly listed conglomerate, operating with ex-Liberal Party treasurer Peter Costello as its chair. Network 10 is owned by Paramount Global: its interests and approaches are different to the other key players, but its influence is still there.

The mainstream media, including the ABC, ran a negative campaign against the Labor Party—generally, a positive one towards the Coalition—and extended this negativity towards the Australian Greens and teal independents. Despite this, Labor won the election. Following on from other recent state election results, where Labor governments easily won those elections in the face of hostile reportage, it's clear that the mainstream media's ability to influence election outcomes, is not as strong as it once was.

LACK OF SEPARATION OF CHURCH AND STATE

Religion has played a role in Australian political discourse, but not to the extent it does in the United States, for example. The first Catholic elected to the prime ministership was Labor's James Scullin in 1929. This did cause some controversy but had mostly died down within the first few months of his term. His successor, Joe Lyons, was also Catholic, but there were few objections, especially given his electoral success.

The Labor Party has split twice over proxy wars related to religion—in the conscription referenda of 1916 and 1917, Catholics tended to oppose military conscription, while Protestants tended to be supportive, and the narrow defeat of both referenda caused the party to split and led to the expulsion of prime minister Billy Hughes from the party. The 1956 Labor split was primarily a debate between atheist Marxism and

Catholic social justice but, essentially, religion has not been at the forefront of Australia politics.

Many people in the electorate were probably unaware that during their periods in office, former prime ministers Bob Hawke, Julia Gillard, John Curtin and Ben Chifley were atheists, or that John Howard was Anglican, or that Paul Keating was Catholic. Aside from Howard, who reintroduced the Lord's Prayer to commence parliamentary sittings, appointed an Anglican bishop to the position of governor–general, and referenced Australia as a society founded on the principles of Judeo–Christianity, there were few direct references to churches and religion. Scott Morrison changed that: he openly displayed his Pentecostalism, and his time as prime minister appeared to be strongly influenced by prosperity theology.

There was a problematic relationship with his mentor and leader of the Hillsong Church in Australia, Brian Houston, who was accused of covering up allegations of child sexual assault; Morrison's personal religious values seemed to influence his actions in government: development of personal wealth, indifference to asylum seekers, homophobia (Morrison abstained from the vote on same-sex marriage legislation in 2017), sexism, hostility to recipients of social security payments, and a commitment to the Religious Discrimination Bill, which provided legal protections for churches and religious schools to discriminate against women and the LGBTQI+ community.

The Australian electorate doesn't tend to care too much about the religion of any politician—performance is the issue that matters the most—but there was a sense of unease of Morrison's promotion of Pentecostalist beliefs, and behaviours such as the unwanted 'laying of hands' and praying for people. The schism between Morrison's promotion as a man of religion and many of his 'un-Christian' behaviours as prime minister was too great a gap for many people to reconcile.

IT WASN'T JUST MORRISON

Australian elections are traditionally fought over 50 or so seats, once the more obvious safe seats that are highly unlikely to change hands, are excluded. That number, of course, has started to slowly shift, with more seats contested by independent candidates in areas that were considered safe for the Liberal Party—such as Kooyong, North Sydney, Mackellar, Goldstein and Curtin—and safe Labor seats, such as Fowler. These seats have been lost for the major parties and might be lost for some time to come.

While it's expected that most of the focus during an election will be on the leader of the party, there were many other problems within the Liberal Party, with poor candidate selection being one of them. In previous elections, the independent candidate Rebekha Sharkie twice defeated Georgina Downer, daughter of former Cabinet minister, Alexander Downer, in the safe seat of Mayo. Independent Cathy McGowan defeated Sophie Mirabella in the safe seat of Indi. Zali Steggall defeated Tony Abbott in the safe seat of Warringah. These were seats safely held by the Liberal Party and choosing better candidates in these cases may have secured victories for them.

Treasurer Josh Frydenberg was a poor campaigner and was not closely engaged with the community in Kooyong. Other Liberal Party members, such as Dan Tehan, are also poor performers. Peter Dutton comes across as a brutal roughneck, but it is a public image that he has cultivated after many years as the minister for immigration, home affairs and defence. Senator Michaelia Cash is a performative irritant and public nuisance, who seems to revel in these irritations. Sussan Ley seemed uninterested and, even one of the better performers within the party, Senator Simon Birmingham, struggled with the more complex issues during the campaign.

INTRODUCTION: ELECTION NIGHT, 2022

Candidate selection is key for any political party but it's only possible to choose from the people who come forward. The Liberal Party has been overtaken by the hard-right members, and many of the moderates have been purged from the party. This is a tragedy, not only for the party, but for the Australian political system. True liberalism isn't a process of 'win at all costs', attacking the disadvantaged people in the community, supporting the wealth class, fearing the *other*, engaging in personal enrichment and enabling corruption that favours political donors. This is a major issue that will need to change for the party.

The Liberal Party has strayed too far away from its Menzian roots and has become an illiberal rump of hard-line conservatism. While Morrison must take most of this blame—as the leader—a stronger Cabinet and party structure would have ameliorated his worst excesses in government and his ignorance of long-established parliamentary protocols and precedents.

LABOR WON, BUT DID THEY UNDERPERFORM?

The Labor Party ran a patchy campaign, not helped by Anthony Albanese's earlier mistakes on day one and contracting COVID in week three. The media's hard-nosed campaign against Albanese also didn't help—magnifying a day one 'gaffe' which ultimately turned out to be meaningless—and rendered irrelevant by Australian Greens leader Adam Bandt snapping 'Google it, mate!' when a journalist tried to catch him out with another 'gotcha' question on an irrelevant and arcane economic statistic.

Labor though, while it won enough seats in the House of Representatives to govern—77 seats—and has received very workable numbers in the Senate, underperformed. Given the poor performances by successive Coalition governments over the past nine years, the weak state of the economy, mismanagement of the pandemic, flaws in foreign affairs policy, and the general stench of corruption, Labor should have achieved a landslide victory.

Albanese played cautiously in this campaign, with no difficult policy announcements, no radical changes, preferring to focus on convincing the electorate that he was a 'safe pair of hands'. It's possible to see why Labor chose this course: the 2019 election campaign offered too many targets for the Coalition to attack, and the character of former Labor leader Bill Shorten was the focus of attention, with many in the media only too happy to take aim and push issues relating to his likeability and trustworthiness. Albanese was not prepared to make these same errors and, in any case, the attempts by the media and the Coalition to smear his reputation fell flat and were less effective.

By not offering too much of a target and playing too cautiously, Albanese didn't inspire the electorate in the same way that Gough Whitlam, Bob Hawke or Kevin Rudd were able to but, sometimes, for a party that has been in opposition for most of the time since Australia's federation in 1901, perhaps it's better to secure the victory first—irrespective of how narrow that victory might be—and then build on that to secure a platform for election victories in the future. However, Albanese has at his disposal, one of the best debut Cabinets in Australia's history, rivalling Menzies' Cabinet in 1949 and Hawke's Cabinet in 1983. There are many seasoned performers in the new Albanese Cabinet, with strong parliamentary and ministerial experience and a healthy combination of ambitious younger ministers who are preparing Labor for a longer term of government.

The 2022 election confirmed a shift away from the major parties—Labor is in an unusual position where its primary vote has also slipped, but still managed to achieve a net gain of eight seats and form a majority government. The previous term of Labor government between 2010–13 was rife with personality and factional issues, leadership changes, which made them an easy target for a rabid media and a maniacal leader of the opposition, Tony Abbott—who was only too happy to feed into the daily chaos and mayhem. This chaos continued after the Liberal–National Coalition returned to office in 2013, which became a daily cycle of controversy, scandal or another esoteric issue which they could then use to whip a frenzy in their continuing conservative culture wars. It was not a recipe for good government.

There is a low level of public trust in politics and it will take a long time to restore this trust after a long period of disillusionment with a political system that voters see is not working in their interests. The 2022 federal election was an important turning point. Australia has changed and this was one of the more important elections from over the past 50 years or so. The damage to Australia's political system and the economy will take a while to repair but Australia has made what appears to be the right choice, even if it will take time for the merit of this choice to reveal itself.

***

FEBRUARY

A SUMMER OF DISCONTENT AND THE BEGINNING OF THE END FOR SCOTT MORRISON

5 February 2022

When the New South Wales government removed all COVID restrictions on 15 December 2021, there were 2,800 new COVID cases across Australia. Fast forward one month and on 12 January 2022, the number had escalated to 175,000 daily case numbers, before easing to the current number of around 37,000. How did these numbers move so rapidly and spiral out of control?

Having so many sick people with COVID opened a wide range of other issues and having that much illness within the community meant that many people couldn't work, including supply chain workers, providers of services, and essential workers in hospitals and aged care homes. In addition, rapid antigen tests—which would have assisted managing the outbreak of COVID—were in short supply.

It's difficult to think of how the New South Wales government could have mismanaged this crisis further. The statements from the New South Wales premier, Dominic Perrottet, and prime minister Scott Morrison, that 'nobody saw Omicron coming' are not accurate, with many health experts and epidemiologists predicting that fully removing restrictions without an adequate support system in place, would result in these outcomes, and they also warned that an unhealthy community riddled with coronavirus would result in many essential workers unable to work, with disruptions in supply chains. Which is exactly what occurred in New South Wales during late December and January, with COVID spreading throughout all other states and territories across Australia, except for Western Australia. Should the New South Wales government have listened to the experts, rather than the business community?

Of course, it's always easier to be wise after the event, but the evidence was there, and presented in a forceful way by the medical community: a new strain of the coronavirus was coming; it was far more virulent; it was far more contagious. There were many warnings that a high increase in COVID case numbers after removing restrictions would result in a far higher hospitalisation rate, more people in intensive care units, and more deaths—the Doherty Institute predicted 80 deaths per day within six months after lifting restrictions, if the appropriate systems of control were not implemented, claims that were ridiculed at the time by some media commentators and senior politicians. On 31 January 2022, Australia reached a seven-day average of 86 deaths per day, exceeding earlier predictions.

This contributed to a summer of discontent experienced by many people. Morrison promised a safe holiday when he said "the restaurants are opening and a big Christmas is coming for all of us" in his 2021 Christmas message. "Big", yes, but not in the way Morrison anticipated. Many people in Sydney spent their Christmas in isolation, either because they had coronavirus, or were waiting for their PCR test results—which were taking around four or five days to come through—and many aged care facilities were locked down for several weeks.

The expected retail bonanza failed to material, people were afraid to venture out and many supply chains were disrupted, primarily because the government failed to understand that

COVID doesn't discriminate and high numbers of cases meant the chances of supermarket workers, forklift drivers, essential workers in hospitals and aged care homes becoming afflicted with COVID would also increase.

The outbreak in New South Wales—which then spread to Victoria, Queensland, Tasmania, South Australia, the Australian Capital Territory and Northern Territory—wasn't directly caused by the Morrison government: that was primarily the fault of the New South Wales government, which had its third incident of COVID mismanagement, following on from the *Ruby Princess* disaster in March 2020, and its failure to adequately manage the Delta outbreak in June 2021. However, the actions of the New South Wales government to remove restrictions on 15 December were fully supported by Morrison and the business community.

To be sure; if a government is ideologically committed to removing restrictions and opening the community, the least it can do is prepare for the inevitable health outcomes. There is an expectation that the government would increase testing clinics; open more vaccination centres and hubs; adequately source, secure, and supply rapid antigen tests and make them widely available.

But the New South Wales government did the opposite. They removed restrictions—only for them to be re-instigated one week later after their mistake was realised—many testing clinics were closed for the Christmas period; many vaccination centres were closed during January; and rapid antigen tests were impossible to find for consumers; the prime minister also suggested individuals should manage their own health and implement a "greater level of self-regulation". The management of this crisis was inadequate and the actions of the New South Wales and federal governments seemed to be an act of pushing the spread of Omicron through the community—not that governments could publicly reveal this, although the Queensland chief health officer, John Gerrard, came close when he suggested the spread of Omicron was "inevitable and necessary"—and if it wasn't intentional, it was in the words of former prime minister Malcolm Turnbull, the "worst failure of public administration in Australian history".

Many other developed countries are providing rapid antigen tests for free or at cost price to make these more affordable to the public. In Australia, the tests are being sold for at least $15 per test, at a mark-up of around 400–500 per cent. There are also Australian companies—AnteoTech and Lumos Diagnostics—currently awaiting approval from the Therapeutic Goods Administration to supply their testing kits to the domestic market but, instead, are supplying their products to international markets.

In this environment, it would be reasonable to expect the Morrison government to step in and fast-track the approval process and support a local production sector, which could then offer supplies domestically—rapid antigen tests were approved for use in the United States in February 2021—but it's difficult to comprehend why approvals have not yet occurred in Australia and why the government is keen to import rapid antigen tests, and deny local manufacturers the option of producing and supplying to a local market.

What was clear, however, was the supply of rapid antigen tests was used as yet another political tactic, and a tool to provide favours for the business community. Aside from the issues of whether the tests should have been provided for free, the actions seemed more consistent with a *de facto* business stimulus package, where rapid antigen tests appeared in some unusual locations—phone repair shops, tobacconists, electronic stores, Harvey Norman—at heavily marked-up prices.

And, of course, this is the result of governments ideologically linked to the desires of the business sector, and not the community.

Towards the end of 2021, many businesses—large and small—complained about the need to ease restrictions in late 2021 and open the economy up again as soon as possible. On 15 December 2021, they were granted their wish, but when COVID case numbers started to rise and shoppers deserted the malls, they then started to complain the government removed restrictions too soon and weren't receiving the number of customers they expected.

Perhaps the main message to government in this case is that stakeholders and vested interest will complain—even if they are a government's most vocal supporters—and it's best to ignore those voices, listen to experts and proceed with what is in the interests of the community. Essentially, the New South Wales government ended up with the worst of both worlds: a sick workforce and a sick economy, and a lesson in politics: it's best to take in the bigger picture and not just stick rigidly to ideological pursuits or listen to political donors.

This followed on from the continuing bungles in many aspects of the management of the pandemic by this government, which would have hoped that these issues could be resolved in time for the next federal election, due in May 2022. But there are limits to how much memory can be erased by the electorate. A mistake can easily be forgotten if a remedy is applied and quickly resolved: that is the role and function of good government.

The Morrison government appears to be making mistakes followed by more mistakes, never implementing a solution until it's far too late, and unable to learn from its mistakes. A missed Christmas or a miserable holiday spent in isolation from everyone else and suffering the effects of COVID are events that are not easily forgotten.

More people have died from COVID during January 2022, than died throughout all of 2021. The federal government managed the supply and delivery of vaccines according to an election timetable, rather than when they were needed in the community, and this factor will not play out well for them in the lead-up to the federal election campaign.

And it is apparent that the federal and New South Wales ministers with these responsibilities, are not equipped for the tasks required of them, and seem to lack the experience, wisdom and leadership qualities. More bizarre ideas were coming into consideration, such as Morrison's thought-bubble of children under the age of eighteen obtaining licences to drive forklift trucks to rectify supply-chain issues and fill empty supermarket shelves. The leaders that lack foresight and created the problems in the first instance, are hardly going to have the skills required to solve those problems.

In this case, business leaders proposed a loosely considered idea, which then ended up at the discussion table of the National Cabinet. After the idea was rejected by National Cabinet, it was lampooned as Morrison's 'onion-eating moment' (in reference to an incident in 2015, where former prime minister Tony Abbott ate a raw onion) and, with it, the political narrative Morrison is so desperate to control, started to quickly unravel into national ridicule.

Every prime minister wants to control the 'narrative' and their political messaging, and one key message Morrison has been cultivating is nobody could "have seen Omicron coming", his government was "blindsided" and could not have done much to stop its spread. But these are excuses and covering over a failure of leadership and a failure to take responsibility.

Governments are the largest organisation in any country and have the resources and the personnel available to assess these situations: the community can't take on these tasks by themselves and it's the critical reason why governments exist.

Governments also perform risk assessments and consider the merits of each decision before they proceed. *That's what governments do*. Perhaps this federal government had the high-level risk assessments and strategies in place but decided to ignore those risks because it didn't adequately reflect its political and ideological needs.

The Omicron variant first appeared in early November 2021 in South Africa, and this should have provided enough time for the government to clearly assess the situation and reduce threats as much as possible. This government failed to do this: they've had two years to prepare for new quarantine centres in Perth, Sydney, Brisbane and Melbourne but these tasks have not been completed yet, in some cases, not even commenced. If there are problems in implementing any of these tasks, governments could fast-track resources and ensure problems are resolved in the best interests of the community. *That's why governments exist.*

However, an incompetent and lazy government, with little pressure placed upon them by the mainstream media, a government which feels that it can lie its way out of any predicament, will produce results of this kind: chaos in the community, chaos in the economy, and a government that has almost lost its entire bank of political capital. If only the Morrison government performed the work that was expected of them in the first place, they wouldn't be in the political trouble they currently find themselves in: behind in the polls, and widely expected to lose the 2022 federal election.

The community is discovering that this type of ideologically driven, libertarian and 'anti-government' government is not suited for these times. If this government is so committed to "removing government from people's lives", they should vacate office at the next election and let those who are committed to strong and effective government, manage the pandemic instead.

The Morrison–Perrottet style of 'hands-off' government has failed, primarily because they've adopted an extreme neoliberal model that can never work effectively, even when the political circumstances are suited this style of thinking, as they were in the 1980s and 1990s.

In 2022, there are by-elections in New South Wales (February); a general state selection in South Australia (March); a federal election (May); and a general state election in Victoria (November). It will be a year that provides opportunities to the electorate to choose what it expects from government: a *laissez faire* approach to political management which has been disastrous and ineffective; *or* a more constructive, effective and responsive approach to implementing solutions in the interests of the wider community, not just to the select few.

A COMPLETE PSYCHO

Every election year commences with presentations from the prime minister and the leader of the opposition at the National Press Club in Canberra and, this year, their respective presentations seemed to mirror how these leaders are performing in the current opinion polls. The Labor leader, Anthony Albanese, had an image makeover during the holiday period and did his best to present himself as a credible alternative prime minister, whereas the actual prime minister, Scott Morrison, was taken to task by journalists over mismanagement of the pandemic and his poor performances, and was asked the kinds of questions he was not used to receiving:

> Peter van Onselen, Network 10: Prime minister, at the start of your speech, you mentioned your close friendship with Marise Payne [minister for foreign affairs]. I wanted to ask you about another close friend, Gladys Berejiklian [former New South Wales premier]—and that's somebody that you wanted to run actually at the next election. I've been provided with a text message exchange between the former New South Wales premier, and

> a current Liberal Cabinet minister... she described you as "a horrible, horrible person", going on to say she did not trust you, and you're more concerned with politics than people. The minister is even more scathing, describing you as "a fraud", and "a complete psycho". Does this exchange surprise you? And what do you think it tells us?
>
> Scott Morrison: Well, I don't know who you're referring to, or the basis of what you've put to me. But I obviously don't agree with it. And I don't think that's my record.

Of course, this is the classic 'gotcha' question and journalists shouldn't be presenting unverified material to any political leader. But it was a sign of the media smelling the 'blood in the water' and deciding to attack a prime minister, even if he is from the side of politics they usually refrain from attacking too strongly.

In an election year, the responsibilities of the leader of the opposition are not the same as those of the leader of government. But in his address, Albanese combined valid points of attack on the government and the broadbrush strokes of what a Labor government might look like if they manage to win the 2022 election. He looked comfortable, whereas Morrison appeared to be a leader under immense pressure for the first time in his prime ministership and seemed at a loss about what to do next. The first question after Morrison's National Press Club address from the moderator set the tone:

> Laura Tingle (journalist and moderator of the National Press Club): Thank you prime minister for that very extensive address. It's a new year. So, a good opportunity to clear the air. You acknowledge today you didn't get everything right, and that you understand the frustration people have felt over the summer. But do you want to take this opportunity to actually say 'sorry' for the mistakes you've made as prime minister, not just about COVID,

everything from going to Hawaii during the bushfires, through to not having enough rapid antigen tests in place, even as you foreshadowed the switch to a greater use of them, and for failing to live up to your pledge to hundreds of thousands of people on the NDIS, that you will make sure the scheme was fully funded, and kept and demand driven? And will you apologise to people who've had the hundreds of people who've had funding arbitrarily cut under the scheme?
Scott Morrison: Well, thanks for the question!
Tingle: ...always happy to ask you questions, prime minister...
Morrison: ...yep. We're all terribly sorry for what this pandemic has done to the world and to this country. These are the times in which we live and I've set out today, I think, very clearly, the challenges that we've faced.

For most of the National Press Club address, Morrison was fuming, barely concealing his anger; he seemed to be flustered and unable to respond adequately. An election that is going to be held in May is never going to be won with the dynamics playing out in February during an exclusive media reception in Canberra. But it was a sign that with only five months before the federal election, the Coalition was worried about their prospects of success.

However, it can never be underestimated how strongly a government will act to remain in power. Conversely, it can never be underestimated how badly the Labor Party can stumble at the large hurdle, as has occurred many times in federal history, most famously, at the 2019 federal election, when all evidence suggested a Labor victory.

There's a wide range of reasons for why last-minute surprise election victories can happen: the electorate that has been disengaged with politics, becomes engaged with the issues as it gets nearer to the election date. Morrison, as prime minister, usually portrays himself as the 'daggy dad' persona, inoffensive and masking his true character. This was the intention with his Australia Day address in Canberra, when he read a poem penned by his school-aged daughter at a citizenship ceremony: he was making a connection with Australian families. It's the same connection he's trying to make by cooking a Sri Lankan curry on a Saturday night or building a chicken pen on a Sunday afternoon at Kirribilli House.

The issue with these actions is that these are not the roles of a prime minister and, especially after two years of pandemic-related hardship within the community, the electorate wanted to see more substance in the role. While all prime ministers engage in vaudeville to engage the electorate and make themselves more appealing to key demographics—Morrison uses these performative aspects of politics to distract from his incompetence. If there are ever any difficulties in government, he looks to blame other people, other agencies, or other governments: nothing is ever his fault, and there is little acceptance of responsibility. This might be acceptable for some in the electorate, but at time of heightened distress, eschewing responsibilities and seeking to blame others was, for many, unacceptable.

The opinions polls—even if they were as wildly inaccurate as they were in the 2019 federal election—also were not offering any succour to the Coalition government. And while there were some suggesting that a landslide such as the 2021 Western Australia election result was in the offing—where the Coalition won only six seats in a parliament of 59 seats—the federal election seemed on track to replicate the preceding 2017 Western Australia election: a large swing, but not large enough to cause a wipe-out of the Liberal and National parties. It was becoming more evident at this stage that the areas of lower north Sydney were becoming a problem for the Liberal Party, with several independents in key seats looking likely to snatch these seats, and even the chances for

Labor in the long-held Liberal seat of Bennelong were starting to look promising. And the perceptions of Morrison's credibility as prime minister and the competence of the Liberal and National parties seemed to be set within the electorate, and once these perceptions are set, they are difficult to shift.

The mainstream media is very helpful when it comes to shifting these perceptions, especially when most journalists generally side with the conservative side of politics—including the ABC—but many at the National Press Club address were lining up to ask the difficult questions of Morrison and critique his performance in government, quite often with hostility.

The favourable reception from the media up to this point of electoral cycle placed Morrison at a disadvantage, ironically, by not asking those hard questions in the past, and for not being too critical of the Morrison government. When the real and justifiable pressure was applied to Morrison, he had no means to defend himself. At the National Press Club, he was flummoxed; he was shown to be out of his depth; and because he hasn't had that practice and experience of dealing with a hostile media that a prime minister could usually expect, he just appeared as not being across his brief, frazzled and under pressure. And this is not a good sign for any political leader, especially several months away from a federal election.

A difference in tone can be seen in the respective leaders:

> Anthony Albanese: Australia can emerge from this once-in-a century crisis better, stronger, more fair, and more prosperous and [this] requires leadership that brings Australians together—protecting the health of Australians will be a defining issue in the upcoming election. And a critical choice will be this: who do you trust to keep Medicare safe?—only Labor will protect Medicare. The states have done a great job in picking up the slack from the slackest government in living memory. In a recent profile, when

asked to reflect on his time in office, Mr. Morrison suggested that he is not interested in leaving a legacy. For him, leaving no legacy is a conscious choice. I find this pretty remarkable. If given the opportunity, I want to make a real difference for the people of our nation, and to strengthen the nation itself. It is beyond comprehension that this government has actively refused to learn from this pandemic. This government has failed repeatedly on testing, tracing, vaccinations and quarantine, the Grand Slam of pandemic failure.

Scott Morrison: It has been tough, raising your family, keeping your job, doing your job. And I don't doubt many have stayed awake at night after telling their kids or those they care for, or those they employ, it's all going to be okay, but wondering themselves in the quiet of that night, whether it really will be. We're all terribly sorry for what this pandemic has done to the world and to this country.

When I say we haven't got everything right, let me reflect on a couple of them for you. Because we went into the summer, I think we were too optimistic perhaps. And we could have communicated more clearly about the risks and challenges that we still faced. And I think in raising those expectations about the summer, that we heightened the great sense of disappointment that people felt...

Laura Tingle: ...you don't have to say sorry about any of those things?

Morrison: I explained my answer fairly fully. I haven't got everything right. And I'll take my fair share of the criticism and the blame. It goes with the job. But with hindsight, the view does change. And lessons are learned, lessons that will continue to be invaluable to me and so many of my team are here with me today, and those who are out there with Australians in their communities to deal with the challenges and uncertainties that are still definitely ahead.

It does seem that the media has started to turn on Morrison, after offering their support for as long as possible. However, it also must be remembered that very few people watch National Press Club addresses—glimpses of them will be shown in news broadcasts for a fortnight or two. Without a doubt, the message of the prime minister asked whether he was called "a complete psycho" by one of his ministers wasn't the best way to commence an election year—these are the media grabs that do cut through. It's unfair for a prime minister to be hijacked like this, but these are the political hazards that can appear out of nowhere.

But the fact that this material is being leaked to the media—whether these are factual or not, and in the field of politics, the truthfulness of whatever is being claimed doesn't seem to matter—but it does bring into question the judgement of the Liberal Party to actually choose a leader of the calibre of Morrison, where he is held in such strong contempt by key members of the ministry and of the party. Morrison consistently put out the message of his great friendship with Berejiklian—he's hardly going to do otherwise—but it's clear that this friendship was not reciprocated.

One issue that is clear is the last vestiges of Morrison's credibility are disappearing, and that can be traced all the way back to that time in December 2019, when he flew to Hawaii in the middle of one of the biggest crises Australia has ever had—the bushfires crisis, and perhaps his credibility had been slowly diminishing from that time. However, it was clear at the National Press Club that Morrison has lost the support of the mainstream media, and, without their support, it was unclear how he was going to survive.

THE DIRE OPINION POLLS CONTINUE

Although the opinion polls in the lead-up to the 2019 federal election were wildly inaccurate and predicted an easy victory for Bill Shorten's Labor Party—only for the reverse to occur: a comfortable victory for Scott Morrison and the Liberal–National Coalition—whenever polls are released, the figures and data are analysed to see if there are any clear advantages for either side of politics.

The Newspoll figures released in early February confirmed all the recent polling from many other polls and showed the Coalition polling at 44 per cent in two-party preferred voting and 56 per cent for the Labor Party. Morrison's net approval rating is minus 19 (the number of people who approve, subtracting the people who disapprove), whereas Anthony Albanese's rating is at zero (neither positive or negative), and the preferred prime minister rating was almost equal.

Statistically, these were not very good numbers for Morrison and while there is the adage that the only polls that count are the ones on election day—this was certainly the case in the 2019 federal election—these were numbers that were also causing serious concerns for the Liberal Party. Whenever a politician claims that they're not even looking at the polls, it's a lie: politicians live and die through opinion polls, irrespective of whether they are accurate or not. Opinion polls are like school report cards in the lower years: they might not provide a final result; they might not even be a true indication of knowledge and skills attained but they do indicate performances relative to peers. In politics, it's a public assessment of how well a political party is travelling and to this stage, the performances of the Liberal and National parties have been poor.

There were also issues causing problems for Morrison within this home state: New South Wales. It was the key state the Liberal

Party was hoping to either hold or gain seats at the federal election, and several preselection issues have arisen in several seats, especially in the northern Sydney seat of Warringah, previously held by Tony Abbott, but now held by an independent member of parliament, Zali Steggall. Several Liberal Party candidates had withdrawn from the race amid an ongoing battle between moderates and the religious right-wing of the party, dominated by a combination of Pentecostals, Opus Dei Catholics and other conservative Christian groups.

These groups—fundamentally undemocratic in their outlook, with an obstinate desire to install conservative social values in government—had achieved a strong presence within Liberal Party branches in Victoria and South Australia, and were hoping to extend their reach into New South Wales and other parts of Australia. This battle suggested the Liberal Party was not in the best condition to contest the federal election—at least in New South Wales—and difficult to see how these issues could be politically beneficial to them.

There were also rumours circulating that the New South Wales premier, Dominic Perrottet—only in office since October 2021, following the resignation of Gladys Berejiklian—was to be replaced due to internal battles within the New South Wales branch of the Liberal Party. There didn't seem to be much substance to these rumours but the fact they existed suggested there were many deep problems within the party.

All political parties face internal battles where the various competing factions seek to dominate the party and hold more influence, and it is essential for political parties to renovate and modernise their internal structures—and their ideological make-up—to maintain relevance to the electorate. But this is difficult to achieve from within government—there is no time to carry out this thankless task and the active role of government masks over any difficulties that might exist within a party. And it's only the release from the burdens of government that highlights and exposes glaring problems within a party and offers them the opportunity to reform—if they're inclined to do this.

The Labor Party learned this process the hard way. After the tumult of the Rudd–Gillard years, where they threw away a hard-earned return to government in 2007 due to internal factional and personality-based conflicts, Labor stabilised the party, worked on policy reforms that were palatable for their membership—albeit offering housing and share franking credits policies that were rejected by the electorate in 2019—and appear to be well prepared for a return to government. The issue for Labor is that it has taken nine years of life in opposition before they could discover a successful political formula.

Every political party will have its difficulties. The Liberal Party, federally and in many state branches, is currently managing some very difficult ideological and structural problems, and this is reflected in opinion polls. But aside from the opinion polls that have suggest a Labor victory at the federal election, there are the real-life events of actual elections in this parliamentary term that support those published opinions polls. Four state by-elections held in New South Wales in February 2022 had large swings against the New South Wales government—in the seats of Willoughby (20.4 per cent), Bega (12.0 per cent), Monaro (6.4 per cent), and Strathfield (0.8 per cent)—and these wholesale changes in voting patterns suggest a change of government is a strong possibility at the federal election in May.

And along with the rumours of a challenge to Perrottet's leadership in New South Wales, there was also speculation that Morrison could face a challenge himself, irrespective of how difficult it might be to instigate a change—thanks to the rules that Morrison implemented soon after he became prime minister, which requires a two-thirds threshold to spill the Liberal Party leadership positions.

But a change of prime minister several months before an election has never worked—the Labor Party removed Kevin Rudd late in the electoral cycle in 2010 and installed Julia Gillard, and was reduced to a minority position at the 2010 election; they repeated the same mistake by replacing Gillard with Rudd, and suffered a humiliating loss at the 2013 election.

Three months before the 2022 election, it seems the Coalition under Morrison are waiting for circumstances to change; perhaps an issue that appears from nowhere and changes the dynamics of the election year. No government had ever recovered from such a dire electoral position in opinion polls 100 days out from an election, and then gone on to win that election. Of course, there are different factors that could come into play to alter this historical fact. It's unclear how the pandemic and COVID restrictions will affect campaign strategies, including how to campaign at a time when there is likely to be vastly higher numbers of postal and prepoll votes.

There is always the possibility of the arrival of external factors—such as those that affected the 2001 federal election, when Kim Beazley's Labor Party was expected to win that election but was overtaken by the *MV Tampa* asylum seeker incident in the Indian Ocean, and the 9/11 disaster at the World Trade Center in New York; both incidents heavily exploited by John Howard. Paul Keating won an election from a worse position in 1993. John Howard won two elections from worse positions in 1998 and 2001. But not as close to an election date as Morrison is to the 2022 election.

But in the absence of these factors, Morrison continued with the performative politics: cooking a curry for his family; baking a barramundi; referring lovingly to "Jen and the girls"; splashing cash for the Great Barrier Reef and kissing the noses of koala bears, as shown in an ABC news report.

Jessica Ross (ABC reporter): When it comes to meeting the nation's leader, it seems there's quite a lot a koala can bear. Australia Zoo's star, 'Brandy', was given cuddles, pats, even a nose kiss.
Scott Morrison: Yes, you have a lovely nose!
Ross: ...as 50 million was pledged to help the rest of her kind.
Morrison: We love to throw arms around koalas. And what this is about is continuing to throw our arms around our koala population.
Ross: Numbers have halved in Queensland in the past two decades, dropping nearly 60 per cent in New South Wales. The Black Summer bushfires claimed six and a half thousand little lives and urban sprawl continues to take a heavy toll. Experts fear the national icon could be extinct by 2050. Twenty million will go towards habitat restoration...
Sussan Ley: To use drones to seed trees in new koala habitat.
Ross: There's 10 million for community projects and two million towards health outcomes, including the chlamydia vaccine rollout. $1 million has also been allocated towards expanding national training for veterinarians and nurses to ensure they had the most up to date skills to treat and triage koalas. But as always, prevention is better than cure. And it's hoped the other measures will say less in here and more out in the wild. But the opposition says the government's just trying to up its green credentials. This crowd pleaser coming a day after its $1 billion reef funding commitment.

This was classic Morrison: a puff-piece item of propaganda prepared by the national broadcaster, using many of the government's talking points and sounding more like a government media release. The ABC should be producing better material than this, which seemed more in keeping with a state-controlled media outlet, rather than a publicly funded broadcaster acting in the public interest.

But this kind of public relations promotion, morphing into a mini-lifestyle documentary and masquerading as a government funding announcement—as a political tactic—is over. At this stage, the electorate had worked Morrison out. Certainly, this type of political messaging influences some people in their voting intentions but, overall, and especially after what they'd been through over the past two years with the pandemic, the electorate wants something different from their political leadership. And it seemed Morrison wasn't prepared to, or able to, offer that difference.

***

LOSING YOUR RELIGION

12 February 2022

Federal parliament returned for the year and because there's an election coming up, it was that time of the year when the government started moving some issues off its plate and removing some of its long-standing problems. They announced the lifting of an indexation freeze for ABC and SBS funding—which was, effectively, a funding boost of $84 million to the ABC. The government also decided to target aged care workers with a promise of an $800 bonus but there were so many exceptions and clauses attached to these funds, that it was unclear how much would finally filter through to these workers.

The government has put in great effort to make sure the Religious Discrimination Bill gets through parliament, a piece of legislation few people in the community want and a bill which seemed more about trying to wedge Labor on cultural issues and create division within the community. But this period of parliament is also notable for what's *not* being done. The attorney-general Senator Michaelia Cash announced there won't be enough time to create a national anti-corruption commission before the election, even though prime minister Scott Morrison promised this commission all the way back in December 2018, and three-and-a-half years later, the public is still waiting.

There are so many other areas that have been overlooked: there's little action to mitigate climate change, there's no action against the minister for aged care, Senator Richard Colbeck, who decided to go to a test cricket match on the day he was meant to front up to a senate estimates committee to look at all the critical issues within his portfolio. There are genuine refugees still incarcerated in a Melbourne hotel after nine years of detention. The government is still paying lip service to women's safety issues. The process of removing difficult political issues before an election is colloquially known as 'clearing the barnacles', but it seems the federal government isn't intent on moving on any of these key issues before the next federal election.

Since it was elected in May 2019, the federal government has had a record of being big with announcements but not with the follow through. Morrison mentioned he was pushing through with the Religious Discrimination Bill because the Liberal Party had promised it, even though there was a raft of other areas that had been promised—most notably, the anti-corruption commission—which he had little intention of delivering. This was a reminder of John Howard's 'core' and 'non-core' promises from 1996—except in contemporary politics, there's not even a mention of core promises: policies seem to be removed at whim and forgotten about.

The promise of religious discrimination legislation will appeal to Pentecostal churches—and many other church groups—but even though the Liberal Party has suggested there are thousands of votes to be gained from many congregations, these might be votes that are already parked with the Liberal Party. The current opinion polls are suggesting a Labor landslide, and the Coalition will need more than just the religious vote to win the next election.

This is also the time—several months before an election—that the disengaged parts of the electorate, the people who rarely tune into politics, start to engage with key issues that might influence the result. Of course, governments will choose to focus on the legislation that provides the best electoral outcomes for them, especially this close to an election, but a focus on religious matters might not provide the result they're after. The Morrison government was one of the more lazy governments in recent history, with only 83.6 per cent of bills passing parliament (compared to 91.8 per cent by the Gillard–Rudd governments during 2010–13 and the Howard government between 2004–07 with 93.7 per cent). Morrison's prime ministership was also a time of low parliamentary productivity rates (highest numbers of acts passed per day of prime ministerial term: Julia Gillard, 0.51; lowest—Morrison, 0.39; Tony Abbott, 0.39, Malcolm Turnbull, 0.35).

And this figure—while it might not mean much to the electorate—is a key indicator of diligence and competence in government. The Coalition generally didn't seem too interested in passing legislation, perhaps thinking that passing legislation meant more accountability, and it was evident this government wanted to avoid scrutiny. Morrison also held a disappointingly low number of sitting days—also another way of avoiding scrutiny—and although this number was affected by the earlier parts of the pandemic, there was no attempt to seek other ways to hold parliamentary sittings, either through remote attendance or technological solutions—but, either way, a low performing government, especially one so reluctant to improve its performance, isn't deserving of re-election, and the current opinion polls are reflective of that.

While the government wasn't intent of spending much time in parliament, it decided most of its attention was going to be put into the Religious Discrimination Bill—and although it was claimed that it's a bill required to stop discrimination against religious institutions and schools, it seemed to provide these institutions, schools and people of faith, the legal protections to perpetrate their own forms of discrimination against people they dislike: in particular, the LGBTQI+ community and young adults considering gender transitioning. When taking all the key points into account, it's an abhorrent proposal and, if ever enacted, would take Australia a step back into the dark ages. The former olympian, Ian Thorpe, was quite forthright in his condemnation of the bill:

> "Taxpayers contribute, to make sure that we actually have a healthy society. And if we actually have independent schools that have different beliefs, I'm supportive of all of that.
> But I don't think it's appropriate that we're actually funding these schools in the way that we are, if that actually goes against what has been recognised in this country—we had a very successful campaign with marriage equality, which if it was an election campaign, which we're coming up to one very soon, we would have had a 100-seat majority in the lower house.
> And it shows that most communities in Australia actually support this. When we look at religious groups, and the largest one that we can talk about in Australia, is Christians—65 per cent of that group actually support making sure that there is protections for people that happen to be in the LGBTIQ community.
> And then when you consider all of the minority religions in this country, is they're fearful of what the repercussions can be from this bill. So it isn't just faith against people that might be gay.
> There's a complexity to this, that also includes people that may have a disability, to someone who may be pregnant. It goes far beyond this.
> And when you get into the detail of this bill—and this is the third iteration of this bill—it isn't right, and it isn't a step forward. And in any way that you discriminate against one group of people in favour of another, it's not a step forward.

> If I were the prime minister, I would not want to go to an election on this. And I actually encourage everyone, the sensible people that are in the middle, in this group, not only from one side... from the government side, but also from Labor's side—and encourage them to actually make sure that this bill does not go through.
> This is a bill that has no friends in Canberra and probably has no friends around the country."

The irony here is that Labor proposed a referendum in 1988 to add protections of religious freedom and expression to the Australian Constitution, and the Liberal Party campaigned strongly against it, resulting in a comprehensive defeat at the referendum. In 1988, it was all about politics, as it is in 2022: as the former New South Wales premier Gladys Berejiklian said of Scott Morrison, he's "more concerned with politics than people".

There were some suggestions that the focus on the Religious Discrimination Bill was a way of moving public discussions away from comments made by Australian of the year, Grace Tame, and Brittany Higgins at the National Press Club, where Higgins asserted that Morrison's comments after she alleged she was sexually assaulted in a minister's office were "shocking at times" and "a bit offensive". Tame referred to a senior member of an organisation that was funded by the government asking her during a "threatening" phone call to not to say anything damning about Morrison.

Morrison has a pathological desire to control the political narrative, but it's an awkward strategy: to avoid the issues that he doesn't want to focus upon, he finds another conversation piece or a different narrative that creates even more uproar, and appeals to an ugly part of the Australian psyche that doesn't like the 'other' and prefers to 'punch down' at the more marginalised parts of the Australian community.

Again, it's a focus on the wrong issues: the Religious Discrimination Bill is part of a conservative wish list, just so that some right-wing churches obsessed with sex can expel LGBTQI+ students and staff. Whereas the issues which are far more important to Australian society, such as an anti-corruption commission and the many unresolved issues with the aged care sector, are being ignored.

There was a report into the many managerial and funding issues within the aged care workforce completed in September 2021, yet the government refused to release it—of course, if the report did contain favourable news, the government would have released it immediately, so it can be assumed that it's predominantly negative and would be damaging to the government several months before an election campaign.

No action on aged care, no action on anti-corruption, no action on women's safety, but all the attention on providing exemptions for religious institutions and schools to be able to discriminate. This is the behaviour of a government which has lost legitimacy, with no real direction for the greater good, or for the greater benefit of the Australian people: a government working in favour of very narrow and powerful interest groups. It's evident that Morrison's own personal Pentecostal faith is driving the Religious Discrimination Bill and it's a bill targeting a small and marginalised group of people in the transgender and gender diverse community—around 1.2 per cent of the population. It's not the religious institutions and schools that need protections—some of the most wealthy and powerful institutions in Australia—it's the people who have been traditionally discriminated against by these institutions, the LGBTQI+ community, who need it the most.

And this discrimination can have dire results, as revealed in parliament by Labor's Stephen Jones:

"Last week, my family said farewell to my nephew Ollie. He was just fifteen when he took his own life. No mother or father should have to endure this sight. No brother should have to clean up afterwards. He was a beautiful, creative, courageous young man. He was loved and accepted by his parents, by his family, by his friends and community. His mum and dad are in anguish, we all are. He was gay, he was uncertain about his gender. And he struggled with his mental health. But now he's gone. And we're no longer going to be able to love and support him on his journey through life. Clearly, the love and acceptance of his family and friends, was not enough.

My own son is also a beautiful, creative, intelligent, fourteen-year-old. He designs and makes his own clothes. He's a gifted makeup artist. He moves seamlessly between the wardrobes of men and women, he wears heels that give me vertigo, and has more handbags than his sister. He has more courage than any other boy of his age that I've ever met. He swims against the tide. I love and support him unconditionally. But I worry myself sick every time he leaves the house. Because I know that the love and protection that he enjoys with his mother, and his friends and his family, is very different to the reception that he may receive in the outside world. Could this be the day when we received the call that says something has happened, that he has been attacked for just being who he is?

Yep, this is about my kids. But it's not. It's about all of our kids. It's about the families of those kids, every child that has had the courage to swim against the tide, just to be who they are. You know, earlier today, the prime minister said we should exercise our power in this place with love. I'm asking the prime minister to reflect on those words, as we consider the bill. I'd asked the prime minister and every other member in this place to put themselves in the shoes of the parents, or the heels of their kids. As they step out in public, what message do we want this parliament to send to these kids? Are they as loved and cherished and respected as every other kid? Surely, we aren't saying to them: 'It's okay, if you're gay, just so long as we don't see it'? Surely, we can do better than that."

These are avoidable, unnecessary deaths, and arise because certain people in the community cannot accept that other people are different. It's no different to racism; it's no different to misogyny; or any other form of bigoted opinion. But this is a federal government with a bill that entrenches this form of discrimination and seems keen to use the issue to try and create political benefit in the lead-up to an election campaign. That's the real travesty.

A FOCUS ON SEXUAL HARASSMENT

There's was a surprise announcement from the federal government that the ABC is set to receive a funding boost—but on closer inspection, it's the removal of the funding freeze from the ABC, which ultimately means an increase of $84 million in funding, an amount the ABC should have received anyway. Since 2013, the Coalition has defunded the ABC by $526 million in real terms, or $793 million if the indexation freeze is included, so, essentially, the government is returning funds they removed in the first place, which has been a typical announcement by the Coalition in office, and by prime minister Scott Morrison. But it's more than likely to be an election stunt to woo back disaffected Liberal Party voters—the party has railed against the ABC over the past thirty years, especially since 2013—and it must be remembered that the Liberal Party membership voted to privatise the ABC in 2015.

Announcements for the federal government seem to be one part of the political process but the other part—the delivery—rarely occurs. Ideologically, the Liberal Party has little intention of increasing funding to the ABC or to SBS, especially considering the defunding and privatisation of both the ABC and SBS is high on the list of the Institute of Public Affairs' 75 radical ideas to transform Australia. The institute is the primary think-tank behind the Liberal Party, so it's clear the party wants to move in this direction with the ABC.

The other factor behind the announcement was that it was clearly an attempt to divert from the other issues that were creating problems for the government, which seemed to be growing daily. These problems were exacerbated when Nationals MP Barnaby Joyce revealed he sent a text message to Brittany Higgins—for reasons which have yet to be adequately explained—when he outlined he didn't get along with Morrison, suggesting he was a "hypocrite" and "a liar" and he had never trusted him. Joyce, who was leader of the National Party at the time, also revealed that after he released the details of these text messages, he offered his resignation to Morrison—and suggested that Morrison was magnanimous and a man of forgiveness for not accepting his resignation.

But this was just messaging directed to the public—as the leader of the Liberal Party, it's not up to Morrison to accept a resignation from the leader of the National Party, it's up to the National Party and the mainstream media overlooked this key fact. Again, it was yet another political stunt.

Morrison also used his forgiveness of Joyce's comments in the media: but it seemed to be more in line with the specific kind of Christian who uses forgiveness as a weapon—in politics, forgiveness is usually offered because a politician has managed to wrench an advantage. It has been known for many years in political circles that Joyce and Morrison do not get on, either politically or personally, although sometimes in politics, opposites are attracted to each other. But in recent times, there have been leaked text and

WhatsApp messages critiquing key figures within the Coalition, especially Morrison. All political parties tend to do this, but it's not the best way to run government. Personalities within parties need to be based on an element of trust, even among the figures who do not get on either personally or ideologically. But backgrounding about their colleagues to the media is a certain sign that the federal government is on the way out at the next election.

The conflict between Joyce and Morrison were peripheral to the main issues of the day: women's safety, harassment, and domestic violence; and the prime minister decided the best way to show that he understands women was to go to Cocos hair salon in Mount Eliza, a suburb in south-east Melbourne, and wash a young woman's hair. This was part of a political stunt to support the Liberal candidate for Dunkley, Sharn Coombes, but it was awkward and it seemed inappropriate for a male politician to be doing this—in the same way if any other male politician, whether it be Adam Bandt, Anthony Albanese, Warren Entsch, Richard Marles, Mark Butler, Mark McGowan, or Daniel Andrews. It just didn't seem the right place for a man in a suit to appear, and even if it was, it was the wrong type of man.

It was obvious that Morrison was doing this to make a connection with women and provide the impression that he understands the plight of working women, but it lacked dignity, and it lacked gravitas. Political leaders need to develop ways of making a connection with the electorate, and this is exactly what Morrison was doing, but it seemed to be a too-obvious reaction to the criticisms he received at the National Press Club address by Brittany Higgins and Grace Tame.

> Brittany Higgins: I didn't want his [Morrison] sympathy as a father, I wanted him to use his power as prime minister. Some of his language last year was shocking and at times, admittedly a bit offensive. But his words wouldn't matter if his actions had

measured up then or since. I wanted him to wield the weight of his office and drive change in the party, and our parliament and out into the country. And one year later, I don't care if the government has improved the way that they talk about these issues. I'm not interested in words anymore. I want to see action.
Grace Tame: I received a threatening phone call from a senior member of a government funded organisation asking for my word, that I wouldn't say anything damning about the prime minister on the evening of the next Australian of the year awards. 'You're an influential person, he'll have a fear', they said. 'Fear? What kind of fear?', I asked myself: 'a fear for our nation's most vulnerable, a fear for the future of our planet?' And then I heard the words, 'you know, with an election coming soon'. And it crystallised a fear, a fear for himself and no one else, a fear that he might lose his position, or more to the point, his power.
Higgins: For all the fear, and anger and sadness that my time in politics has brought me, it didn't take away my belief in Australia, my faith in our democracy. I know our country can do better for women and girls.
Tame: You see me here standing tall, if a little bit broken, standing on the shoulders of giants. Side by side with Brittany, side by side with all of you, together, making change, making history, but above all else, making noise!

Morrison did make an apology to Higgins in parliament after she made criticisms of him at the National Press Club:

Scott Morrison: I am sorry, we are sorry. I'm sorry to Miss Higgins for the terrible things that took place here. And the place that should have been a place of safety and contribution turned out to be a nightmare.
But I'm sorry, for far more than that, for all of those who came before Miss Higgins and endured the same, but she had the

courage to stand. And so, here we are, so we are sorry for all of these things. And in doing so, each of us taking accountability for changing these things.

The leader of the opposition, Anthony Albanese provided his observations as well:

Anthony Albanese: We owe a debt of gratitude to everyone in this building, as well as every former staff member who stepped up to share their experiences of workplace bullying and misconduct of sexual harassment, and most traumatically, of sexual assault. I also acknowledge, particularly the women who bravely stood up and called out a culture of mistreatment that brought this issue into the light. And I particularly pay tribute to the courage of Brittany Higgins, who is with us today.
You have torn through a silence that has acted as the last support system for the most odious of status quos. To describe your experiences is to relive them. I say to everyone who took part: that took a level of courage that you should never have needed to show. But you did. And we thank you for it.

The speeches from Higgins and Tame at the National Press Club were powerful and ensured that the important issue of women's safety remains on the agenda in the lead up to the next federal election. Having outspoken people speaking about these important issues is the way to make sure that the powerful people that just want the issue to go away, end up doing something about it and not just offer apologies and sweep it under the carpet.

Morrison' apology to Higgins in parliament was appropriate, but it's a pity that he didn't apologise for the Liberal Party covering up the incident of alleged rape in April 2019, just a few days before the 2019 federal election was announced. It's also a pity Morrison didn't apologise for the slow movement on these issues. Morrison delayed the release of a report by the sex discrimination commissioner for over a year; he was slow to acknowledge there are serious gender balance issues, sexual harassment and abuse that takes place in parliament and within the Liberal Party. Morrison also barred Coalition members from attending the National Press Club address by Higgins and Tame. His apology was more about being seen to be dealing with a political problem in the lead up to an election campaign, rather than dealing with the issues, so typical of Morrison as prime minister: make an announcement or make the appearance of doing something about the issue, but offer no action to address the issue.

And this also highlights the main concern for the Liberal Party in its re-election chances—there is a veneer of action, but not the action itself. In the case of Higgins, there was no attempt to find the perpetrator or discover what happened in April 2019: there was a cover up. There's been little attempt to introduce sweeping reforms into parliamentary behaviour, or at least make Australian parliament house a safer workplace for women and allow that to become a model for other workplaces across Australia. It was a missed opportunity.

BURNT BY THE SPECTRE OF VICTORY

There have been many suggestions that because the Labor Party was in a similar position electorally in the lead up to the 2019 federal election compared to where they are now, and, because they ended up losing the last election, there's a strong chance they could also lose the 2022 election. irrespective of how well they're positioned now.

Of course, that may end up being the case, but confirmation of this theory won't occur until the night of the election. Comparing opinion polling from mid-November in 2018, with mid-November in 2021, the figures are the same, with Labor leading the Coalition in two-party preferred vote at 53 per cent to 47 per cent. After mid-November 2018, opinion polls started to move towards the Coalition, narrowed dramatically in the final weeks before the election, and the Coalition ended up winning the election in May 2019.

However, there is a difference this time: since November 2021, opinion polls have started moving away from the Coalition and towards the Labor Party. There's still an understanding that this will be a difficult election for Labor to win—as is every election—and many factors still need to fall into place for Anthony Albanese to be able to give a victory speech on election night.

Australia, generally, has a good and fair system of voting through preferential voting, and delivers the general will of the electorate. Britain has a first-past-the-post system, which works well if there are only two candidates in a seat, but when there are many candidates, it means that a large proportion of voting intention is excluded. It's not a perfect system—no system is—but Australia's preferential voting system provides for a fairer and more democratic system. However, there are still ways for the system to be 'gamed' by Astroturf parties, or political parties such as One Nation, or United Australia Party—generally right-wing parties—who act as preference harvesters for the Liberal and National parties. And this is where elections can be influenced or affected, which did occur in the 2019 federal election, although there were many other factors that also contributed to the Morrison government's victory, rather than minor party preferencing; if anything, the preferences directed towards the Labor Party from the Australian Greens are far more influential in election results.

And while these factors are still in play, the election outcome for 2022 is still difficult to predict, irrespective of what the opinion polls are suggesting—it's the main reason why Labor insiders are still skeptical of their chances, and why Liberal insiders are still confident of a last-minute turnaround: they've done it so many times in the past—1998, 2001, 2004, 2019—so why wouldn't it happen again in 2022?

Labor needs to win seven seats to form government at the 2022 election but, mathematically, there are many factors that come into play, which suggests a more difficult task than it appears on paper. There's a band of four ultra-marginal seats held by the Coalition, with a margin of less than 1.5 per cent in two-party preferred terms. One of those seats—Wentworth—if it does fall, would fall to the independent Voices Of candidate, Allegra Spender.

After this band of ultra-marginal seats, there are five others in the 3-to-4 per cent margin and a swing of 3.7 per cent to the Labor Party on election day would give it a two-party preferred vote of 52.3 per cent, and that level of vote is usually a landslide victory in Australian elections. But if this swing was uniform across Australia, it would only give Labor 78 seats—which is still a victory, but only a narrow victory, and it's also possible that the Labor Party could receive 52.3 per cent of the two-party preferred vote and not win the election. That's never happened before—the highest level of the two-party preferred vote without winning the election was Kim Beazley's Labor Party in the 1998 federal election, when they received 50.98 per cent. In state politics, the Liberal Party obtained 53.0 per cent of the two-party preferred vote at the South Australia election in 2014 yet failed to win enough seats to form government.

Of course, this analysis is moot if there is a bigger swing against the Coalition government—there are six seats in the 4-to-5 per cent band, and then a further six seats in the 5-to-6 per cent band—and a larger swing, albeit unlikely, means this speculation becomes irrelevant. But the deeper analysis of these seats provides a better understanding for why there is a reluctance by many media commentators to be confident of a

Labor victory, and also helps to explain why they're suggesting a Coalition victory is still the more likely result.

While the 2019 opinion polls were disastrously wrong, it's not a case where they are deliberately wrong—it's not a good business model for opinion polling and behavioural research companies to be wrong with their data, and they've put in a greater amount of research and development into correcting their modeling and methodology for the 2022 election.

What is not widely understood about opinion polling companies is that while political polling is their most identifiable work, it's only a small component, and most of their work involves consumer behaviour and sentiment for commercial products. However, being wrong with their political polling suggests there's something wrong with their commercial consumer testing, and manufacturers and providers of goods and services are less likely to use these research companies if their methodology is shown to be wrong.

Aside from opinion polling, it also must be considered that every election is a series of smaller elections in different states, and in different regions—in the 2022 election, there will be 151 individual elections. Although there are national issues that will affect every single seat, sometimes it's not possible to predict regional differences or specific events that cause unusual swings and results.

Sometimes, a strong incumbent in a seat might be able to withstand a national swing against their party, and it could also be because a government or opposition has promised a certain benefit: a new hospital or a new road, renovations to parks or sporting facilities, or some other salient issue which could be enough to tip the vote from one party to the other.

This is the role the independent candidates will play at the next election: Dave Sharma in the seat of Wentworth will have difficulties holding onto the seat for the Liberal Party. In the seat of Kooyong, the treasurer Josh Frydenberg is also under pressure from the independent candidate, Monique Ryan. Morrison is likely to suffer a swing against him, although there's little chance of him losing the seat of Cook. There is a swathe of Liberal-held seats in the northern Sydney area that is also under pressure. It's a difficult election to predict—whenever it is to be held—although there is feeling of a change in the air.

While the election is yet to be called, it feels that the campaigns for all parties have already commenced. There are still many areas that need to be prepared by the parties but, based on their behaviour and the regions they are travelling to, it's possible to see where they will direct their resources. Labor is heavily targeting four seats in Queensland, four seats in New South Wales, two in northern Tasmania, one in South Australia, and three in Western Australia. And if it wins those seats and it holds all the seats it currently has in parliament, there's their election victory and it doesn't really matter what the swings are in all the other seats. But the difficulty for the Labor Party—and this is an issue in every election—is that the Liberal Party will also be focusing on those same seats and sandbagging them as much as possible, to ensure they don't slip away.

Sometimes in elections, the final result might end up the same as the previous election but with a different configuration of seats, which was the case in the 2019 federal election, which replicated the numerical results from the 2016 election, with seats won and lost for both sides.

The economy will be a key feature of the next campaign—as it usually is—as well as health and education. The coronavirus pandemic is an unusual factor in this campaign, because the management of this one-in-a-hundred-years' event will be an issue, although it's unclear how the electorate will respond.

Perhaps it's an indication of why Morrison is keen to focus upon the future, because the past three years of this parliamentary term do not look very good for him. It also explains why he uses analogies such as "we're not looking at the rear vision mirror", while using a marketing stunt of driving a racing car at Mount Panorama to highlight this. To extend this analogy, drivers not looking at the rear vision mirror are lacking in a general awareness of their driving conditions: to assess whatever may be ahead on the road, the view behind needs to be assessed as well. This is symbolic of the Morrison government: a lack of overall awareness and responding to issues when it's far too late. And it's also symbolic of the main battle during the next federal election: Morrison wanting to look forward into the future so electorate will forget about the past, and Albanese focusing on the government's record as a reminder of what that future might look like, if the Morrison government is re-elected.

One critical aspect of elections is that it's easier to win an election with a united team—it's still possible to lose an election with a united team, but it's usually the team in disarray that loses. The side that was in disarray—the Liberal Party—didn't lose the election in 2019, despite all the personal enmities and divisions that existed. Usually, a winning election can make those divisions dissipate but, in this case, the divisions seemed to have exacerbated these ideological and personal differences.

There are other bad-faith actors, such as the Liberal–National Party's George Christensen in the seat of Dawson—retiring from politics at the next election—who is fueling the fires within the anti-vaccination communities, as well as pushing his pro-mining and climate change denial agenda. It's primarily an attempt to undermine every aspect of science, just for the sake courting extremists in the election and hoping to get their vote. It's hoped that there will be enough time before the election to focus on these players and send a strong message that these behaviours—which go way beyond the point of ideological preferences and opinions—are not conducive to a normal and functioning democracy.

***

CHASING THE APRIL SUN IN CUBA

17 February 2022

The talk of the town has been ukuleles, *60 Minutes* and trying to find the April sun in Cuba. This week, there was a continuation of the classic distraction from the Morrison government and the strategy of deflecting from the important issues of the day. Politicians will always try and humanise themselves and present themselves in the best way possible, and in the lead up to an election campaign, what better way for the prime minister to present themselves to a national audience than doing a little sing song with his wife Jenny and two children at Kirribilli House, forgetting the words of a song—'April Sun in Cuba'—and playing the wrong chords on a ukulele.

> Scott Morrison (singing): *Take me to the April sun in Cu-ba, oh ho ho... take me to the April sun in Cu– ...* I can't remember the words ... *oh oh oh...*
> Karl Stefanovic (motioning to Jenny Morrison): Come on Jen, get into it! Ha ha ha ha ha ha ha harr!

There was speculation that Scott Morrison was going to announce the election date on Sunday afternoon and have the soft interview on Nine Media's *60 Minutes* on Sunday night to kickstart the election campaign but, it didn't turn out that way.

Politicians crave a media spotlight but sometimes the concept of 'less is more' is more useful, and Morrison became the focus of attention for all the wrong reasons. The public doesn't need to know too much about the private lives of politicians, and it should primarily be on a 'need-to-know' basis—the names of their spouses and children, only so the public can see if any family members are receiving undue benefits by virtue of being related to the prime minister. But that should be where it ends.

The role of prime minister's partner has been an interesting one in Australia—for the first thirty years or so after federation in 1901, the spouse of the prime minister was a relatively unknown figure, and it wasn't until Dame Enid Lyons—wife of Joe Lyons—who also went on to become the first woman elected to the House of Representatives and the first woman to enter the ministry, that a prime minister's spouse became recognisable within the public and political sphere.

Since the time of Enid Lyons, the exact role of the spouse of the prime minister has been unclear. In the United States, there is the title of 'first lady', although the position is not codified or officially defined, but in Australia, there isn't a clear definition, so it's up to the incumbent to define the role. Morrison is very good at wheeling out 'Jen©™' whenever he's in political trouble, but Jenny Morrison isn't the political fix he requires, and nor should she.

She has been used as a political shield by Morrison, as have his two daughters, and using them as a cover to let the public know that he really does 'understand women', especially in the context of all the issues that have been surrounding parliament over the past year. Morrison couldn't articulate the correct sentiment surrounding the allegations of rape that occurred in parliament house in 2019, so he inserted 'Jenny and the girls' into the political narrative, by asking "what would she do", and then reporting this information to the media.

There will always be a public curiosity about the family of the prime minister, but it would best for them to keep away from the public eye—they are not the ones who appear on the ballot paper on election day and are not the ones who are elected by the public. But if a prime minister decides to insert their family into the political framework and allow them to be used as their 'secret weapon', then whatever scrutiny follows—fairly or unfairly—has to be expected.

Anyone who makes public commentary—irrespective of who they are—can and should be held to account, but that doesn't mean they should be subjected to personal abuse, although that is one risk that occurs when politicians parade their families in public.

Former prime minister Tony Abbott faced criticism in the 2013 federal election, when he suggested the electorate should vote for him, because he was "the guy with the not bad-looking daughters". What does this mean? His opponent at that election, Kevin Rudd, also has a daughter. Was it a peculiar *Handmaid's Tale* or *Penthouse*-style ranking? Did it mean Rudd's daughters, were not as 'good looking' as Abbott's daughters? And should a father be commenting on his daughter's appearances anyway? Morrison has faced a similar level of criticism for using his daughters in a similar way, albeit not in the crass manner used by Abbott, but there is a fine line that must be navigated between the personal aspects of a politician and the political.

Morrison's issues were not only limited to the use of family members: his musical skills were also brought into question, when he unsuccessfully strummed the chords to 'April Sun in Cuba' on the ukulele. It's not often that politicians are shown playing musical instruments, and Morrison's performance was a reminder of another politician's performance all the way back in 1992, when United States presidential aspirant Bill Clinton played the saxophone in a live television performance:

> Arsenio Hall (addressing Bill Clinton after performing a rendition of 'Heartbreak Hotel'): Did you ever think about playing professionally?
> Clinton: Yeah, and I liked it tonight, I like being on the other side of the posse. You know what your drummer said? He said if this music thing doesn't work out, you can always run for president.
> Hall: You twist Chuck!

Clinton's performance was one of the key moments in the 1992 presidential campaign. He was trailing in the polls against the incumbent president George H. Bush but managed to turn the polls around and won the election. The difference is that Clinton can play the saxophone and Morrison cannot play the ukulele, or even remember the words to the 'April Sun in Cuba'.

It's difficult to know what Morrison and his minders were thinking—and it was hard to know how this could benefit him politically. It's not a big deal to not know how to play a musical instrument, or forget the words to a popular song, but it reinforced the big issue that seemed to be reflective of Morrison's term as prime minister: competence.

However, there were other political motivations at play. The appearance on *60 Minutes* kept Morrison in the spotlight, and if the focus was on whether he can play the ukulele or not, and whether he can remember the lyrics to a song, that was surely going to distract from all the other important issues which were detrimental to Morrison's political stocks: the poor management of the pandemic; issues in the aged care sector; his 'women problem', and his collapse in opinion polls.

And the other important way that such a family appearance works politically is that it gave Morrison's enemies an opportunity to attack him and his family, which would then activate Morrison's supporters either within the Liberal Party, or within the media, to engage in 'sympathy trolling' and 'outrage journalism'. The subtext in these circumstances was: 'how dare *they* attack Scott Morrison for just being a family man' or 'how dare *they* attack Jenny Morrison for being a supportive wife', which was then weaponised against Morrison's opponents.

In media strategy terms, it also offers an insight into why family photographs were published in 2019 with Morrison's left foot Photoshopped in the wrong position. It's also the reason for the release of photographs Morrison breaking protocol, alighting from a RAAF plane and walking onto the red carpet at Williamstown in Newcastle. Or the photograph of Morrison holding up a barramundi at the Lodge. Morrison's opponents get outraged, and the image—and the issue—is magnified. It occupies the time and energy of his opponents, as well as getting the free publicity. It becomes a discussion point, people who dislike Morrison get outraged by it.

Then Morrison supporters start attacking people on 'the left' and start claiming that they're being obsessed with the insignificant issues. This is a clear tactic borrowed from other populists, a relatively new tactic in conservative politics: it was a tactic used by Boris Johnson in Britain; it was the tactic used by Donald Trump in the United States. But ultimately, it's an ineffective tactic. Johnson is floundering as the British prime minister (and subsequently resigned); Trump was ousted in the 2020 United States presidential election. Morrison seems to be heading towards a similar outcome, but instead of resorting to media stunts and gimmicks, perhaps it would be wiser to just do the job of the leader.

However, the performative aspects of politics seem to be here to stay, although if a leader is prepared to go down this path, it's important to do it well and effectively: Morrison didn't. 'April Sun in Cuba' is a well-known song for a particular demographic, performed by the Australia–New Zealand band, Dragon, in the late 1970s, but Morrison botched it badly. He also performed the song with a ukulele, a reminder of his holiday to Hawaii during the bushfire season in December 2019, when half of Australia was facing a fire emergency. The song itself is a lament about wanting to be somewhere else—while most people wouldn't have picked up this reference, it was a poor choice by Morrison: *I'm tired of the city life, summer's on the run*. Of all the songs to choose, Morrison chooses 'April Sun in Cuba'. Of all the instruments to choose, Morrison chooses *a ukulele*. Of course, it was unlikely for Morrison to choose a Midnight Oil song, or strum a death metal guitar, but surely there could have been different choices made.

There were also other criticisms of the *60 Minutes* episode: it aired on Nine Media, a network sympathetic to Liberal Party interests, and chaired by the former treasurer and Liberal Party member, Peter Costello. Of course, there is a symbiotic relationship between mainstream media owners and the Liberal Party—most notably, Kerry Stokes and Rupert Murdoch—and it's obvious that a puff-piece promotion of Morrison and his family, especially in an era of infotainment, was going to appear on their networks under the guise of serious analysis.

Labor prime ministers are rarely afforded these opportunities: Kevin Rudd, Julia Gillard, and Paul Keating—the last three Labor prime ministers—were endlessly attacked by the media closer to their respective election campaigns. Albanese is rarely afforded the same coverage as Morrison. It was predictable for Morrison to be inserted in an episode of *60 Minutes*, in the same way other prime ministers have done so in mainstream media and popular culture: Malcolm Fraser appeared in an episode of the ABC's *Countdown* in 1979. Bob Hawke made an appearance on *A Country Practice* in 1986. Morrison's understanding of Jean Baudrillard and Jacques Derrida might not be deep, but perhaps he understands more about cultural theory and post-modernism than he is given credit for.

It wasn't so long ago that another cultural theorist, Marshall McLuhan, suggested 'the medium is the message', and it's becoming more apparent within contemporary politics that this is certainly the case. Former prime minister John Howard refused to appear on the youth television program *Rove Live!* arguing that there were not many votes to be gained—possibly correct—whereas his opponent in 2007, Kevin Rudd, appeared and received an electoral boost within a key demographic.

The 'medium is the message', but it can't just be the only message, and the only act of the leader. Media engagement and stunts are the fun and games of politics, and they're mostly a part of an irrelevant sideshow: however, it's the area that mostly engages the electorate, and the main reason political leaders adopt these tactics. But it's also a sign of desperation, and desperate governments engage in these tactics to deflect from other issues.

Morrison and the minister for defence, Peter Dutton, have been ramping up the anti-China sentiment recently and for a relationship with a two-way trade value of over $100 billion each year, this was not a clever move. Of course, these relationships are never just about the money, but Morrison and Dutton have been pushing the idea the Chinese government will be "barracking" for an Albanese Labor government at the next election—and why wouldn't they after all the diplomatic garbage that has been thrown at them by the Coalition government over the past three years, and the damage caused to the Australia–China relationship.

However, if the Liberal Party is going to criticise the Labor Party—who haven't been in federal office since 2013—for failures in the Australia–Chinese relationship, it's best to look at what the Liberal Party has been up to in government: they created a 99-year lease of Port of Darwin to a company owned by the Chinese government for the low fee of $5 million per year. Former Liberal Party minister, Andrew Robb, secured an ongoing consultancy with this company worth $880,000.

The Liberal Party member for Chisholm, Gladys Liu, received a secret $1 million donation from a Chinese businessman. The 'Julia Bishop Glorious Foundation' funneled hundreds of thousands of dollars from Chinese mining interests into the Western Australia branch of the Liberal Party.

To back up their claims of the Chinese government preferring a Labor victory at the next federal election, Liberal Party members Josh Frydenberg and Tim Wilson pointed to the endorsement of China's *Global Times* newspaper, which promoted Albanese as a "safe choice" and said Morrison is a "clown". This might not be a sentiment in China alone though: 55 per cent of the Australian electorate is dissatisfied with Morrison's performance as prime minister, and opinion polls have steadily registered this dissatisfaction over the past three years. But if the Liberal Party wishes to engage in this type of racist anti-China sentiment, they must be very careful because these issues will come back to bite them. Karma, when unleashed in politics, has a terrible whiplash and devastating consequences.

There are many people in the Australian community with Chinese heritage—5.5 per cent of the entire population, and 10.6 per cent and 8.3 per cent in the larger cities of Sydney and Melbourne, respectively—and it's probable that these heavy-handed attacks on China will have a significant electoral effect in those seats with a high proportion of the Chinese community: Reid and Bennelong in New South Wales; Chisholm and Kooyong in Victoria. Those seats provide ample opportunity for the Labor Party to attack this issue head-on in the election campaign, in addition to the growing list of other material they can already use against the Morrison government.

The Liberal Party—like all political parties—is opportunistic but takes this to extreme levels when it comes to race-based politics: they'll use the Chinese community when it suits them; but then attack the Chinese community when they can gain political points. In the 2019 federal election, they displayed 'Vote 1 Liberal' signs in Mandarin that replicated the colours and fonts from official Australian Election Commission signage. On one hand, they accept illicit donations from key figures with close contacts to the Chinese government but, on the other, they'll attack the Chinese government to curry favour from racists and right-wing elements in the Australian electorate.

It is very dangerous for a senior minister such as Dutton, to start spreading anti-Chinese rhetoric. Australia would never want to enter a war with China, despite this ill-informed rhetoric, but even if it came to this, Australia would be seriously overwhelmed and underprepared. Just recently, Australia sent a warship to Tonga in the Pacific Ocean, to assist with their recent *tsunami* event—the warship broke down, and needed assistance from the Tongan navy, and then spread the coronavirus to the island nation, triggering a five-day lockdown. If Australia couldn't manage a smaller peacetime event with a friendly neighbour, how effectively could it deal with a military conflict with China?

It's a very dangerous line for Dutton to walk upon, and if he has ambitions to be a future prime minister, or the leader of the Liberal Party, it would be wiser for him to think past the ambitions of winning a federal election and think about the broader international consequences.

It's an unlikely scenario, but Morrison and Dutton would dearly like to see Australian tanks rolling onto the streets of Beijing at some point before the election, and they're clearly attempting to link every negative connotation about China back to the Labor Party. While China has been the focus of their attacks, they've strayed into other areas: Morrison accused Senator Kristina Keneally of supporting violent abusers and rapists and also said Albanese is "clearly on the side of criminals". This is in the context of the government security and immigration character test rules, and it's a style of rhetoric which is the basic 'bread and butter' issue for conservative politicians, not just in Australia, but all over the world. It's essentially a tactic used to cover over their incompetence, mismanagement and corruption: they play the race card, they wheel out national security, they wheel out immigration, and the basic fear of 'others'. But the tactic has limitations: while it might appeal to certain parts of the electorate, it repels others.

The anti-Chinese rhetoric in Australian politics is not new: it has been seen here since European invasion and settlement in 1788. It was ramped up in the 1830s, in the 1850s, and continued through the twentieth century. If China wanted to invade Australia, it would have done it long before now: the early 1950s was possibly the most propitious time. Other opportunities were presented in 1989, when prime minister Bob Hawke—bravely—granted asylum to Chinese students living in Australia who didn't want to return after the Tiananmen Square massacre.

Australia is not large enough within geopolitics for China to be worried about, and the existence of the Australia–China relationship has been highly beneficial to both countries. Chinese immigration has improved Australian culturally, economically, socially and politically, and despite suffering some of the most hideous racism—casual, subtle and not-so-subtle—the Chinese community thrives in Australia, with some members existing as fifth or sixth generation Australian. The Coalition is drawing on some dark periods of Australia's history to win the next federal election. It does so at its own peril.

A SIGN OF THINGS TO COME

There were four by-elections over the weekend in New South Wales, and while there are clear distinctions between federal and state politics, all sides of politics were viewing the results to assess what lessons there could be for the federal election. There was a major swing of 11.9 per cent against the Liberal Party in the seat of Bega on the south coast of New South Wales, resulting in the loss of the seat for the Liberal Party, and a lesser swing of 6.4 per cent in the neighbouring seat of Monaro. These two state seats overlap the federal seats of Eden–Monaro and Gilmore but, as these seats are already held by the Labor, a swing of a similar magnitude won't be beneficial for the Labor Party.

A bigger issue for the Liberal Party is the 20.4 per cent swing which occurred in the North Shore seat of Willoughby, previously held by former Premier Gladys Berejiklian, who resigned after corruption hearings at the New South Wales Independent Commission Against Corruption. The North Shore is Liberal Party heartland, and it's the heart of affluence in Sydney. If an unknown and last-minute independent candidate—Larissa Penn—can inflict such a damaging result in a safe Liberal-held seat, what could it mean for other areas in the federal election? The seats of North Sydney, Goldstein, Kooyong, Flinders and Wentworth where Liberal members are facing strong challenges from independent candidates, have similar characteristics to Willoughby, and the result in the seat—even though it was marginally won by the Liberal Party candidate, Tim James—shows that the Liberal Party should be very concerned about their prospects there.

The result also doesn't bode well for the Liberal Party in the 2023 New South Wales election. Of course, it's always possible for a political party to turnaround their political fortunes but, for Morrison, the next few months are looking dire. The New South Wales Liberal Party is facing many problems: an ultra-safe seat in its heartland region has been pushed to a marginal position. There are factional problems between the hard right and the moderates. And it's not an issue restricted to New South

Wales; there are also factional problems in the Victoria and South Australia branches of the Liberal Party, which have been infiltrated by hardline conservative Christian and Pentecostal evangelists. It's not quite the recipe for electoral success.

Willoughby was previously held by a large margin of 21.0 per cent, and that's been reduced to 3.3 per cent. The seats of North Sydney, Goldstein, Kooyong, Flinders, Wentworth are held by reasonably safe margins, but far less that the 21.0 per cent margin that existed in Willoughby. Even if half of that swing is achieved at the next federal election in those seats, that will be enough for the Coalition government to lose its majority in parliament.

The state seat of Bega was won by the Labor Party for the first time, further proof that the Liberal Party brand is on the nose, at least in New South Wales. The seat of Bega was at the centre of the bushfire affected areas in December 2019 and is still in recovery mode over two years later, and there were residual feelings that the area had been neglected, especially from the federal government.

While it's difficult to compare different elections in different jurisdictions, aside from the 2021 Tasmania election victory, electoral outcomes have not been favourable for the Liberal Party ever since Morrison won the federal election in May 2019: a by-election loss in Eden–Monaro in July 2020; a swing of 3.3 per cent in the Groom by-election in November 2020; a 4.1 per cent swing in the Queensland 2020 state election; a massive 14.1 per cent swing in the Western Australia state election, where the party was reduced to two seats in a 59-seat parliament; and large swings against the party in these recent New South Wales by-elections.

The next set of elections will be held in South Australia on 19 March, yet another litmus test for the federal Liberal Party. On the surface, the Marshall government appears to have handled the pandemic well, but it has also been caught with a series of scandals, several ministers are facing the anti-corruption commission, and there are hospital management issues, with ambulance 'ramping'—where patients are triaged and treated in the back of an ambulance in hospital carparks—one of the key concerns for the South Australian electorate. It is a first-term Liberal Party government, but there is opinion polling to suggest that it could be in some trouble. There is a consensus that the coronavirus pandemic has been favouring incumbent governments—a belief that the electorate is reluctant to change a government during a crisis—but as the electorate tires of the pandemic, they are returning to those key issues of competence in government, and this could create trouble for both the Marshall and Morrison governments, possibly becoming the first governments to be removed from office during this pandemic.

Of course, South Australia and New South Wales are different states, with different political concerns. But because there is spate of elections occurring within a short period of time—February and March, followed by a federal election due before the end of May—it's possible to pick up on the national mood and what this will mean for Morrison's electoral prospects. The most realistic result for the Labor leader in South Australia, Peter Malinauskas, is to achieve a minority government, with the seats required to form government hovering in the 6-to-7 per cent margin. It is possible, but unlikely. Whatever the result is in South Australia, there are not enough federal seats in this state to make a difference at the federal election—ten seats from a total of 151—but it should provide for clearer understandings of what could occur in the federal election: if South Australia Labor can secure an unlikely victory in the state election, it will be another signal pointing to the end of the Morrison government. There is only one federal seat that is likely to change at the federal election—Boothby—but it means one less seat Labor needs to gain in other states, if it is to win the election.

Conversely, Morrison's main hope will be that most of the voter anger directed towards his government will be tapered by the New South Wales by-elections and the South Australia general election and dissipate by the time of the federal election. Sometimes, savage by-election swings can satisfy the hunger of the electorate to inflict pain on a government but, sometimes, it can create an appetite for further electoral carnage. Of course, Morrison will be hoping to avoid the latter, but it appears increasingly unlikely that he'll be able to do this.

***

MORRISON'S WAR AGAINST EVERYTHING

26 February 2022

The Coalition government has decided that the upcoming election campaign might best be won through the fog of war, and it's ramping up all the rhetoric on China. *China!* And they're trying to magnify the conflict between Russia and Ukraine as an issue that is highly relevant to Australia's geopolitical interest and make it seem like Australia is *actually* at war. Every key point of difference between Australia and China will also be magnified over the next couple of months as prime minister Scott Morrison tries to focus upon national security issues and portray leader of the opposition, Anthony Albanese, as weak on border protection, and not being able to guard Australia's national interest.

There was a maritime incident during the week when a Chinese military vessel shone a laser beam at an Australian Defence Force aircraft—the full details were not apparent, although this didn't stop the media from depicting this as a major incident. And, of course, Morrison was also quick to claim that this was a major incident with China and provided a platform to explain to the public why only someone like him could protect Australia from the Communist Party of China—even though he damaged the perceptions of his competence by almost burning his eyes out during the week while using an arc welder in yet another publicity stunt in the Northern Territory.

There was so much material to unpack in this incident: a fear of foreign aggression; the fear of China. There was also some anecdotal information from people of Asian backgrounds starting to get worried that Australia was heading back to its racist ways of the past, where people were being stigmatised and called out for being different to mainstream Australia. Of course, the Chinese government should be held to account, and criticised when its behaviour doesn't meet the standards expected of the international community, regarding human rights abuses, corruption and authoritarian behaviour. But it's an extreme behaviour for the Liberal Party to use race to try and force an election victory: this was a key characteristic of election campaigns throughout the early parts of Australia's history, but in modern Australia, this is a destructive path for the Liberal Party to take. Alongside the damage their actions could cause to Australia's social fabric, there's also a strong chance it will severely damage the Australia–China trade relationship, and that's a damage that could take decades to repair.

The Australia–China relationship has taken a battering over the previous eighteen months, where Morrison and Peter Dutton have attacked the Chinese government and accused them of created the COVID crisis, to which China retaliated by imposing tariffs on a range of imported Australia products. And it seemed the Coalition government wanted to damage this relationship for political gain, although it wasn't apparent that these issues were gaining too much traction within the electorate.

That didn't stop Morrison wanting to ramp up this recent maritime incident, even though the details were sketchy, and although the incident did occur in Australia's exclusive economic zone—details which the media magnified—it occurred in international waters, in which the Chinese vessel had every right to be in: these details were overlooked by the media, and by the prime minister. The incident occurred in a maritime area that was closer to Papua–New Guinea than Australia; again, details that were overlooked.

This is not to condone the actions of the Chinese military vessel, but the media ran with very scant details, and produced a one-sided narrative which suited the Coalition government. Morrison and Dutton then ramped up their attacks on the Chinese government, which of course, segued into attacks on Albanese and the Labor Party.

There is no question that an incident did occur. But anyone who raised questions about the incident—which is the job of political journalists—was labeled as a Chinese government apologist; a conspiracy theorist; or just 'a nutcase'. Others have suggested that the Australian Department of Defence would never release factually incorrect information and, as an organisation, they need to remain apolitical: a riposte to this is the 'children overboard' incident in 2001, when the minister of defence at the time, Peter Reith, claimed asylum seekers had deliberately thrown children into the sea, and provided distorted photographic material produced by the Department of Defence. That was a lie, and a fabrication. There were also the lies presented by former Prime Minister John Howard in 2003, who claimed Iraq possessed weapons of mass destruction as a pretext for a military invasion: the invasion of Iraq proceeded, but no weapons were ever found.

Looking further afield, there were also the manipulations of the British government in the lead up to the Falklands War in 1982, when Margaret Thatcher's Conservative government, behind in the polls, gave ambiguous diplomatic messaging to Argentina in their quest to reclaim the disputed *Malvinas*, which they then proceeded with. Thatcher then went on to claim this action was an invasion of British territory, went to war against Argentina and then won a general election a few months later. Governments lie: departments of defence lie as well: sometimes a simple lie; sometimes an egregious lie, but these are lies that result in wars and mass casualties. Morrison is known as a leader who is loose with the truth—lying about issues, even when he doesn't need to—and the manipulation of this incident with the Chinese vessel fits into this pattern.

While it would be ideal for government departments to never become politicised, there are certain areas that should definitely remain neutral—defence, foreign affairs, intelligence. All departments should serve the government of the day with free, fearless and frank advice, although that notion seems to be a quaint expectation from yesteryear, when the public service had more autonomy.

***

Major Bennett Marco [from The Manchurian Candidate]: *Made to commit acts too unspeakable to be cited here, by an enemy who had captured his mind and soul. He freed himself at last, and in the end, heroically and unhesitatingly gave his life to save his country.*

This maritime incident also introduced new terminology that many in the Australian electorate might not be aware of: Labor members were accused by Dutton of running as 'Manchurian candidates' on behalf of the Chinese government—a reference from *The Manchurian Candidate*, a movie starring Frank Sinatra and released in 1962. The electorate was also hearing the words 'socialism' and 'communism' for the first time in many years, and Albanese's name was linked with these ideologies, even though it was unclear what level of resonance this would have with the public: half of the electorate wasn't even born when the Cold War ended in 1989, and the Soviet Union dissolved in 1991.

What is forgotten is that one-fifth of the world's population still lives under communism—mainly in one country: China. But using these labels doesn't have the same potency as they might have had during the Cold War period, and it's also an unusual political tactic to use. Morrison using the spectre of communism to attack 'the left' and continue with his ongoing cultural war: the person most likely to succeed Morrison if he loses the next federal election, treasurer Josh Frydenberg, has publicly stated that his political and economic views are highly influenced by former British prime minister Margaret Thatcher and former United States president, Ronald Reagan.

These were the ideological wars played out almost 50 years ago, and they're irrelevant today. There are also the mixed and confusing messages about national security and the Chinese government. And it's all falling on deaf ears: the public isn't listening to these messages, and they don't consider them to be relevant to their daily lives.

There are certain players within the media, most notably, News Corporation, who are fixated in this ideological mindset. The terms 'left' and 'right' have changed so much over the years, as have the people who occupy these spaces, that the definition is almost meaningless. Some people on the traditionally demarcated 'left' also want free markets, but they want markets that are just and equitable. Former prime minister Malcolm Turnbull, a merchant banker, multimillionaire and entrepreneur, was labelled a 'socialist' by his enemies within the Liberal Party, just because he suggested people who don't earn as much money as he does, could pay a lesser amount of tax.

This is part of simpleton's mindset and a move back to the rhetoric of 'communists: *bad*; everyone on the right: *good*'. It's a dangerous rhetoric because, only a few years before the second Cold War commenced in the late 1940s, there was World War II. The earlier cold war, or 'The Red Scare', was between the 1920s and 1930s—the 1917 revolution in Russia frightened the establishment in countries such as Australia and Britain, and there was nearly a military coup in the United States led by the grandfather of George H. Bush. In Australia, there were secret armies being amassed, ready to put down any communist uprising, circa 1931 and 1932.

This is the historical context, but the main point is that this is 2022, not 1931, or the 1950s. There have been communist parties throughout Australia's history and, indeed, the Communist Party of Australia still exists today. Morrison alluded to Albanese reading articles from communist journals in the early 1990s and has described him as the "most left-wing leader since Gough Whitlam"—which in some sense is correct, but it wasn't intended as a compliment. Morrison's commentary is primarily based upon fear, an American-styled discourse lifted from the playbook of United States billionaires who are worried about having to pay more tax, or have their guns taken away. It's a rhetoric that has no place in over there, let alone in Australia.

Politics, of course, is always based on double standards—sometimes even more—but there have been a few different anomalies in the public sphere. The 2022 Winter Olympics have concluded in Beijing and, by all accounts, it was a very successful sporting event. If China is so big, bad and dangerous—which is what the federal government would like the public to believe—why were Australian athletes competing in these Winter Olympics? And if China is so big, bad and dangerous, how is it that China is Australia's largest trading partner, with $100 billion of two-way trade each year? Why doesn't Morrison call for a trade embargo on China and encourage other countries to do the same?

There also other anomalies: two major ports leased or part-leased by companies affiliated with the Chinese government—most infamously, the Port of Darwin, which was a strange strategic choice to make to a foreign power, which is likely to be a more aggressive foreign power than others; and the port of Newcastle in New South Wales, only two hours away from Sydney.

Australia, along with many other countries, does need to be wary of China and its global ambitions, but it needs to engage with their leadership constructively. Good diplomacy means that it's possible to engage with the countries where differences exist, and work towards securing common goals. There is no doubt that some people in the electorate will be swayed by the anti-China racism promoted by Morrison and Dutton. But there are many other people in Australia who will accept that the relationship with China is far more complicated than two testosterone-driven men shouting from the sidelines with their political megaphones, trying to score domestic political points and win their next election contest.

If attacking China with over-the-top rhetoric doesn't work for the Coalition, there's always the Russia–Ukraine conflict. Again, it's a complex dispute and involves a great deal of history. It's a leftover of political issues from the old Soviet Union, and the age-old issue of different groups of people living in the borders of the country they don't necessarily want to be a part of.

It's an issue related to nationalism, control of resources and economics. The conflicts between Russia and Ukraine essentially commenced as soon as the Soviet Union dissolved in 1991, initially as a cold war for most of that time, until it became a hot war in 2014, when Russia annexed the Crimea peninsula.

It's a war which seen some of the worst atrocities in Europe that have not been seen since the war in Bosnia in the early 1990s. But the upshot is that not many people in Australia understand what it's about, and most people probably wouldn't be able to point to Ukraine on a map. And that's what Morrison is hoping for—for him to make the electorate believe that it's in Australia's field of interest, even though it's not. The issues that resulted from America's 9/11 incident assisted prime minister Howard in the 2001 election, and because it was a major atrocity that occurred in New York, and to a close ally, with people culturally and linguistically like Australia, Howard was able to position it as an event that closely affected Australia.

Ukraine doesn't offer many of those domestic relationships and while many people in Australia would be shocked by these events, they'd also be questioning how the events in Ukraine relate to Australia. Of course, Australia should take an interest, and be concerned about Ukraine, but it's not in Australia's field of interests. Politicians enjoy wrapping themselves in nationalist flags during election times and surrounding themselves with the sound from the drums of war, and it wouldn't surprise as all if Morrison deployed Australian troops to Ukraine to invoke the image of 'Australia at war'. If he does do this, there might be an electoral boost from this act, but it won't be a repeat of the events from 2001.

Australia has typically fallen in line with international military requests ever since 1885, when a contingent from New South Wales and Victoria was sent to Sudan. Then another contingent from the states was sent to the Boer War in the 1890s. World War I, which includes the disaster of Gallipoli, was promoted as a victory for Australia; the horrors of the French front at Villers-Bretonneux and the Somme; through to World War II. Korea and Vietnam; Iraq in 1991 and 2003; Afghanistan, primarily wars that Australia didn't need to become involved with but still attended. This is not to disparage the bravery of individual troops, or the professionalism of the job Australians did at those times, but it is to question whether Australia should have expended so much time and resources.

Ukraine is probably another similar circumstance. There is a Ukrainian population in Australia as well as a sizable Russian population, and it would be more worthwhile to ensure that these groups are not marginalised or stigmatised, but sending troops to Ukraine? It would likely be a political ploy in a location halfway around the world that will provide Australia with very little material benefit in either the short, medium or long terms.

STRIKE ACTION

For conservative governments failing to find traction with an international conflict in Ukraine, or from overt race baiting with the Chinese government, what better way to cause division than pick a fight with an old enemy: the unions.

Both the New South Wales and federal governments are in a great deal of political trouble, and it seems they've worked out a joint plan to start attacking unions—during the week, the New South Wales government orchestrated a shutdown of the Sydney train system.

The Rail, Tram and Bus Union and the government have been in a protracted dispute over safety provisions, working conditions and privatisation concerns, and there has been rolling industrial action for several years. But this was the first time the network has been shut down and while this was instigated by the New South Wales government, it didn't stop the prime minister, Scott Morrison, attacking the unions:

> Scott Morrison: Honestly, the disrespect being shown to their fellow Sydneysiders who are going about their day, kids trying to get to school, parents trying to get their week underway, aged care workers, nurses, police officers, fire-ies, ambulance officers, or having to deal with the unions carrying on like this in the middle of the night, to cause such terrible disruption.

Morrison went on to claim that the shutdown was an example of what life would be like under a federal Labor government. Not much is going right for the Morrison government at the moment, but it seems like the prime minister is road testing different themes and lines of attacks against the Labor Party and Anthony Albanese—China, socialism, communism, national security and now, the unions—and this might end up being the end of the road testing before the federal election is announced: after unions, there's not much more he can attack.

Conservative politics is a brand that uses 'the other' and 'difference' within the community to leverage and create division: homophobia and attacking single mothers and the unemployed has reached its use-by date, so other issues need to be found. It's also a sign of desperation—the train shutdown is a Sydney-centric issue, and it has Morrison's fingerprints all over it. He was quick to draw Albanese into this issue, even calling out the name of Victoria premier, Daniel Andrews, as if he somehow had something to do with this union, even though his office of power is in a different state of Australia. The *Sydney Morning Herald*—owned by Nine Media—didn't acquit itself very well either, by running large front-page headlines that it was a strike instigated by the union and hiding the fact that it was caused by a New South Wales government lockout, and not a strike.

The New South Wales and federal governments are similar ideological beasts and thrive on division—a specific kind of conservative government that uses all the clichés in its attacking points: national security; outsiders; people that don't belong; people on welfare; pensioners; unions. And they attack all unions: nurses, teachers, train drivers, even the unions that are more sympathetic to the Liberal Party, such as the Pharmacy Guild and the Australian Medical Association.

Blaming the unions is not a new tactic; it's been used all over the world by conservative governments and sometimes even Labor governments use the tactic, such as the time when Bob Hawke attacked the Federation of Air Pilots union during the 1989 pilots' strike. The tactic was fine-tuned by the Thatcher government in the 1980s, during the miners' strikes in 1984 and 1985, and the printer's strike in 1986, orchestrated with the help of Rupert Murdoch: create chaos and then blame the unions for it. The Greiner government also used this tactic in New South

Wales against the Teachers Federation in the late 1980s, as did the Court government in Western Australia during the 1990s. There was also the Patrick dispute on the waterfronts in 1998, a manufactured crisis created by minister Peter Reith and John Howard, and then blamed on the unions.

But it seems that this time around, the public isn't buying it. They're blaming the New South Wales government for causing this shutdown and not the unions. The other issue here was the transport minister, David Elliot, said that unions were engaged in "terrorist-like activity", probably not the smartest choice of words for a minister involved in negotiating an outcome that avoids industrial action, and it seemed to be the words of a minister who was keen to promote conflict, rather than seeking a resolution. It was obvious that these actions seemed to be a test run to bring out a few clichéd political lines—a day where the Sydney public was inconvenienced by the lockdown of the train system, just so that the prime minister could see what the electoral response would be to a few anti-Labor and anti-Albanese sentiments.

These actions were also about Morrison attempting to fill in the picture for those 25 per cent of people in opinion polls who say that they are still undecided about Albanese. Morrison is happy to let these undecided voters that Albanese is a communist; a Chinese sympathiser; a socialist; that he's part of a future Labor–Greens alliance and, therefore, it follows that he's a unionist who will allow train strikes every single day of the week in Sydney, if he manages to become prime minister. Of course, no prime minister can control the events of a union in a state or territory, but it doesn't matter if what Morrison says about Albanese is true or not; it's just a question of whether enough people will believe it and, at this stage, it doesn't seem to be the case.

Morrison's credibility has diminished remarkably. Former prime minister John Howard rarely lied; he obfuscated; he was deceptive; he suggested words in a way that perhaps meant something else to what he said. But there aren't too many instances of a straight-out and provable lie. Morrison seems to be the one prime minister who lies when he doesn't have to, as though he's playing out a macabre political game where he feels the public is not worth telling the truth to. And the public is starting to see that everything he's attempted in the past three weeks has backfired: washing a woman's hair in a Coco hair salon came across as creepy and weird. A spot-welding stunt, where he almost burns his retina away. Claiming that Albanese is a dangerous communist because he read the *Tribune* or a socialist youth weekly newspaper back in 1992. And nothing has really stuck in the public mind because the rhetoric has been so overblown.

There was also the perception that Morrison has a series of political tricks up his sleeve and when he reveals them, everything will fall into place for the Coalition government, and they will be returned at the next election, as many in the mainstream media have been predicting, despite what the opinions polls are suggesting.

Of course, this may end up being the case. However, it's clear that Morrison is struggling badly, and his government's behaviour and performances are consistent with other governments in political history after they've achieved a surprise election victory—which it clearly was for the Coalition at the 2019 federal election. And there is a believe that another surprise victory will occur, even though there is no previous evidence of a government achieving two consecutive narrow victories against all expectations.

This was the result expected of former prime minister Paul Keating and for Labor at the 1996 election: they had an unexpected victory in 1993 and had been a long-term government in office for thirteen years. And the expectation was that Keating would win again—much like the expectations of

Morrison today. But that never happened for Keating. The 1993 election result was the Labor Party eking out one final victory they didn't deserve, and this showed up in their performances during that final term. The final Keating government between 1993–96 was a relatively poor government and didn't perform well. It became complacent as a 'natural government' and expected that all it had to do was turn up on election day in 1996 and it would continue its stint in office.

There are similar features between the Keating and Morrison governments: the Coalition is a tired long-term government that didn't expect to win in 2019 and eked out one extra term it didn't deserve. And its performances have been abysmal during this parliamentary term. Of course, that's not to say that Morrison can't win or won't win the next election, but electoral history does have a habit of repeating, especially when it's least expected.

There is also a pattern of electoral behaviour in Australia, where the electoral doesn't like to change a government, until it feels it's entirely necessary, and it's the reason why there hasn't been a one-term government since James Scullin's Labor government was voted out of office in 1931. Generally, a new government is provided with a second term, and this period of Coalition government has lasted three terms, even though they haven't got much to show from the past nine years. If this current term by the Morrison government was the electorate providing them with second chance, they've really squandered the opportunity.

Two areas the Morrison government was clear about at the 2019 election, have not come to fruition: the federal anti-corruption commission, which was first announced in 2018; and their Religious Discrimination Bill—the former was promised, even though it was obvious by their delay and obfuscation that they had no intention of introducing the commission; the latter was left hanging in the breeze as a promise to the hard line

Christian conservatives, but also as a mechanism to attack non-conservative politicians.

While religious discrimination legislation is hardly the sign of great government achievement, it does go to the heart of the productivity of this government. It's not a government deserving of re-election, although 'deserving' in politics is never a clear indicator of who will win an election. Labor's issue is one of complacency, an issue that affected their 2019 campaign, which they were highly expected to win. In hindsight, for all of Bill Shorten's strengths—Labor's leader in the 2019 election—he never really captured the imagination of the electorate. Albanese is a more palatable and electable candidate, but whether this will be enough to take Labor over the line is still up for debate.

***

MARCH

THE CONTINUING CRISIS IN UKRAINE

3 March 2022

The Russian invasion of Ukraine is continuing, it's one of the more serious international events in recent times, and it's difficult to know exactly what the endgame is. The federal government has committed $100 million of support to Ukraine—with the usual caveats here for the Morrison government—that's the amount that has been announced, but whether it's delivered to Kyiv or not is a different matter. But it is a start and part of the international efforts to end this conflict as soon as possible. Australia does have to do something and be seen to be doing something about the Russian invasion in Ukraine but, ultimately, all politics is local, and Australia's actions now are playing to a domestic audience, especially in the context of the upcoming federal election.

While this international support to Ukraine is to be acknowledged and congratulated, the current government has not been the most nuanced thinkers or the most competent executives of policy and diplomacy. But it is a war that has attracted the attention of most of the world and, of course, with a Ukrainian community in Australia, the government had to act in some way.

Russia is a major power; Ukraine is a middle power. There are issues that relate to membership of the North Atlantic Treaty

Organisation; there are issues related to nationalism within both Ukraine and Russia; there is a wide range of historical and geopolitical issues at play as well. It's a difficult issue for the world community, and the Ukraine–Russia war means that the world is sitting on a precipice, waiting to see if this develops into a Spanish Civil War-like situation, which then acted as a precursor to World War II.

The Morrison government has done what it likes to do best, which is: make announcements, make promises, which it may or may not keep—and to be fair, these promises may not need to be kept. Germany, for example, a country that is trying to raise its defence budget to 2 per cent of its GDP, has sent arms to Ukraine. Switzerland has closed off Russian transactions within its banking system, an unprecedented act for this country, which usually remains steadfastly neutral in international conflicts. The Russian Ruble is worth less than one cent in US currency, so the Russian economy has collapsed. Australia may not need to do anything, but the focus of this action has been to try and posit prime minister Scott Morrison and his team as a 'wartime' government, even if it isn't directly involved in the Ukraine–Russia conflict.

Australia is a key part of the international community but it's nowhere near the critical lynchpin that it thinks it is. But it had to take some action and do whatever it can, despite the limits of needing to go through existing international structures, such as the United Nations. And it's right that Australia does become involved somehow in a positive way but it's hard to avoid thinking that if a federal election wasn't coming up soon, there would have been a much lower level of government support for Ukraine.

It's important to compare the actions of the Australian government now, with the actions of the Keating government during the breakup of Yugoslavia in the early 1990s, and the conflicts which mainly occurred in the republics of Bosnia and Croatia. These were conflicts which lasted for over three years, and when considering all the different geopolitical factors, the wars in Bosnia and Croatia are similar to the Ukraine–Russia war, albeit on a smaller scale. Australia's involvement at that time was virtually non-existent, and there was a belief that these conflicts would be resolved by the major world powers and European countries through the United Nations. Australia wasn't even asked to provide peacekeeping forces and offered $10 million of assistance over five years.

The civil war and the breakup of Yugoslavia was seen as a distant conflict and most people in Australia didn't know what it was about—much like the current Ukraine–Russian conflict—and Australia did keep its distance.

Australia's response when Russia annexed Crimea in 2014 was also minimal: the Abbott government instigated several financial and travel sanctions against eleven unnamed Russian political figures and, realistically, that was probably all they could have done. But essentially, there was no promise of funding to the Ukraine government, there was no promise of the 'lethal aid' that Morrison is promising now. But at least it has given the prime minister an opportunity to talk tough:

> Scott Morrison: Today, to further increase the support we're providing to Ukraine and to the NATO, and all the members of NATO. We will be answering the call from president Zelenskyy. President Zelenskyy said: "Don't give me a ride, give me ammunition". And that's exactly what the Australian government has agreed to do. We will be committing 50 million US dollars to support both lethal and non-lethal defensive support for Ukraine. The overwhelming majority of that, that's some 70 million Australian dollars, will be in the 'lethal' category. We're talking missiles; we're talking ammunition; we're talking supporting them

in their defence of their own homeland in Ukraine. And we'll be doing that in partnership with NATO. I'm not going to go into the specifics of that, because I don't plan to give the Russian government a heads up about what's coming their way. But I can assure them, it's coming your way.

This is all very welcome, but the war in Ukraine didn't just commence last week—it commenced in 2014 in those republics of Crimea and Donbas within the Ukraine borders. And, of course, on a more serious level, this current situation is an invasion, whereas the actions preceding have been proxy wars within Ukraine supported by the Russian government: proxy wars are more difficult to define and delineate. However, it's an invasion that should have been avoidable—there have been long-standing border issues, and there is an abundance of natural resources in Ukraine that Russia would like to gain access to. But to be brutally honest about this political situation, none of this really matters to Australia. Morrison wants to be seen as a wartime leader, in the mold of Robert Menzies, or John Howard during the 9/11 disaster and the associated 'war on terror' initiated by United States president, George W. Bush. Of course, many in the electorate will 'rally around the flag' when it comes to a wartime situation, even if not many seem to be buying the idea of Morrison as wartime leader. Morrison wants this to be perceived as a wartime effort that is in Australia's interest, but it's difficult to make the war in Ukraine fit into the narrative that he wishes to weave.

The Ukraine–Russia is a conflict that could be drawn out for a long time: this is a very complex international situation and complex situations in international politics take time to resolve. But in some ways, Russia president, Vladimir Putin, has already lost this war: sanctions have been applied, the economy is collapsing. This war is costing Russia almost $US1 billion per day; there's been the loss of face for both Putin and the Russian federation as well. There has also been the loss of World Cup qualifying football games, a setback to a populist dictator who attaches great importance to sport as a tool of propaganda.

More sophisticated leaders can achieve their goals through non-military means but this type of Russian invasion is nineteenth-century imperialism and, ultimately, it's bad politics in the twenty-first century, and trying to achieve political goals using military might is a sign of foolish leadership.

There have been suggestions that Putin wants to return to the pre-1991 Soviet Union-styled structure but that is a situation that is, realistically, never going to happen. No one in the world political circles ever talks about the return of the Austro–Hungarian empire, the Ottoman empire, or Yugoslavia, and even if Putin attempts a *de facto* Soviet Union setup—an ambition he'd achieve by establishing a puppet regime in Ukraine to complement the control he already has in neighbouring Belarus—the international community won't allow it to happen. It also reveals the mindset of a leader such as Putin: he's only 69 years old, but this invasion is the action of an unstable leader. And this situation could ultimately see him deposed by a *coup d'état*, or through the start of a civil war within the Russian federation.

It's likely Putin has lost his grasp on reality as the tension has ramped up and surrounded by 'yes' men. In such a high-pressure situation, leaders need to be surrounded by wiser heads, people who can calm a crisis down, and look at broader perspectives. Russian is losing the war, not just from a moral standpoint but from a tactical standpoint, too. If the reported numbers are correct—and there is the adage that truth is the first casualty of war—the Russian military has lost more soldiers than the Ukrainians. And the lessons from the Vietnam and Afghanistan wars are that a large standard army cannot defeat a highly motivated civilian army. The United States and its allies attempted this for twelve years in Vietnam, and for over twenty years in Afghanistan, both ended badly. The Soviet Union also had this lesson with its occupation of Afghanistan as well, between 1979–89. In 2022, Putin is playing a very high-stakes games with long odds and a weakened hand.

The other issue to consider is the relationship between Putin and Rupert Murdoch—a close, albeit a fraught relationship. Putin provided many favours for Murdoch to access the lucrative Russian billboard market in the early 2000s, by facilitating the purchase of very profitable advertising companies in Russia and, in some cases, competition was *literally* killed off. The Murdoch empire was having financial problems at this time and gaining access to the Russian billboard market was considered a major coup for Murdoch. And in recent times, Fox News in the United States, owned by Murdoch's News Corporation, has pushed pro-Russia propaganda through their primetime opinion host, Tucker Carlson:

> Tucker Carlson (Fox News): Why is it disloyal to side with Russia, but loyal to side with Ukraine? They're both foreign countries that don't care anything about the United States—kind of strange. Since the day that Donald Trump became president, Democrats in Washington have told you, you have a patriotic duty to hate Vladimir Putin. It's not a suggestion; it's a mandate. Anything less than hatred for Putin is treason. Many Americans have obeyed this directive, they now dutifully hate Vladimir Putin, maybe you're one of them. Hating Putin has become the central purpose of America's foreign policy. It's the main thing that we talk about. Entire cable channels are now devoted to it. Very soon, that hatred of Vladimir Putin could bring the United States into a conflict in eastern Europe.
> Before that happens, it might be worth asking yourself, since it is getting pretty serious: 'what is this really about? Why do I hate Putin so much? Has Putin ever called me a racist, has he

threatened to get me fired for disagreeing with him? Has he shipped every middle-class job in my town to Russia? Did he manufacture a worldwide pandemic that wrecked my business and kept me indoors for two years? Is he teaching my children to embrace racial discrimination? Is he making fentanyl? Is he trying to snuff out Christianity? Does he eat dogs?'

These are fair questions, and the answer to all of them is 'no'. Vladimir Putin didn't do any of that. So why does permanent Washington hate him so much? If you've been watching the news, you know that Putin is having a border dispute with a nation called Ukraine—now, the main thing to know about Ukraine for our purposes, is that its leaders, one, sent millions of dollars to Joe Biden's family. Not surprisingly, Ukraine is now one of Biden's favourite countries. Biden has pledged to defend Ukraine's borders, even as he opens our borders to the world. That's how it works. Invading America is called 'equity', invading Ukraine is a war crime.

Carlson's sentiments are verging on treason and sedition, it's reflective of the sentiments that have also been broadcast on Russian state-controlled television stations, and it follows on from Murdoch's support for former United States president Donald Trump, who is also a supporter of Putin. It's evident that the pro-Russia material broadcast on Fox News is a payback from the time Putin assisted Murdoch in the early 2000s; Murdoch is repaying the favour twenty years later. And this also creates the situation where the man whose company owns 64 per cent of the newspaper market in Australia, as well as substantial media and television interests—and is a major supporter of the Liberal Party and the federal Coalition government in Australia—is actively campaigning and propagandising on behalf of the Russian government in a war where the Australian government is offering support to the other side.

The support for Putin from certain American interests is an extension of 'Trumpism', and continues the relationship that Trump had with Russian sources that provided funding to these political campaigns. In some cases, United States Republican Party supporters of Trump were suggesting they'd prefer to live under Putin's dictatorship in Moscow than a Democrat president in Washington, and one wonders what Republican luminaries such as Barry Goldwater, Richard Nixon or Henry Kissinger would have thought about how the Republican Party has changed.

However, Murdoch and News Corporation are clever enough to know there's not a great deal of public support for Russia, irrespective of how much effort Fox News is using to rehabilitate Putin's image, so it's a process of walking a fine line by supporting Putin through its pro-Russian theme but also recognising that presently, Ukraine president Volodymyr Zelenskyy is a very popular international figure.

Australia's reportage has been different, although there have been queries about how the Russian–Ukraine conflict will affect Australian politics in the lead-up to the next federal election, and based on recent opinion polling, it won't play a large role. The Newspoll results recorded between 23–26 February showed there is 55 per cent support for the Labor Party in two-party-preferred voting, and 45 per cent for the Coalition, a slightly worsening position for the Coalition, and this is a contrast to suggestions an overseas war would play to the Coalition's strengths on national security, although it has to pointed out that these are *perceptions*, rather than reality: all Australian national governments have been strong on national security since federation in 1901, if anything, Labor's performances may have been superior. It's a moot point, however; governments of all persuasions can't afford to be seen as 'weak' on national security, although there are the residual memories of the *MV Tampa* asylum seeker incident in the Indian Ocean in 2001, closely followed by the 9/11 disaster in the United States, which give the impression that Coalition governments are stronger on national security.

Morrison is desperate to be seen as the 'wartime leader' to partially play into this narrative, even though the Russia–Ukraine war is on the other side of the world, and not close to Australia's national interest. Politically though, it provides an opportunity to also portray the leader of the opposition, Anthony Albanese, as weak and unable to respond to an international crisis—an impossible test, as Albanese is not the national leader and not in a position where he can present his credentials in this field.

The Ukraine–Russia conflict is still in its early stages, but the sad fact is that the longer it does continue—and it is expected to be a protracted conflict—the less likely it will affect and influence the Australian public. Warfare in the televisual age is remote for populations in the Western world and audiences become immune to the death and misery they see through the media and, primarily, these audiences are glad that it's a situation that's not happening to them or their families—it's happening somewhere else in a remote part of the world and, they move on. This was exactly the case with the wars in Croatia and Bosnia—a war in another part of the world which most people in Australia couldn't comprehend, were shocked by the daily news footage but then, over time, became immune to the conflict: the shocking war footage didn't have much effect after a while.

And unless there's a major escalation of the war into other parts of Europe, the conflict is unlikely to influence the outcome of the next federal election. Of course, Morrison would be keen to commit Australian ground troops, but it's not a case where a prime minister can make a unilateral decision—there are geopolitical considerations; there are practical considerations; it has to part of a joint international action. While there might be a political advantage for Australia to provide troops to Ukraine, there is no practical or long-term advantage. Elections can focus the mind of a political leader, but they can also lead to rash decisions in that quest to win an election at any cost. Former prime minister John Howard was a more subtle political thinker on these issues and navigated that pathway between military engagement overseas and political victories during elections. But Morrison is not in the same league as Howard.

A war in Ukraine is disastrous and debilitating—for the people of Ukraine—and every measure of support should be provided to end the war, reduce the effects of this war on the local population, and ensure that it doesn't spread into other parts of Europe. But there are already too many issues going on in Australia; recovering from the effects of the pandemic, facing an economic recovery—Ukraine is an issue many Australians should be concerned about, but it's a conflict, unfortunately, that's too far away for too many people to be concerned with here.

THE CLIMATE CHANGE FLOODS

Looking at the modern history of flooding in Queensland, there were major floods in 1893 and 1974 in Brisbane, and then again in the summers of 2010 and 2011. At the time, the consensus was that these events occurred once-in-a-generation but since 2011, there have been floods in this region in 2012, 2013, 2017, 2019 and now in 2022.

These major flooding events are becoming more frequent, and the electorate is making that link between these more frequent flooding events and climate change management—or to be more precise, *mismanagement*. And this is the link the Coalition government isn't keen to make and would prefer to avoid discussions about climate change in the lead up to the next election. The government has gone so far to avoid these conversations by covering up a government report assessing high risk weather events and their effects on eastern Australia up to April 2022, and the action the government needed to take to alleviate some of these effects before that time. This report was prepared in November 2021 and presented to Cabinet but no action has been taken. Of course, governments can't stop floods and extreme events, but they can prepare when these events do occur and, based on the contents of this report, the government had months of warnings about these events and they failed to act: another dereliction of duty by this federal government.

It's an ideology consistent with the notion of 'less government', and an extension of the message that National Party member Barnaby Joyce espoused in his 2019 Christmas message of being "sick of the government being in my life", and the expectation of the individual to deal with life situations on their own. To the unemployed: *get a job*. If there are no jobs: *the unemployed are at fault*. Those with a disability: *they can sort it out themselves*. An older person with care needs: *the private market can sort that out as well*. It's an anti-government nihilism and, unfortunately, the two largest governments—federal and New South Wales—are afflicted with this ideological perspective, and the results are evident: communities have been left behind through the slow delivery of financial and practical support.

Although the media is generally reluctant to criticise Coalition governments, even their patience is starting to wear thin:

> James Wilson (Nine Media reporter): ...they can't access their stores because there's still floodwaters right in the heart of Lismore. But we're still talking about dozens and dozens, if not hundreds of businesses that we've seen this morning, in a similar predicament to this. Where do you start? How do you rebuild? I don't think these things have even crossed people's minds at the moment. But certainly, it's a long journey ahead. And as I

mentioned, what we're seeing here is just absolutely devastating at the moment. You look at this and you think "how", and you look across the road and there's petrol stations, and there's automotive stores, there's the Woolworths, there's the KMart, there's the Big W, there's literally every single store in Lismore has been impacted by floodwater in some way or another. So you have to ask yourself: "where are all these people are going to go to get their groceries for the next few months? Where are they going to go for their essential services? How can Lismore realistically survive and rebuild from this in a short period of time?" The answer is: they can't. And we haven't even really been exposed to the full picture here. From what we're seeing on the outskirts of the CBD, it's complete devastation. And something like this, the enormity of this ... it's not a thing that's going to clear up over a couple of days; we're talking about a timeline of several weeks and months just to get back up and operational. So, what that means for some 50,000 people who call Lismore home? It's a very scary picture.

The government's slow response is confusing: why allow an issue that will dominate the news cycle and create political problems for the government if it's ignored and left to fester? There were suggestions that this approach related to Morrison's Pentecostal faith—that the Pentecostal god will reward adherents of the faith and punish those who are not. It's not clear if this is the case, irrespective of how tempting it is for the anti-Morrison forces to believe this, but it's more likely that it's linked to the libertarian notion of small government and allowing corporate interests into the space that is usually occupied by government.

And these corporate interests are only following their own interests, not the national interest. When there are times of national emergencies—such as a pandemic, natural floods and bushfires—the corporate sector can't compete with the resources and financial capacities available to government. Morrison and, to a lesser extent, New South Wales premier Dominic Perrottet, are implementing less action that would normally be required to address a crisis because they share an ideology that suggests that it's not up to governments to intervene and, of course, this has led to the political problems they are having now: it's hard to see either of them winning their respective elections with a strategy such as this.

In general, climate change is a negative issue for the federal Coalition: they undid all the work the previous Labor government initiated on climate change, including repealing carbon pricing; repealing the minerals resources rent tax; abolishing the Climate Commission. Key Liberal Party members, including Greg Hunt, Christopher Pyne, Peter Dutton and Kelly O'Dwyer, celebrated on the floor of parliament when these repeals were made. The Coalition government has done very little on climate change, except for produce a series of campaign brochures, advertising campaigns and overplay their limited achievements.

But whether there is a belief about climate change within this government, or not, and despite the arguments about what is causing climate change, the effects are very real, and it's best for governments to be prepared for these situations. It's evident this government doesn't even want to be prepared: in November 2021, the Bureau of Meteorology briefed the National Cabinet—comprising the prime minister, state premiers and territory chief ministers—and outlined the high-risk weather events that were facing eastern Australia in the short-term period. There was also a presentation from Emergency Management Australia, outlining the increased chances of widespread coastal flooding, erosion, tropical cyclones and heat waves.

Of course, it can't be suggested that the effects of climate change can be acted upon within two or three months. But the national leaders present at these presentations, including Morrison,

Perrottet, and Queensland premier, Annastacia Palaszczuk are claiming that these floods are 'once-in-a-lifetime' events, and they've been completely caught by surprise, even though they were warned about the possibility of these events by the Bureau of Meteorology and Emergency Management Australia. A better national leadership could have acted upon these warnings: emergency response teams; preparing the community in those areas; contingencies for evacuation; emergency funding protocols. While a government can't do anything to stop these events, there is much that they can do to alleviate the crisis when it does occur, but the Coalition government failed to implement any meaningful action beforehand, even though they received ample warnings for the possibility of these severe floods, as well as attempting to suppress the reports which outlined those warnings.

This reluctance to act is even more bemusing when considering the quality of the Australian public service, and the emergency management resources available to them. There is a $4.8 billion fund that was allocated to the recovery program from the 2019/20 bushfires disaster, a fund that is largely unused and earning $800 million in accrued interest, three years after the event. In a further act that highlighted the dissonance of the federal government, the minister for defence, Peter Dutton, created a GoFundMe crowd-funding page with a limit of $25,000. Dutton is a senior minister within the Liberal–National Coalition, and Queensland—the location of these floods—is his home state. He should have been able to not just to lobby the government but demand and make the instructions to offer a substantial support package for his home state. Instead, he opted for the gimmick of a crowd-funding page to entice and extract funding directly from the public, a process which collected an insubstantial amount of revenue.

The minister for emergency management, Senator Bridget McKenzie, continued with these inadequate levels of support, where she offered $180 per person for relief funding—not per day, but in total. To place this amount into context, the minister's meal and travel allowance for the day that she traveled up to the region to make these announcements is $609 per day. A minister of the Crown can't be expected to stay in a local backpacker hotel, but relative to what McKenzie received to travel and make the announcement, $180 in relief funding is miniscule.

There are other areas of government waste: in addition to a $4.8 billion fund for bushfires relief that has barely been used, $1.4 billion has been paid to Canstruct—a company which donates to the Liberal Party—for managing offshore asylum seeker processing in Nauru, even though Nauru hasn't received any arrivals since 2014. A $4.8 billion fund which is sitting idle and collecting interest; $1.4 billion to a Liberal Party donor for essentially managing a political problem for the government, but very little for the people affected in floods.

These are the events when government should step in—whenever there's a national emergency or disaster, governments need to act—the community can't resolve these issues by themselves. But this is a government that wants communities to resolve these issues themselves, even if they are ill-equipped to do this: it's an extreme part of that liberalist ideology that individuals need to look after themselves and not expect any support from the government. It's also the message Morrison has been pushing in recent months about ending COVID support for the community, where he suggested that it was time for the government to "get out of people's faces" and manage their own health—a peculiar agenda that seems to combine Calvinism and prosperity theology, which doesn't appear to be the correct approach at this stage. Government should be about helping people, not avoiding them or punishing them when they face a crisis.

The experiment of neoliberalism in government has failed to support and create opportunities for communities. It's a corporatist ideology that favours large businesses such as News Corporation, Amazon and Harvey Norman, where they almost compete as a badge of honour to see who can pay the least amount of tax. It's an ideology that favours the wealth class and shows indifference to those people outside this class. McKenzie complained it would take many weeks to negotiate with state governments to implement the correct method of support but, in reality, what is there to negotiate? Emergency funding is based around assessing immediate need, implementing adequate resources and finances as soon as possible, and negotiating the finer details of subsequent or longer-term funding later.

This has created a strange juxtaposition: a federal government which wants the electorate to believe they can protect Australia from external threats such as China and Russia, and talks up these threats at every opportunity. But when it comes to local issues, whenever there's a disaster, they're slow to act and reluctant to distribute funding when it's needed. A prime minister who goes away on holidays during a disaster—flying to Hawaii for a family holiday in December 2019—or seeking photographic opportunities to present himself as the hero who rescues the community, even though this is the exact opposite of what he achieves. A government which claims to be the solution to every problem, whereas in reality, it compounds the problems by doing very little to address the problems it created in the first instance.

The Coalition government can talk up its credentials and alarm the electorate about national security and the threats posed by China and Russia—or sensationalise Albanese as a worthless leader and one soiled by reading communist manifestos when he was a student—but if the rhetoric doesn't match up to people's real-life experiences, then these political attacks will be futile. The electorate will not engage with issues that are occurring in China and Russia or be too overly concerned about Albanese's past if they can see that in a time of crisis, the government is failing to act and support people in need: international events in far-away countries are abstract; floods in local communities are real.

The events in China and Russia are real too, but only for the people living in those countries. Australians do need to be concerned about events in other parts of the world, but these are not the issues that affect their voting habits. Cost of living issues, including the price of petrol, consumer goods and groceries: stagnant wages—the energy prices that were promised to go down with privatisation, but have increased significantly instead. These are the issues that matter to the public, as well government support if there's an emergency from a flood that might have washed away a family home, a business, or the hopes and dreams of a community. And unless the Coalition government can do something to address these issues over the next few months, its election prospects will continue to be grim.

***

ON WATER MATTERS

10 March 2022

The floods are continuing to have a major impact in eastern Australia and the flows which started off in Queensland and continued through to northern New South Wales, are now hitting the streets of Sydney. And there is a belief that governments don't generally engage in any serious responses until disasters affect a major city and tend to forget about them when they occur in smaller regional areas. This was the case with the floods in Lismore, where the New South Wales and federal governments have been slow to act in providing support to people affected by this disaster, and this is contrary to the reason why governments exist—assisting people in need—both governments have ignored their responsibilities, leaving angry communities behind:

> Lismore resident: It's neighbour helping neighbour... we've got strangers turning up with hot food, tea, biscuits cakes. We don't know who these people are.
> Where's the army? Why isn't the government taking responsibility?

The events in eastern Australia are the direct costs the community is paying for the decades of inaction on climate change. There's been many authoritative reports published over the past thirty years suggesting many areas of Australia will become uninhabitable because of extreme flooding and weather events: there were the major bushfire events from 2019/20; the government has done very little since that time, and it's apparent with these major floodings, the government is making the same mistakes.

The New South Wales and the federal governments both believe in that diminished role of government, epitomised by the YouTube clip from National Party member Barnaby Joyce several years ago, where he says: "I just don't want the government any more in of my life, I'm sick of the government being in my life". And of course, the riposte to this is that it's very easy for Joyce to not have the government any more in his life—he should resign from his seat and remove himself from government, although current indications suggest the electorate will soon act to do this on his behalf.

Both governments seem to protect the interests of the wealth class and business interests, but not much more. Of course, they want government in people's life when it comes to social issues: women's health; marriage rights; the rights of LGBTQI+ communities. But when it comes to appropriating public funds to political friends and directing those funds to vested interests and corporations, they're happy to vacate the field and let those corporations do the work. Essentially, the reason why the people in those flood-affected areas of Lismore and south Queensland are being left behind is because there is an ideological commitment from these two governments to avoid these responsibilities.

The former Country Liberal Party chief minister of the Northern Territory, Shane Stone—and many people were surprised to learn he was the head of the National Resilience and Recovery Agency—revealed this ideological commitment with his first response to these floods: that people shouldn't be living in these areas and it's time for them to move away. Of course, this could be a discussion that can be held when dealing with the future of these regions but this message from an agency that is based on emergency recovery wasn't the best message to put out to a community that has lost housing and suffering from traumatic shock.

One other aspect that revealed itself again during this flooding emergency—a feature which has been prominent for the entire duration of this Morrison government—is the practice of political marketing as a replacement of government action: making the appearance of doing the work, rather than doing the work itself. In politics, if the electorate believes the government is fulfilling expectations—even if it isn't—this is the best outcome for such a government, until the word gets out that nothing is being done about a crisis.

There is also a feeling that the lack of response so far has been politically partisan. The floods primarily appeared in seats not held by the Coalition, and this lack of action appeared to be an extension of a corporatist brand approach to government: why should government offer support to the people who didn't vote for it and, likely, would never elect a Coalition member in those seats? It was a cynical approach and a practice adopted by conservative governments around the world, especially the Conservative government in Britain, where voting and the support offered by government is akin to a brand or a political company: if a voter doesn't elect a Conservative member, they won't receive any support from the Conservative government, even if there is crisis: the 2017 Grenfell Tower fire in London is a case in point—the fire occurred in a seat which had been lost by the Conservative government in the preceding election, and the support offered to this community in this crisis was minimal, because it was no longer a seat held by the government. The message is that if a voter wants any kind of support for their community, they must vote for the incumbent government, and hope their entire electorate follows that voting pattern.

Of course, governments will always offer more support to the seats that provide them with a member of parliament—that's how politics functions, but this is taking the partisanship to the next level. This was a conservative style of thinking in the lead-up to the 2019 federal election during the 'sportsrorts' affair, where 70 per cent of all funding was distributed to Coalition-held seats.

It's disgraceful politics, of course and the public doesn't appreciate this style of largesse and pork barreling, especially when it comes to emergency funding. It doesn't really matter which party an electorate has voted for, government is there to support as many people in the community as possible—that's how the process of government is meant to operate, but it appears to be a notion the Coalition doesn't quite understand.

> David Koch (Channel 7, Sunrise): Are you embarrassed that ordinary Australians are having to do so much work in this, having to get themselves to remote areas in their dinghies, wading through floodwaters to help people to take them food and to make sure they're alright?
> Peter Dutton: No Kochie, I mean, that's the Australian spirit. That's what you and I would do for our neighbours...
> Koch: ...absolutely...
> Peter Dutton: ...it's what people do in extremes...
> David Koch: ...we want the ADF to do that for us as well?
> Peter Dutton: No, I'm not embarrassed, but I'm not embarrassed by that. And the ADF is doing it and I'm just not going to cop criticism of the ADF.

The Australian Defence Force received a substantial amount of criticism for not acting quickly in the northern New South Wales floods, and the minister for defence, Peter Dutton, engaged himself in large doses of political sympathy trolling, continually suggesting he wasn't going to let people question the bravery of the ADF. But very few people were doing this; rather, they were questioning Dutton's performance as minister for not engaging the services of the ADF, but when the ADF did arrive in Lismore, it wasn't clear what they were meant to be doing and seemed to be more concerned about video recording their activities and posting choreographed photographs for Instagram:

> Lismore resident [describing the events on his street]: ...they're [the ADF] filming themselves ... look at them ...emptying out a trailer full of rubbish onto the side of the road with the rubbish ... this is what's happening, they're filming themselves, look at them! This is unbelievable... doing a good job guys! That trailer ain't gonna empty itself is it? Make sure you get it filmed!
> This is incredible ... unbelievable ... well done fellers, you're earning every penny ... look at that trailer ... save the trailers everybody!

It was also evident the government was starting to lose their supporters within the media, who had reached their limits of tolerance and criticised them over their mishandling of the floods.

> Barnaby Joyce: Speaking to Kevin Hogan [National Party member] just before this—this is a one in 3,500 year event... for his area in Lismore. So, it is beyond something that is naturally able to be planned for, this is monumental, this is diluvian...
> Channel 7 host (Natalie Barr): ...Barnaby, this whole one-in-a-hundred, one-in-a-thousand, one-in-three-thousand... sounds to most people to be BS, to be quite frank. We've heard the Bureau of Meteorology say that's not right. And we've heard that a minister in New South Wales or the minister for western Sydney saying it's actually a 1 per cent chance of it happening every year. So we've had it last year, and we've had it this year and it could

happen again... next year. So, I think we need to drop all that stuff, don't we? It can happen, so what do we do about it?
Joyce: I'm either going to listen to the member of western Sydney or listen to the local member, Kevin Hogan, who actually lives there. And I'm going to do...
Barr: ...or the Bureau of Meteorology ...we don't want to argue about it, but we just have to...
Joyce: ... get them to talk to them. And if they got another reason where they say that something that's 2.1 metres higher than the last record, the biggest record known in history, then they can explain that to you on television, 'cause I don't know what the answer to that one is.
David Koch: Yeah... we went to the experts for the answer rather than a politician...

Many people in these electorates are frustrated with the lack of action from the government on these floods and it seems the lack of action on climate change management over the many years is beginning to catch up, politically, with this government. The other issue is that media figures such as Natalie Barr or David Koch are not radical or even progressive figures. And it's when these figures—who are normally supportive of a conservative government's agenda—start to attack the Coalition for their lack of action on floods and climate change, it's clear there's a momentum against the government and a political problem which will be difficult to shift.

One of the main roles of government over the past thirty years should have been to reduce the risks from climate change and adapt to new climate change situations and, primarily because of political posturing and opportunism, these solutions haven't been adopted. As a result of these floodings, there has been some thinking within the government—and repeated by the head of the National Resilience and Recovery Agency—that these locations shouldn't be rebuilt and people need to move elsewhere. Perhaps if there had been some creative solutions implemented over the past thirty years—such as an incentives program for high-risk communities to gradually move to other regions—this could have reduced the amount of people affected by these current floods, but it's all a bit too late at this stage.

There have been many high-level reports produced over the past thirty years, indicating that many parts of Australia might become uninhabitable because of climate change, through floods, fires and higher temperatures. And it has been over 50 years since the first major international research produced by the Club of Rome on the effects of climate change was first published, so this information is not new. But there has just been so much political grandstanding and misinformation on climate change, not just in Australia, but in many parts of the world. For as long as this grandstanding and procrastination continues, it's the community and the environment that will pay, not the political leaders who have been making poor decisions over many years.

It can't be certain that simply a change of government will make a difference—Labor in opposition has indicated to the electorate that it will act on climate change if it wins government and, until that time that Labor *is* in government, it won't be possible to see if they will be any different to a Coalition government: one aspect for certain is that it surely could not be any worse. But the starting point for the role of any government is to act preemptively—based on all the knowledge and information that is already out there about climate change mitigation—so when the crisis does arrive, the impact is not as severe. The floods are symbolic of the Coalition government overtaken by events that it can't control, either politically or practically. The floodwaters will recede at some point, but so are the chances of this federal government winning at the next federal election.

If Morrison hoped the electorate would forget about the bushfires debacle of 2019/20, then surely that hope was removed when he appeared on *60 Minutes* playing—of all instruments—the ukulele, the national musical icon of Hawaii, and also the location of his family holiday at the height of bushfires. Perhaps he was signaling to his audience that, yes, he does take responsibility by taking a residual issue head on and… *playing a ukulele*. Or hope that the appalling management of the pandemic might be forgotten, as well as his low standing with women in the electorate.

There are too many issues circulating for the electorate to become afflicted with collective amnesia, especially this close to an election. There are also too many seats that can be lost in New South Wales, Victoria and Western Australia, where the memories of the mismanagement of these issues are still too raw for the electorate to simply ignore and provide Morrison with another chance at government.

THE GREAT SUBMARINE ILLUSION

The prime minister has made an announcement that the Liberal–National Coalition government intends to build a nuclear submarine base on the east coast of Australia and the usual caveats should apply—this is an announcement only and based on the experiences of Scott Morrison since he became prime minister, it's a base that is unlikely to be built.

These are the issues that need to be considered: ostensibly, this base is a part of the AUKUS arrangement that was made late last year in the wake of the cancellation of the submarines project with the French government. The eight nuclear-powered submarines under the AUKUS deal—and that's assuming that they are *actually* built—are not due to arrive until 2040 and one of the locations that Morrison has suggested—Brisbane—doesn't have the right maritime conditions to house nuclear powered submarines.

Brisbane and two other locations Morrison announced as possible locations—Newcastle and Wollongong—were not even in the top five locations suggested by the Australian Department of Defence. The multiple locations suggest yet another announcement influenced by political considerations: by not defining an exact location, Morrison has given the appearance of a facility coming to *all* of those locations. Of course, there are no surprises to learn there are key seats in all those areas Morrison announced and giving the appearance that a submarine servicing hub may appear in those locations, along with all the economic and employment opportunities that arise from this, could just keep some of the marginal seats in those areas in the Liberal Party ledger on election day.

In 2002, the United States president George W. Bush, made a declaration that Iran, North Korea and Iraq constituted the "Axis of Evil" and in his announcement, Morrison—as if to replicate Bush's words—outlined the "Arc of Autocracy", a more banal and bureaucratic epithet, but one that left many people confused: what exactly is an "Arc of Autocracy" and what does it mean?

There was also criticism of the locations of these nuclear submarine base—what if the area of the final location becomes a nuclear target? Brisbane has a population of 2.3 million people. Wollongong and Newcastle are closely located to Sydney, which has a population of 5.3 million people. While there was a debate from the respective mayors of those cities, which essentially ruled out the possibility of hosting a nuclear submarine base, most of Morrison's announcement was moot: submarines are not like a car dealer's yard on Parramatta Road; there's a long production waiting list, and the construction of the first submarine won't commence until 2030, eight years away. Governments need to prepare for future developments in military hardware submarine but warfare technology is moving more towards underwater drone and clustering technology—these massive submarines could become redundant, even before they're delivered in 2040.

Of course, many people will have different opinions about this announcement, but even supporters of the Coalition government were scathing. Greg Sheridan is foreign affairs editor for *The Australian*, and provided this analysis:

> Greg Sheridan: Talk is cheap, actions count. And what did the prime minister announce? He announced that a defence committee will look at a location for a base to take a shape over the next twenty years. So, the $10 billion for the bases to cover the next twenty years, for subs which don't exist, we haven't ordered, and god knows when we'll ever get. There is no way on god's green earth we'll get this fleet of nuclear subs in under twenty-five years. If we can spend $70 million on missiles for Ukraine, how about a couple of billion dollars for long range ground-based missiles for Australia, instead of which, the army is buying tanks and heavy armour we could never use.
>
> The nuclear subs, they exist in science fiction time. This is a kind of a *Star Trek* capability. Now, even allowing that all these things in some bizarre alternate universe makes sense, why isn't the government giving us some extra capability in the next five to ten years? And the answer is: it's doing absolutely nothing. I'm no natural enemy of the Morrison government.
>
> But I am just flabbergasted that in this big national security speech and in the hundreds of billions of dollars that Josh Frydenberg has flushed down the toilet with COVID, we've got not one new missile, not one new warship. Nothing. I just can't believe it... perhaps I'm strange, but it just strikes me as unbelievable.

To add to Sheridan's criticisms, there's no nuclear industry in Australia, aside from a small unit at Lucas Heights used to produce low-grade nuclear-based medicines, so this industry and its related infrastructure would need to be built, which wouldn't be required for at least another eighteen years. It wasn't entirely clear where the political benefit would lay for Morrison, but it appeared to be yet another announcement for the sake of making the announcement.

Morrison's announcement also provided an indication of the mindset of the Liberal Party and a belief that their prospects of winning the federal election were dire. Such a nebulous announcement which included three regions with a large swathe of marginal seats the Coalition needed to hold or take from the Labor Party, revealed a random scatter-gun strategy to try and save a few Liberal–National held seats, or hope for a miracle result that replicated the 2019 federal election victory.

The report produced by the Australian Defence Force listed the best ten locations to house nuclear submarines in Australia—but the three locations nominated by Morrison were not even in their top five recommendations. The top three locations according to the ADF are Sydney Harbour, an unlikely location because of political and strategic reasons, and two separate sites within Jervis Bay on the south coast of New South Wales. Jervis Bay already has a military presence and is one of the best harbours in the world for submarines.

But it was typical of this Morrison government to not seek an outcome in the national interest, but the best political benefit for himself and the Liberal–National Coalition, and try to win marginal seats in Queensland, the Hunter region, and the south coast of New South Wales.

It was also unusual for Morrison to make such a critical announcement without the involvement of the minister for defence, but it appears Dutton is keeping busy with other matters. During the week, there were allegations of impropriety surrounding his relationship with Brisbane-based companies SCD Remanufactured Vehicles and Boss Holding Capital—both companies are significant donors to the Liberal–National Party in Queensland. Dutton also appeared in an SCD advertisement in the lead up to the 2019 federal election, an unusual engagement for a politician.

The allegations involved Ryan Shaw, who was employed by SCD and was the Liberal–National Party candidate in the Queensland seat of Lilly, and there have been allegations of widespread cocaine usage within the company and sex parties such as those made popular in Stanley Kubrick's *Eyes Wide Shut*. While there is nothing illegal about politicians involved in sex parties—and it wasn't clear if Dutton had been involved—it must be remembered that the prayer room at Australian parliament house was used by conservative staffers and members for drug usage and sexual activity.

Shaw was shown in photographs to be snorting what appeared to be a white powder, and while the photographs only appeared in independent media outlets, it did raise questions about the types of personal contacts Dutton keeps, as well as the links between the Department of Defence, private companies and donations made to the Liberal–National Party in Queensland. There's also the relationship between Dutton and Paladin, a small company which received $532 million from the federal government for managing asylum seekers on Manus Island. The auditor–general reported that it was unclear what work Paladin performed within this contract, and did not represent "value for money". It's behaviour reminiscent of the corruption from former Queensland premier, Joh Bjelke-Petersen, during the 1970s and the 1980s, the difference in the current era is that the corruption is on public display, with nobody wanting to do anything about it, except for a few independent journalists attempting to alert the public from the sidelines. And events such as these make the arguments for a federal commission against corruption even more compelling.

The Coalition government did promise a commission against corruption in December 2018, even before this parliamentary term commenced. And in the shadows of the final days of this term, it's clear Morrison has no intention of creating such a commission, even though the enabling legislation had been prepared. It's these types of activities that Dutton appears to be involved with that could be the subject of an inquiry by a commission against corruption, but this is a moot point: such a commission doesn't presently exist.

Dutton has other immediate issues to deal with: he is facing a challenge to retain the seat of Dickson, facing a strong opponent in Labor's Ali France, but it must be remembered he also faced a strong challenge from the same candidate in 2019 but actually increased his margin to 54.6 per cent of the two-party preferred vote.

It's important to look at the role of the mainstream media here. When these allegations of drug usage were made by independent journalist Jordan Shanks-Markovina (a.k.a. Friendly Jordies), Shaw resigned as the Liberal–National Party candidate, the mainstream media announced he resigned because of mental health issues and post-traumatic stress disorder from the time he worked as a sniper in the Australian Defence Force. No reference to allegations of drug usage or corruption—usually a goldmine for media outlets—and that was the end of it, the media remained silent.

It's clear that Shanks-Markovina has influence within the political landscape, with a substantial number of subscribers to his YouTube account—over 600,000—but a small independent shoe-box-sized production outfit with a team of four, uncovered more material than the entire eco-system of the mainstream media, with its thousands of reporters, resources, finances and a bevy of Walkley Award-winning investigative journalists. Of course, this material on Dutton could have easily been explored, but the media decided not to, and failed to make a powerful politician accountable to the public.

INTERNATIONAL WOMEN'S DAY

It was International Women's Day during the week, the global day to commemorate the cultural, political and socio-economic achievements of women, work towards gender equality and eradicate violence and abuse against women. Here's what the prime minister Scott Morrison had to say about gender equity on International Women's Day in 2019:

> Scott Morrison: We're not about setting Australians against each other, trying to push some down to lift others up. That's not in our values. That is an absolutely liberal value that you don't push some people down to lift some people up, and that is true about gender equality.
> So, we want to see women rise but we don't want to see women rise only on the basis of others doing worse.

Morrison really chooses his moments: here's what he had to say on International Women's Day in 2021:

> Morrison: Today, here in many cities across our country, women and men are gathering together in rallies, both large and small, to call for change, and to act against violence directed towards women. It is good and right, that so many are able to gather here in this way, whether in our capital or elsewhere, and to do so peacefully, to express their concerns and their very genuine and real frustrations.

This is a vibrant liberal democracy. Not far from here, such marches, even now, are being met with bullets, but not here in this country.

In 2022, Morrison didn't say anything at all about International Women's Day: there was no public comment; no message on his social media channels; but, based on his past performances, it was probably best for him to say nothing at all. There are many gender-based issues within the Liberal and National parties that are lingering and it appears that they are hoping all of this will just go away. Only 21 per cent of Coalition Senators and members are women—compared to 47 per cent of Labor's—a number unlikely to change after the next election. It must be acknowledged, however, that the National Party is doing much better in achieving gender equity than its senior Coalition partner.

The Coalition has decided not to talk about gender-issues at this stage of the electoral cycle, because it will just remind the electorate about their failings in these areas.

Former Liberal Party Minister, Amanda Vanstone, raised eyebrows when she suggested women's equality will have been achieved once incompetent women started to receive promotions in politics, to which there must have been a collective silence all around Australia when she made this statement. The world has changed and in many areas of business, politics, education—all sectors, in fact—women have been shown to as competent as men, if not more, and society and culture is reflective of those changes, albeit there is still more work that needs to be done.

Vanstone, who represented South Australia as a Senator, was spruiking the credentials of the Liberal Party, not just federally, but also for the upcoming state election in South Australia on 19 March, where she suggested the incumbent Liberal Party premier, Steven Marshall, was deserving of a second term in office. However, it is likely to be a one-term government, a phenomenon which is rare in Australian politics, but has become more common in state politics over the past decade. This occurred in Victoria in 2014, after Labor defeated the Baillieu–Napthine government, and then again in 2015 in Queensland, when the Newman government was defeated by Annastacia Palaszczuk, an election which also saw premier Campbell Newman lose his seat.

There is a good chance Marshall will repeat this feat, with a strong possibility of losing the election, as well as losing his own seat in Dunstan. Current opinion polls for South Australia suggest a 5 per cent swing against the government in two-party preferred voting, and the Liberal Party has several issues they're dealing with: allegations of corruption; in-fighting; and they're currently governing in a minority position, hardly the recipe for a successful re-election campaign. This is not a good look for the prospects of successful re-election campaign for the Morrison government either.

Marshall had been beset by some bad luck but in politics, bad luck is often from your own making and that's an issue that beset the Rudd and Gillard governments federally during 2007–13. During the coronavirus pandemic, there has been a perception that governments of all persuasions have been re-elected because of their management of COVID, and a reluctance of the electorate to change a government during a crisis—the crushing victories of the Palaszczuk government in Queensland and the McGowan government in Western Australia, during 2020 and 2021, where they were able to secure election victories with increased majorities, underline these factors. The fact that the Marshall government is facing the opposite of this in the South Australia election, suggests there are many political problems with the Liberal Party brand, especially in context of the federal government's poor handling of the pandemic.

An election loss for the Marshall government will go against the key narrative pushed by the mainstream media: a reluctance of the electorate to change a government during a time of crisis. It's not a case where all an incumbent government has to do is arrive on election day and their work is done; there still has to be a level of competence and performance for the electorate to re-elect that government. It was also a narrative used to undermine the re-elections of Palaszczuk in Queensland and McGowan in Western Australia—that these were governments that were only re-elected because they happened to be in office when the pandemic arrived. But the same formula of electoral success still applies: governments are re-elected if they are competent and unified; and are usually defeated if they are incompetent and disjointed.

While the electorate was still waiting for the announcement of the federal election date, new opinion polls confirmed the information from preceding polls—that the Coalition government was going to be tipped out of office. One statistic from a recent Essential poll was that almost 50 per cent of the electorate indicated it was time to give 'someone else a go' at running government, while only 32 per cent felt the Coalition government deserved to be re-elected, a marked drop from polling completed in August 2021. If almost half of the electorate is suggesting it's time for 'someone else to have a go' only several months before an election, it's going to be very hard for the government to change those perceptions, although it must be remembered that governments can go from being highly unpopular to being popular, if the right circumstances prevail.

Former prime minister John Howard knew how to massage the election cycle to get re-elected, as did Bob Hawke. Governments tend to make the decisions they feel will be unpopular with the electorate in the early-to-mid parts of the parliamentary term, and the skew the more favourable decisions towards the end, although, quite often, they can't navigate this field perfectly, as there are always events outside of their control that arise. This Coalition government has had too many issues go wrong for it, and while many of these issues were out of its control: a pandemic, and the floods and bushfires weren't caused by the government but, as far as the electorate is concerned, it's how governments manage these issues when they do arrive that matters the most: this government has mismanaged these issues.

Prime ministers do have the ability to turn events around and address poor political news during an election cycle: Morrison had the political skill to turn events around back in 2019 and win the federal election. Howard managed to turn around poor mid-term performances into election victories in 1998, 2001 and 2004, as did Hawke on several occasions, and as Paul Keating managed in 1993. But it requires a herculean effort to do this, as well as great political skill. Morrison must announce the federal election by 18 April and hold the election before 21 May. At present, it appears Morrison is using a scatter-gun approach—like his performance in 2019—to see what influences the electorate and gains traction with the media, like a gambler throwing a dice and waiting for the right numbers to arise. These numbers are not appearing for Morrison now, and they might not ever appear.

The announcement of a nuclear submarines base seemed to underline this random approach: make the announcement and see what the reaction is within the media and the public. The war in Ukraine seemed to take on a similar process: announce, and look at the reaction, but this is also an area that's not gaining traction: research suggests that the electorate doesn't see any difference between Labor or the Coalition insofar as who would handle the Russian invasion in Ukraine in a better way. But with his various announcements on Ukraine, it was evident to see Morrison's strategy: loop the messages from a nuclear submarine base back into the war in Ukraine, but the issue didn't resonate with the public. Morrison gambled, he didn't win, so he moved onto another political table to see if his luck would change. But, just like trying to juggle several balls in the air, something eventually must fall, if not everything. The electorate is firmly focused on the floods in eastern Australia and the weather events here, and it could just be a case where the poor management of the emergency response to the floods could be the final straw for the electorate.

The events in Ukraine are important in world political affairs, and there are many terrible incidents and atrocities that are occurring there: the world needs to unite to force an end to the Russia–Ukraine conflict as soon as possible. But the Australian electorate is not going to vote according to Morrison's responses to the conflict and, try as he might to conflate his leadership with an overseas war, he probably understands this factor as well. Morrison travelled up to the flood zones of Lismore but barred the media from recording his interactions with the public, possibly because of the hostile and damaging responses that were recorded during his visits to the bushfire affected areas on the south coast of New South Wales in 2020. And for a prime minister who has nurtured and curated his profile through media appearances, this is instructive.

Election victories help to solidify the reputations of a prime minister, and so it was after the 2019 federal election victory, where many seasoned political commentators labelled Morrison as "a formidable campaigner". But election victories, especially unusual and surprising victories, can mask deficiencies in a leader. Morrison had luck on his side in 2019, but he is not a nuanced or skillful political operator; he's immature; reactive; impulsive; he's a short-term thinker and, as he has admitted himself, he's a 'transactional' politician.

His actions are rarely about the public good; it's rarely about making material improvements for the general community. What can Morrison get out of an opportunity? What does he need to trade to be able to get the advantage he's after? The electorate is starting to realise that this is who Morrison is. The soft puff-piece appearances on commercial television haven't shifted opinions; most of his public appearances and announcements have a tinge of desperation and have the sign of a leader who knows he is way behind but, doesn't know how to get in front again. It's always difficult to suggest a leader is not going to win an election, especially in the context of what occurred at the 2019 federal election, when Morrison was expected to lose, but on balance of probabilities, it's difficult to see how he can turn around another likely election loss into a victory.

***

WHO IS ANTHONY ALBANESE?

17 March 2022

In February, Scott Morrison appeared on Nine Media's flagship current affairs program, *60 Minutes*, and on Sunday night, it was Anthony Albanese's turn to appear. Albanese had nowhere near the same level of promotion that was afforded to Morrison, as if the mainstream media wanted to keep with the narrative they'd been pushing for some time: "who is Anthony Albanese". *60 Minutes* was an important and leading current affairs and political program from the time when it was first launched in 1979, but in the 2020s, it's more of an infotainment format than anything else.

Not too many people watch *60 Minutes*, but they are still the kinds of people that do need to be convinced into thinking Albanese and Labor will be safe to vote for at the next election. The host, Karl Stefanovic, didn't appear to be as enthusiastic with Albanese as his was with Morrison but, in the end, Albanese came across as a relatively innocuous leader, which is the way Labor campaign headquarters wanted to promote Albanese: a 'safe pair of hands' who wasn't going to cause trouble. The audience was perhaps grateful Albanese didn't follow on from Morrison's performances with a ukulele, but he could have boosted his image if rolled out a portable deejay system and grooved away with a Radio Birdman vinyl collection.

The people who had been calling for Labor to release more policy would have been disappointed, however, Albanese has learnt from the harsh lessons in 2019—it wasn't so much that they released too many policy details during the last federal election, but the details they released were too easily weaponised by the Liberal Party, and he wasn't prepared to make that mistake again. Albanese wasn't taking any chances and, while it was frustrating for those in the electorate who prefer to see a genuine contest of ideas, it was perhaps the best action to take, politically.

This part of the election cycle—several months away from election day—is when the people who pay little attention to politics, start to tune in. While they might only hold a casual glance at what might be happening in politics, these are the people who decide election outcomes, and these are the people Albanese needs to hold the attention of, if he is to prevail. In the *60 Minutes* episode, Albanese suggested the election would be held on 14 May—not that it would be up to him to call the election—but there are only two days left, logistically, that the election can be held—14 May, or 21 May, the last possible date.

There was also no perceptible change in opinion polls—aggregate polling suggested 55 per cent to Labor, and 45 per cent to the Liberal–National Coalition in two-party preferred voting, and Albanese and Morrison are level pegging in the preferred prime minister ranking. This latter metric is possibly the least useful statistic—the electorate doesn't directly vote for a prime minister—but on this occasion, it does suggest the narrative the mainstream keeps pushing on the relatively low-profile of Albanese and the question they keep asking—'who is Anthony Albanese'—is not an accurate reflection of the sentiment within the electorate. Either way, it's a statistic that damning for Morrison: his contender is equally preferred by the electorate, and even if Albanese is as 'unknown' as the media would like the public to think, to have an unknown figure as equal-preferred prime minister indicates just how poorly Morrison is performing.

Morrison has not had a good start to the 2022 year, although this could change once the election date is announced. The Coalition also had poor performances during the 2016 and 2019 election years, but then went on to win those elections—which underlines the erstwhile adage: a winning campaign is a good campaign, irrespective of how badly it's viewed by the pundits. Sometimes in elections, a good campaign isn't enough to win an election; conversely, a bad campaign might not be enough to lose. Morrison might be seen as a 'formidable campaigner' by media commentators but he hasn't been able to effectively manage external factors. Flood relief: he mismanaged this. The vaccines program: he mismanaged this too.

Petrol prices are pushing $2.50 per litre in capital cities and way over $3 per litre in regional areas and although a prime minister can't be held responsible for these high prices, they usually get the blame for it. Morrison could lower the fuel excise levy, something the Howard government did in the lead up to the 2001 election, but even that might be viewed cynically by the public. In 2019, the narrative pushed by the Liberal Party and the media was that the Labor leader at the time, Bill Shorten, was untrustworthy and unlikable, a sentiment that has now shifted over to Morrison. For Albanese is to be 'unknown' by the public if far preferable to being untrustworthy and unlikable.

The 'who-is-Anthony-Albanese' narrative doesn't seem to be gaining traction within the media, who also ignored the irony of this narrative: if it's true, isn't it a failure of the media to adequately present the person who is the alternative prime minister of Australia? One failed narrative within the media can always be replaced by another, and Albanese's change in personal appearance and attire over the preceding four months started to become the focus of attention.

Politicians usually change their appearances to make themselves more presentable to the public—and why wouldn't they—a politician is unlikely to be elected if they're scruffy, untidy or disheveled. John Howard trimmed his eyebrows, dyed his hair, and capped his teeth: he went on to become prime minister after this makeover. Of course, the makeover doesn't make the prime minister—it's not a case where peripheral issues automatically result in an election victory—but a potential prime minister needs to remove all the obstacles in an election campaign, and if market research suggests it's time to lose weight, wear a different set of glasses, wear a loose-fitting suit or get a haircut, only a foolish leader would ignore this information: these issues shouldn't matter, but they do. And it also puts out the subconscious message to the electorate that a leader has attention to detail and is focused on becoming prime minister.

In 1980, when Bob Hawke first entered parliament, he decided that if he wanted to become prime minister, he needed to abstain from alcohol. In a slight departure from that, Albanese has decided that if he wants to become prime minister, he needs to refrain from eating Italian cakes, lose weight and be 'match-fit' for the election campaign.

These efforts, regardless of how peripheral and inane they might be, should be commended, but that didn't stop Morrison from attacking Albanese for losing weight and sharpening up his appearances. However, it seemed that these attacks backfired and Morrison's usual supporters in the media decided these attacks had gone too far.

> Karl Stefanovic (Nine Media): Let's talk about the election—it's just weeks away. This was Scott Morrison on Sky News last night:
> Scott Morrison: I'm not pretending to be anyone else... I'm still wearing the same glasses!
> Paul Murray (Sky News): Ha ha ha ha ha ha ha ha!

Morrison: Sadly, the same suits... and I weigh about the same. And I don't mind a bit of Italian cake either. So, I'm happy in my own skin. I'm not pretending to be anyone else...

Stefanovic: All right, the prime minister clearly watching *60 Minutes* on Sunday night, Chris. You?

Chris O'Keefe (Nine Media): I think that was a bit of a low go for the prime minister. That's a bit schoolyard stuff, isn't it, pointing at someone's appearance and having a go at someone's appearance? Albo's lost fourteen kilos because he went on a health kick—good luck to him... that's called discipline... isn't that what you want from a prime minister? It's hard to lose weight—I'd love to lose fourteen kilos but losing that and the makeover—good luck to him. Are we really gonna have a crack at someone's appearance? I think it's beneath the prime minister of Australia... Scott Morrison... how about we ask what the hell is he going to do for us as Australians if we vote for him, because I still got no idea.

Stefanovic: It's certainly going to be interesting. Well, as soon as the election's called, you can see what they're going to go at—the Coalition's completely off its head.

O'Keefe: Australians won't cop that, that's bullying.

Morrison displays all the attributes of a bully, but it might be a case of not knowing any better: these are the attributes that brought him success in politics, so why change? But appearing to bully his opponent in this election campaign was too much for some in the media and wasn't a good way to present himself to the electorate. And the irony of Morrison suggesting that he wasn't "pretending to be anyone else" wasn't lost on people either: so far, Morrison has pretended to be a sheep shearer, hair beautician, racing car driver, carpenter, barre dancer, gnocchi maker, chef, court sweeper, ukulele musician, a pilot. Of course, anyone can do those things if they wish to, but these actions opened Morrison to criticisms that he's trying to be everyone else *except* prime minister; and further, he should stop pretending to be a prime minister, and let someone else do the job who's capable of doing it.

For a prime minister who is reputed to be a marketing expert, with a special skill of knowing how to connect with people, it's unusual to see how far these skills have deserted him. The Coalition will be hoping for a repeat of 2016 and 2019—especially 2019—where lacklustre campaigning was still rewarded with narrow election victories, supporting the adage that the only poll that matters is the one on election day. Morrison's tactics may work on a subconscious level, influencing voting habits at the last minute for a second consecutive election: of course, it's always possible, but it's difficult to see how this last-minute change will occur.

Morrison does have an obsessive grip on political messaging and once he locates the right message, he'll zoom in on that message and keep hammering the point. If a message isn't working, he dumps it quickly and moves on to the next message. But unlike the 2019 election campaign, Morrison as the messenger is the problem, and he is yet to find the messages that resonate with the public.

There have also been discussions behind the scenes within the Liberal Party about can be done about the so-called 'Morrison problem'. Political parties will always hypothesise about different scenarios, and one theory floating around is that Peter Dutton and Josh Frydenberg are angling to take over the leadership of the Liberal Party *before* the election—which, of course, means that one of them would become the prime minister. It also brings up the respective motivations in this situation: would it be to save their own seats from a likely defeat? Frydenberg is facing a challenge in the seat of Kooyong, from a strong independent candidate, Monique Ryan, and Dutton is facing a challenge in

Dickson, from the Labor candidate, Ali France. Would this be the primary motivation, would it be to save seats in other areas for the Liberal Party, or an unlikely rescue of the government itself?

Changing leaders is not the big risk that it once was, as was shown after Malcolm Turnbull and Morrison challenged for the Liberal Party leadership mid-term, and then went on to win the following elections in 2016 and 2019, respectively. And a leader in an election presenting themselves as the actual prime minister, has a significant advantage over their opponent, irrespective of how long they've been in office: that applies to either Dutton or Frydenberg. The Liberal Party changed their leaders, scraped across the line in those elections and that was all that mattered: winning an election, no matter how fine the margin is, or under whichever leader—in most cases—is preferable to languishing on the opposition benches.

Another issue for the Liberal Party is that Morrison changed the leadership rules in 2018, soon after he assumed the position of prime minister: a two-thirds threshold of Liberal Party members and Senators is required to mount a leadership spill, and in the unlikely event of this threshold being achieved, Morrison would ward it off by contacting the governor-general, David Hurley, and call a general election. There's also the great level of instability that this would cause, but given the regular instability created within the Coalition since their election in 2013—which still resulted in two further election victories in 2016 and 2019—it wouldn't surprise if either Dutton or Frydenberg considered these factors if they challenge for the leadership.

The chaos, mismanagement, instability and incompetence created by the Liberal Party was rewarded with election victories; surely the instability created by a further leadership change wouldn't have a negative impact on the results in the 2022 election?

Different rumours have been floating around that Dutton 'has the numbers' to roll Morrison; or Frydenberg has the numbers and, of course, they could both be true or false, and not lead to any material difference. The support a leader has from their own party fluctuates, and if either Dutton or Frydenberg had the numbers to assume the leadership, it doesn't necessarily mean that a leadership challenge will take place. A leadership challenge so close to an election would create so much mayhem and uncertainty that whoever did become the leader, would have one of the shortest reigns on record after a very likely election loss.

Frydenberg's opinion polling in the seat of Kooyong is tracking poorly, with many polls predicting a loss for him, in a seat that has been held by the Liberal Party since 1945, and other conservative parties since federation in 1901. Kooyong is not just any Liberal Party seat, it's a seat held by Robert Menzies, Andrew Peacock, John Latham, senior and important figures within the party's history. While Frydenberg has carried on with this tradition—reaching the position of treasurer is a major achievement—he's a neoliberal and from the right of the party, whereas most of the preceding members for Kooyong have been from the moderate liberal wing, including Petro Georgiou, who retired from politics in 2010. Frydenberg's positioning as a neoliberal—as well as nominating former British prime minister Margaret Thatcher and United States president Ronald Reagan as his political and economic inspirations—may work against him, especially when positioned against Ryan, who appears to be a strong and formidable independent candidate.

Dutton is a different prospect to Frydenberg, with a low electoral appeal and a 'hard-man' image that might be difficult to shake off, after years of being the face of immigration, home affairs and defence, attacking asylum seekers and appealing to the more fringe conservative elements of the electorate. But whoever ends up leading the Liberal Party into the next election—more than likely, Morrison—they will need to perform another miracle to win. To paraphrase John Howard's comment in 1989 that he would be 'Lazarus on a triple-bypass' if he was ever to return to the leadership of the Liberal Party—which he did—winning the next election for the Liberal Party, irrespective of who the leader is, would be Lazarus with a heart transplant; brain transplant; lung transplant; and rescued from a car accident, all at once. A leadership challenge is unlikely to happen, but the rumours that keep circulating within political circles shows the deep level of disarray the party is currently in.

Current opinion polling confirms this predicament. No government has ever come back from this current position in opinion polling, so close to an election date, and gone on to win the election. When governments realise the level of trouble they are in, they look for announcement opportunities or ways to change the dynamics and discussions that are occurring within the electorate. The last opportunity Morrison has to make this change is in the federal budget, which will be held on 29 March. The media tends to be more interested in the budget than the public, but it does offer the government an opportunity to springboard into other big announcements, and one big item that relates to cost of living issues—petrol excise—is likely to be trimmed. The revenue raised by the excise is currently between 44-to-47 cents per litre, and while it will be a substantial hit to budget revenue, it could be the headline issue that allows Morrison to reposition himself and the Liberal Party.

There are more useful issues that could provide relief, such as halving the fares of public transport—an initiative introduced by the New Zealand government—or even make it free, but these are state government responsibilities, not federal. It would be a slow-moving policy change, whereas Morrison is after the immediate headline announcement, and one that directly affects the hip-pocket for many families. All of this could be moot: it could even be a case where it doesn't matter which policy or budget measures he announces, it won't make a difference to the election outcomes. It's reached a case where the electorate seems to have decided, and it's not a very favourable one for Morrison or the Coalition government.

THE DEATH OF A SENATOR

Senator Kimberley Kitching died unexpectedly last week, and parliamentarians dying in office is rare in Australian politics. But the grieving hadn't even commenced when the media—and the Liberal Party—started speculating that her death was caused by Labor Party preselection issues.

Politics is a difficult business and it's difficult with all the different interest groups and stakeholders that either must be balanced or appeased: people who are unhappy with the decisions that are made, and then there's the scrutiny from the media. Kitching was only 52 when she died, and because she was relatively young, it brought up questions about whether the media and the public is too harsh on politicians.

This level of scrutiny is a part of the job of a politician, but it's best if scrutiny is based on facts and policies, rather than personalities, although sometimes these two areas are intertwined. For example, to understand the nature of the policies produced and promoted by the prime minister, Scott Morrison, it is essential to understand his personality, which is also reflective of his Pentecostal beliefs. It's not clear if Senator Kitching had underlying issues; it's unclear whether there were too many pressures placed upon her by the Labor Party, or if there were other factors involved. The anti-vaccination community came out to say that it was another example of COVID vaccinations causing a death of a person aged in their fifties, following on from the death of cricketer Shane Warne in the same week, also at the age of 52.

It was morbid the way the mainstream media tried to weave in a narrative and inuendo about the cause of Kitching's death, with a subtext that the Labor Party is so terrible that it can even kill its own parliamentarians. A similar issue arose when Labor member Greg Wilson, suicided in 2000—at that stage, the media blamed preselection issues and the Labor Party for causing grief on a good family man, even though they'd never taken any interest in him beforehand. The Liberal Party member Don Randall died from a heart attack in 2015 in similar circumstances, but no one in the media discussed the stress of the job or any looming preselection issues, and his family's privacy was respected: and that's the way that it should be. No death in politics should be politicised, but there seems to be more of a habit in the media of somehow blaming the Labor Party when these unfortunate events happen on their side.

Senator Kitching was effective in Senate estimates committees, and in her actions of holding the government to account. She was also instrumental in creating the Magnitsky legislation in Australia—the legislation to implement sanctions against individuals involved in human rights abuses and corruption, with the law coming into effective in December 2021. But it became clear why the Liberal Party wanted to focus on the relationship between the death of Senator Kitching and Labor preselection issues: they had immense internal problems and were trying to do as much as possible to distract the public from these problems.

The New South Wales branch of the Liberal Party had been dissolved, and there was an intervention by the federal Liberal Party branch and, two months before a federal election, this is an issue which deserves more scrutiny.

While this is only a temporary dissolution, Morrison and the New South Wales premier, Dominic Perrottet, are *the* Liberal Party of New South Wales. Three sitting Liberal Party members—Sussan Ley, Trent Zimmerman and Alex Hawke—were facing a revolt from Liberal Party rank-and-file members who refused to endorse them for the federal election and wanted to hold a vote by the members to preselect other candidates. Morrison wasn't so interested in Ley or Zimmerman—who was likely to lose his seat to an independent—but it was Hawke who Morrison really wanted to protect. Hawke is a close ally of Morrison's and, like Morrison, he's part of the Pentecostal cult that has afflicted the Liberal Party and this government, and it was evident that Morrison would do whatever he could to protect Hawke, even if this meant an undemocratic take-over of the Liberal Party.

This intervention into the New South Wales division of the Liberal Party was taken to the Supreme Court and in the lead-up to an election campaign, it's hardly going to make the party more appealing to the electorate, or even give their candidates—who hadn't even been preselected yet—enough time to prepare for the campaign.

Such disorganisation and potentially damaging action—two months before a federal election—should be the front page of every mainstream newspaper, and lead into every home page of a mainstream news outlet's website, but there's been a curious disinterest in the story and is indicative of a media industry keen to fault every perceivable fault within the Labor Party—real or imagined—and overlook and misgivings of the Liberal Party.

A case at the Supreme Court trying to overturn an intervention affects virtually every part of an election campaign: there's no campaign without a candidate. It affects the scheduling of production material, such as corflutes, pamphlets and advertising material, which creates awareness and recognition of a candidate within the electorate. In the unlikely event of the Supreme Court overturning the intervention, rank-and-file membership is less likely to assist a candidate if they haven't had a role in choosing them—members are the lifeblood of the party and do the hard task of putting up campaigning material and posters, handing out how-to-vote-cards at the polling booths. Without their support, winning an election campaign is difficult.

This was the big issue in New South Wales, but there were also issues developing in another state: Victoria. In the division of Deakin, the Liberal Party member, Michael Sukkar, has been displaying election signage without authorisation, as required by the Australian Electoral Commission, a requirement so people in the electorate know the origins of that signage and which political party is behind it. It's obvious to most people that a poster with Sukkar's face on it—in the colour blue—had been prepared by the Liberal Party, but rules are rules, otherwise, why have them in the first place? Complaints about this lack of authorisation were made to the Australian Electoral Commission, and they guaranteed they'll reply within five working days and refer this to the authorisations team, if necessary. But the Australian Electoral Commission is just like any other bureaucracy; it's slow to act, and nothing is likely to be done about this. And in the unlikely event that they will act, it will be far too late. This is a small loophole and a minor matter, but if nothing is done about this, it could lead to a repeat of the unauthorised and misleading election signage that was displayed by the Liberal Party during the 2019 federal election in the seats of Chisholm and Kooyong, which indicated the correct way to vote is to 'Vote 1 for the Liberal Party', using typefaces and colours to replicate official signage from the Australian Electoral Commission.

In the seat of Goldstein, the Liberal Party member, Tim Wilson, decided to go to the Victoria Supreme Court to have the election posters of the independent candidate, Zoe Daniel, removed. The Bayside Council—which covers the seat of Goldstein—has a bylaw, which stipulates that no election material can be displayed unless it's within a three-month period of an election. The latest the federal election can be held is 21 May, and the display of Daniel's posters were clearly within this three-month window, but Wilson argued to the Court that the election can be held as later September 2022—this is technically correct if Morrison decided to hold Senate and House election on separate days, but also close to impossible.

Local critics of Wilson claimed they had never seen him move so quickly: he did very little to campaign for marriage equality laws; he hasn't acted at all on climate change; nothing at all on ending corruption in politics. However, he was active on the franking credits misinformation campaign during the 2019 federal election but was considered to be one of the least effective local members of parliament ever in Australia's history—and there's been quite a few of those. And the most work he's ever been engaged with was an attempt to stop his opponent from displaying election posters: self-interested and focused on all the wrong priorities.

Wilson's actions also showed, perhaps, that as a local member, he really didn't have much to offer: given a safe seat in Goldstein in 2016, ambitious without the talent to support these ambitions and, when faced with a serious political challenge from an independent candidate, didn't really know what to do and had to resort to inane legal challenges over election posters. His time in parliament is in keeping with the style of person who receives well-paid and powerful positions they've never deserved. Before entering politics, he was appointed to the Australian Human Rights Commission, even though he had previously called for the abolition of the organisation. In 2011, he also suggested water cannons should have been used to disperse Occupy protesters in Melbourne, even though he's a libertarian who believes in free speech.

Sukkar and Wilson seem to be reflective of the difficulties of the Liberal Party, both in New South Wales and Victoria:

ineffective politicians who have placed ideology and self-interest first. Seat-by-seat opinion polls are suggesting there will be many seats lost in Liberal Party heartlands—including the seats held by Sukkar and Wilson. It's really a question of whether they can turn around the malaise that is affecting the Liberal Party now. Of course, it's always possible, but it's unlikely.

A FURTHER PROMISE ON NATIONAL SECURITY IN THE WEST

The federal government has imposed sanctions on Russian individuals, organisations and banks, and this is the correct course of action to take at this stage of the Russian military invasion of Ukraine. But just making an announcement is never enough for Scott Morrison and, in keeping with his desperation to find traction on an issue that could resonate with the public, he recklessly warned about an invasion by Western forces into the region, and—for illogical reasons—managed to weave China into the equation, before completing the triumvirate of fear and anxiety on national security, suggesting Australia will be the next target of cyber warfare.

Morrison's focus on national security was an odd choice: a federal government that sent one warship to Tonga to assist during their cyclone disaster, a ship that broke down and then spread coronavirus to the island nation; and couldn't protect its own citizens during a domestic crisis of floods and fires, was somehow going to defend Australia from the ravages of Russia and China.

This conversation on national security neatly dovetailed into an announcement of $4.3 billion to build a naval dry dock shipyard in Perth, and there were no prizes offered for guessing that the announcement was made in an area that the Liberal Party needs to hold seats if they want to win the next election. In keeping with many of Morrison's announcements, there was no supportive policy for this naval base. Where are these naval ships? What are they going to be doing? Where will they be kept? And how does it fit into Australia's military strategies on naval ships? Morrison announced that the building of the docks will commence in two years and be completed by 2030—eight years away.

As the public saw with the cancellation of the French submarines contract in late 2021, announcements can easily offer promises that are never delivered, even after a project is commenced. But that wasn't the point of the announcement—for the political leader, believing something is going to happen, is as good as it *actually* happening: as long as people remember these announcements when they vote and lodge their ballot, in Morrison's mind, that's all that mattered.

***

RUMBLINGS FROM SOUTH AUSTRALIA

25 March 2022

The South Australia election was held on the weekend and the Liberal Party government was removed by the electorate after just one term in office. Peter Malinauskas is the new premier in South Australia after a 7.2 per cent swing to the Labor Party in the primary vote and a 6.5 per cent swing in two-party preferred voting. Labor won twenty-seven seats—it only needed twenty-four to win, and the Liberal Party has been reduced to just sixteen seats. It wasn't a totally unexpected loss for the Liberal Party—opinions polls had been erratic and inconsistent but suggested a loss was a possibility—and certainly the magnitude of the defeat was a surprise.

The narrative in the media over the past two years has been that because of the coronavirus pandemic, incumbent governments should be easily re-elected because of the fear of change within the electorate during a crisis, but this is a moot point: a crisis can help a government, but the electorate still needs to see evidence of competence during an election campaign to reward an incumbent, and the electorate has decided that the South Australia Liberal government was not competent enough. And there's also the other narrative that usually runs in the media: that a result in a state election doesn't have a crossover into federal elections, but with a state election being held so close to a federal election, there are implications in this result for the federal government, and not much of it is good.

There's very much an anti-Morrison atmosphere in the electorate and the fact the prime minister wasn't visible during the South Australia election campaign confirms this. Of course, it's not unusual for prime ministers to restrict their appearances in state election campaigns if they have low approval ratings, and to not appear at all during the main part of the campaign is telling.

Every election—whether it be at a state or federal level—is different: there's a wide range of different issues and different characters in every election, different party structures in each state, different demographics and histories. Realistically, there's only one seat seriously in play for the Labor Party in South Australia in the federal election—the seat of Boothby which has a margin of 1.3 per cent, held by the Liberal Party's Nicolle Flint.

The next seat after Boothby is Sturt, held by the Liberal Party with a margin of 6.9 per cent: even if the voting pattern at the federal election is the same as the South Australia state election, only one seat will be lost by the Liberal Party in South Australia. Going back further in political history, in the 1993 Western Australia state election, the state Labor Party was expecting a massive 10 per cent swing against them, but only received a 3.1 per cent swing against—they still lost that 1993 election—but the prime minister at the time, Paul Keating, decided the swing was nowhere near as bad as it could have been; he announced the date of the 1993 federal election the day after the Western Australia election result, and went on to win. Of course, there were different issues in state and federal politics at the time but real-life election results—such as the Western Australia 1993 state election that preceded the federal election—can provide political leaders with a good understanding of how their party is viewed by the electorate, even if it only within one state jurisdiction.

If the 8-or-9 per cent swing that is being suggested by the opinion polls for the next federal election is applied nationally, there are many other seats in South Australia that could fall to Labor. But South Australia is not the main game for either of the major parties, although a seat lost by the government in the state, means another seat must be gained elsewhere. There are large anti-governments swings predicted for Western Australia and Victoria, with Queensland and New South Wales the only location where the government can hope to hold ground.

Premier Marshall had managed the pandemic reasonably well, and his loss has gone against the grain of election victories by incumbents, and the expectation that the pandemic has inoculated governments from any electoral pain. United States president Donald Trump badly managed the pandemic and lost the 2020 presidential election. New Zealand prime minister Jacinda Ardern managed the crisis well and was rewarded with a rare majority election victory under their mixed-member proportional representation voting system.

However, the Marshall government did experience other issues during its one term: people dying while waiting for an ambulance; ambulance ramping, where triage and medical support was provided within the ambulance, rather than the hospital; scandals; allegations of corruption; interpersonal difficulties with key ministers.

It might not have been the same level of corruption that was alleged against former New South Wales premier, Gladys Berejiklian, but it was enough to have an impact within the electorate.

Those issues related to hospitals, health and corruption had a strong influence in the South Australia election. But research also suggested that two-thirds of people said that they were less likely to vote for the Liberal Party once that connection was made between the Liberal Party and Morrison. And, of course, much of state Labor's election material contained photographs of Marshall and Morrison, emphasising that connection.

A first-term government is usually provided with the second term by the electorate, and the Marshall government was nowhere near as incompetent as other recent first-term state administrations: the Newman government in Queensland between 2012–15, or the Baillieu–Napthine government in Victoria between 2010–14. If a reasonable first-term government such as the Marshall government—albeit with the problems with ambulance services and corruption—are punished with a 6.5 per cent swing against them, what kind of electoral punishment awaits the Morrison government, which has been infinitely worse and mismanaged the pandemic response?

Some commentators have been suggesting a repeat of the 'Western Australian wipeout' from 2021, where the Coalition was left with six seats in a parliament of 59 seats. This is unlikely: the 2021 Western Australia election will be studied for years by psephologists, just in terms of how comprehensive the defeat was, and the circumstances behind the loss. It's likely for the Coalition to suffer a large defeat at the federal election, but it won't be anywhere near the 2021 Western Australia election result. Morrison seems to have played himself into such a corner, that it's difficult to see how he can retrieve the situation.

The effects of the Omicron breakout in South Australia in December, also came into play, with the effects of that still being managed by the time of their election in March. It's difficult to see if there is a causal link between the Omicron breakouts—which have occurred in every state and territory around Australia—and election losses. However, there was a similar pattern in New South Wales, where the state government suffered major swings after their Omicron breakout. If the federal government falls—as expected—at the 2022 federal election, it also suggests that there could be political consequences for the Daniel Andrews in the Victoria election, due in November 2022.

The South Australia election can now be added to the list of election results since the 2019 federal election, that have been unfavourable for the Liberal and National parties: the by-election in the seat of Eden–Monaro in 2020 (won by Labor); a by-election in federal Queensland seat of Groom (a 3.3 per cent swing to Labor); by-elections in New South Wales in 2022; general elections in Western Australia, Queensland, Tasmania, the Australian Capital Territory and Northern Territory. And all those elections—except for Tasmania—have provided poor election results for the Coalition.

There can always be speculation about the Coalition's chances at the next federal election based on opinion polls, or media analysis and confidence of the respective political parties. But it's difficult to ignore all those election results that have occurred over the past three years: real votes cast in the real world, rather than a speculative vote recorded in a pollster's database and weighted with a secret numerical formula that few people understand. Real election results, which don't contain very much good news for the Liberal Party.

Sometimes, the writing on the wall is too clear. There might be some delusion within the Liberal Party that it's always possible to revisit the 2019 federal election—one which very few people expected Morrison to win—and, of course, irrespective of how unlikely a repeat performance is to occur in 2022, it's always a possibility. And that might be the only factor the Liberal Party is banking on at present: *a possibility*. And if that's all a political party is left with—*a possibility*—it's hardly a recipe for success.

FACTIONAL DRAMAS

The issue of Labor Party factions has been highlighted in the week since the death of Senator Kimberley Kitching and highlighted for all the wrong reasons. As is usually the case, many people commenting in the conservative media about the undue role of Labor Party factions have virtually no knowledge about factions and use this to weaponise the case against Labor ever being elected. But the Liberal Party also has factions, despite what prime minister Malcolm Turnbull said at a Liberal Party conference in 2015:

> Malcolm Turnbull: We're not run by factions, we're not run by... [laughter]... well, you may dispute that.
> But I have to tell you from experience, we are not run by factions [more laughter].

Factions play an essential part in being able to manage the differences that do exist when harnessing over a hundred local members and Senators into one political party. To paraphrase former German chancellor, Otto von Bismarck, the public should never see what goes on in the making of laws and sausages; the same applies to factions: it's better to look at the outcomes rather than how those outcomes are made. Factions are based on personalities, political ideologies, and who sponsored the arrival of a particular member into parliament, whether that's a union or a business interest group or any other interest group. Some of these personalities are vindictive and spiteful, and in some cases, would prefer to lose a federal election rather than give up a hold on their personal fiefdoms.

The media will magnify factions into a negative issue for Labor—they rarely actually do this with Liberal Party factions—but should factions be left to lurk in the background and do their dirty work or should they have full workings be exposed in the light of day?

All parties, particularly federal parties, must have factions. For example, the Labor Party in Tasmania is a different party to the Labor Party in Queensland—the reasons for this are partly personalities; the demographics of membership—some might be closer to the Catholic notions of social justice; economically conservative viewpoints; Marxist perspectives. The Labor Party has traditionally been strongly based around factions because it's the best way for it to manage these ideological differences. Labor's factions are more well-known and obvious because it was the first party to make these official, where members could align themselves with a particular faction and be co-ordinated according to the directives of that faction.

The Liberal Party uses factions to organise their members as well, although these processes are not well known to the public and appear to be more fluid than Labor's factional structures. In the 2009 Liberal Party leadership spill against Turnbull, where Joe Hockey was expected to win the leadership, only for Turnbull to counter-challenge Hockey and split the moderate Liberal vote, the leader of the conservative faction, Nick Minchin, shored up the votes and delivered victory to Tony Abbott. The Dutton-versus-Turnbull challenge in 2018 was also a factional issue within the Liberal Party between the moderate and conservative forces, although a disorganisation between the two allowed Morrison to come through and claim the leadership for himself. Liberal Party factions tends to be based more around the personalities of the party—the dynamic between Andrew Peacock and John Howard in the 1980s is example of this—but, essentially, philosophical and ideological differences still remain as the key feature of factions.

In the case of Senator Kitching, the mainstream media used her death to amplify their message against the Labor Party—

much of their behaviour has been totally undignified during this time but knowing how parlous the state of journalism and the mainstream media is in Australia, perhaps different behaviour could not be expected. Journalists at News Corporation reveled in yet another opportunity to attack the Labor Party. Senior political journalist, Samantha Maiden, seemed to be more concerned about using the incident to promote a new book she was planning to publish; politicians such as Simon Birmingham, Dutton, Morrison, Josh Frydenberg all wanted to use the incident as an undignified opportunity to score political points against the Labor Party.

And of course, there must be an analysis of Labor's factions within the media and within public discourse, but the death of Senator Kitching was used by the conservative media to attack other Labor figures such as Penny Wong, Kristina Keneally, Katy Gallagher, and Tanya Plibersek—even though those issues didn't seem to have very much to do with them—but this is a typical conservative media and conservative politician's attacking point. If it's not possible to attack a person's credibility using conventional and reasonable methods, best to use some innuendo and gossip against them, and attribute comments to a person who has died, where the facts can't be directly checked.

The politicisation of Senator Kitching's death has been one of the lower ebbs in politics, and it's not that far removed from the Penny Easton issue in Western Australia back in 1992—an issue used by the Liberal Party against the premier at the time, Carmen Lawrence—accusing her of killing a woman who had suicided. But this is the type of action typical of conservative political parties and of News Corporation: a habit of using the actions and words of people who have died to attack their opponents.

Issues such as this have the potential to create difficulties for the Labor Party in the lead up to the federal election because the Liberal Party in its current form is the expert in being able to magnify a relatively non-existent issue into a massive problem to the electorate, as they successfully managed to do with the franking credits and negative gearing issues in the 2019 federal election. If the Liberal Party can find a negative issue that can be magnified, then that is exactly what they will do: it's primarily a question of whether the electorate is interested in anything related to Labor Party factions, and it's quite possible that they will not. The strategy for the Liberal–National Coalition is to throw as much political mud around, in the hope that some of it will stick for long enough for the electorate to take notice.

The management and interplay of factions are problems, not just within the Labor Party, but in the Liberal Party too but not many people in the electorate understand or care too much about this issue. The media will always be infatuated with factions, especially if the issue can be used to cause damage to the Labor Party, but surely other more important events will occur: it can't be expected than an election will be decided by factional problems in either political party.

THE ELECTION WAITING GAME CONTINUES

Just two months before an election, it's obvious Scott Morrison and the Liberal–National Coalition are keen to focus on all those issues that don't really matter too much, because it distracts from all the other important issues that the Coalition has mismanaged: the floods rescue operation; the pandemic; the economy; climate change. Therefore, Morrison has focused on factions: if the electorate is focused on Labor Party factions and other peripheral issues, they're not focused on the important issues. But in Morrison's case, this won't be so easy. He also announced Australia will send coal to Ukraine as part of the war effort against Russia—how this is to be done; how much coal or even why Australia is sending coal to Ukraine when it would be easier for neighbouring countries such as Poland or Hungary to manage this, is never questioned by the media, and is also an announcement that can't be fact-checked quickly.

Not to be outdone, Peter Dutton also engaged himself in other distractions: announcing a new Australian space agency, even though this was a replica of his announcement of an Australian space agency from almost two years ago, and it's an agency that will probably never be created, only a figment that remains in the realm of election announcements, forgotten about, and then re-announced several years later. Again, no one in the media was wise enough to ask questions about why this is being announced now.

Australia already has a small space agency, although it's unclear what it would do if it was to be expanded. The point wasn't so much about the agency itself, but how it could neatly segue into issues of national security and the Russia–Ukraine war. And it's clear that both Morrison and Dutton are using these issues as distractions from other more important domestic issues.

The issues that have plagued the government over the past three years haven't gone away: the economy; climate change; ongoing COVID management. The cost of living has sharply increased in recent times and Morrison's response to many of these problems is a glib response to say that 'things will always be far worse under a Labor government', even though there's no evidence to support this. It's just mindless political speculation.

But announcements about the future isn't what Morrison should be worried about; he should be worried about the issues that are happening right now. Morrison has been marked down further in the latest Essential poll for his government's poor response to the floods in Queensland and northern New South Wales, but his only response was to claim his government had learned from the mistakes from the past and, because of this, they had the experience to deal with the problems in the future.

An inspection of the evidence suggests this is not the case: they didn't learn anything from the bushfires in 2020 that could then be applied to the flood events in 2022, where the government made the same mistake of either not acting quickly enough or not acting at all. There's been no evidence of learning from the many mistakes during the COVID vaccination rollout; the problems of overpayments within the JobKeeper program; or diplomatic problems that arose from the cancellation of the French submarines program, including a $5.5 billion contract severance payment to the French Naval Group. The Morrison government keeps squandering money and keeps making mistakes, and they're expecting to be rewarded for these mistakes: the electorate is now more wary about the behaviour of the prime minister and his government.

It's a government that has also failed to outline why it should be re-elected, and has had more than enough opportunities to display its competence: in the national bushfires in 2019/20—it delivered almost nothing. There are still people living in caravans after losing their homes over two years ago in the south coast region of New South Wales. Support and rebuilding schedules have been stymied and only a small percentage of a $4 billion emergency relief fund has been released. There was also partisanship in their relief responses during the floods in New South Wales, where Coalition-held seats received support, while neighbouring Labor-held seats received nothing. It was partially a response of favouring those areas that are voting for the government, but equally a philosophy of small government and an ideological response that communities are better in dealing with these crises, even though they're ill-equipped and under-resourced communities: governments are always best placed to manage a natural disaster.

Even if the prevalent political ideology is based around reducing the role of government in all facets of public life, a prime minister still needs to learn from mistakes. The key to former prime minister John Howard's success and his political longevity was that he rarely repeated a mistake—Howard learned from his mistakes and that's one attribute this government clearly lacks.

The political difficulties for Morrison seem to be never-ending, but it's also clear that there's not much that can be done to stop this going into freefall. Qualitative research suggests he's viewed by many in the electorate as an incompetent prime minister and a compulsive liar, and these are issues identified by Essential Research, Newspoll and Roy Morgan research. To paraphrase Oscar Wilde, one batch of terrible research material might be a misfortune; two might be regarded as carelessness; but three is confirmation of a willful disregard of the responsibilities of government.

In the latest Morgan opinion poll, the two-party preferred vote for the Coalition is 42 per cent, while Labor is at 58 per cent—in Australian politics, this is an electoral wipeout. The Morgan poll has historically overplayed the Labor vote in its polling methods, but even if there was an inherent inaccuracy of these numbers, it's a terrible message for Morrison and for the Liberal–National Coalition.

The opinion polling figures are now so poor that it has resulted in continuous chatter—on social and mainstream media—of Morrison being challenged for the Liberal Party leadership. Of course, this chatter is coinciding with the budget announcement next week, when party members will be in Canberra—and available to vote in a leadership spill, if one is to occur. It's unlikely that a prime minister, irrespective of how poor their performance is, will be dumped during the budget week. But the fact that there is speculation about this—and the recent history of prime ministers being challenged and dumped—just emphasises how bizarre this term of parliament has been. Despite the speculation, Morrison is likely to lead the Liberal Party and the government into the next election, however unlikely he is to win the election.

If Morrison did hear of a spill meeting—and he does have a band of loyal supporters within the Liberal Party to alert him about this—he'd rush off to the governor-general immediately and call an election. And given the proximity to the date that he'd need to call the election, he may act quickly anyway. The other factor that needs to be considered is the Liberal Party leadership rules that Morrison introduced in 2018, where two-thirds of the Liberal Party parliamentary team are required for the spill of leadership positions to be called. These rules, of course, could be overturned but the permutations required to reach this point are too difficult to contemplate and given the disorganisation and mess of the 2018 leadership challenges to Malcolm Turnbull—where the manager of the leadership numbers, Mathias Cormann, managed to support three different prime ministerial candidates on the same day—it's an action the Liberal Party would be keen to avoid.

The other factor is the absence of a leadership contender: which Liberal Party member would want to take on the leadership of a sinking ship and lead the party to a historic loss? Of course, any member would jump at the chance of being able to take on the position of prime minister, but both Dutton and Frydenberg are in the position of not having the numbers to challenge for the position, or enough time to muster up a likely two-step challenge, like the events of the 2018 leadership spill. They've run out of time.

***

APRIL

THE LONG NIGHT OF THE BUDGET

1 April 2022

The federal budget was announced this week, and not only was it one of the most political ever, but it was also one of the most expensive job applications in history for the federal treasurer, Josh Frydenberg, who was clearly angling for the leadership of the Liberal Party after the next election, win or lose.

The budget seemed to be magically finding money for those areas that the Coalition hasn't been able to fund over the past nine years—and the mirage of returning money into the programs they had previously cut, hoping the electorate will be impressed by what the government is offering for the future.

The media has been obsessed about whether the budget will do enough for the re-election prospects for the Coalition, rather than focusing on whether the budget is good for the community and the economy, and pondering whether those headline figures about tax cuts and fuel excise reduction will produce an electoral boost in the opinion polls for the Coalition. A pre-election budget is always going to be highly political and based on a re-election strategy for the government, but it appears Frydenberg might have gone too far. Budgets prepared by conservative governments are usually based around spending as little as possible, and veering any benefits towards certain parts of the electorate that will offer political rewards but this budget—especially the halving of the fuel excise levy—is a vote-buying exercise that has the dual purpose of trying to win the next election and, in the event of a likely election loss, leaving a political problem for Labor to clean up.

The Coalition was expecting to lose the 2019 federal election and they produced a budget that also suggested this—spread electoral favours and leave timebombs behind for the Labor Party, only to go on to win the election and deal with the fiscal problems they created—and it seems they are following the same course of action in 2022.

Budgets should always be about the needs of the community and the economy at any given time and with the media commentary focused on whether the budget will be enough to get the Coalition re-elected, this means the bigger issues and the real priorities will be missed. This budget has a $78 billion deficit: deficits and debts aren't inherently a problem—spending cycles need to fit into the circumstances of the times—but there is a question about what this debt is being used for, and it appears that most of the national government debt that has been accumulated over the past nine years hasn't been very well targeted.

Budgets are also a 'smoke and mirrors' process, where funds are shifted from one program and then announced as new money: one such example is the Resilience Effects Defense Space Intelligence Cyber and Enablers program—REDSPICE—a $9.9 billion announcement, which is existing funding shifted from the Department of Defence, and announced as a new program. There are peculiar omissions: a recent announcement by Morrison of a dry dock facility in Perth at the cost of $4 billion isn't mentioned at all in the budget papers. Frydenberg has also managed to find funding for all the programs the Coalition had great difficulty in finding the money for over the past nine years they've been in office: schools, health, mental health, aged care,

Indigenous affairs, the National Disability Insurance Scheme, although in many of these cases, they were simply replacing funding they'd previously cut.

Frydenberg also constantly referred to programs as "fully funded" and "record level funding"—people who are on the National Disability Insurance Scheme program might dispute that idea of "fully funded"—but there's a wide range of aspirations and assumptions within this budget which are unrealistic. One assumption is that wage rises are going to outpace consumer price index increases over the next three years, even though this hasn't occurred over the past decade, and these assumptions were asserted without any underlying analysis to support the claims. Australia has been in the unusual position of budgets being prepared in 2016, 2019 and 2022 on the cusp of an election, and primarily produced as political documents which were designed to distract the electorate and focus on re-election, rather than prudent fiscal responsibility.

There were also several items that were carefully targeted: yet another first-home buyer scheme that sent out the message that this is all available to all first-home buyers, but it's only a carefully targeted program benefitting a small number of people. It's a similar situation with the home purchase scheme for single women with families. Again, it supports only a small number of women, but the headline announcement makes it seem like everyone is going to benefit.

Of course, it's good that first home buyers and single women with families or women fleeing from domestic violence are supported, aside from the inflationary pressures that it places on housing prices and, in some cases, making them more unaffordable. But it's only a small amount of people who will receive the support. These two budget items were also announced in the 2021 budget and the budget before, so it's a tactic that is all about getting the announcement out to the public and influencing their vote at the next election. If the program doesn't exist after election, or if the people who thought they might be eligible for the fund, but then find out that they're not when the time comes, governments aren't too fussed about this: if it's enough to win the election, that's all that matters. It's a cynical vote-buying exercise.

Budgets are usually based around spin-doctoring and presentation of impressive graphs, statistics and acronyms—such as REDSPICE—and confusing references to "employment and real GDP relative to pre-pandemic levels", which Australia is apparently leading the world in these statistics, even though no one is really sure what these statistics mean, or what they relate to. All political parties do this although a desperate government is more likely to do this with an election looming.

This budget also provided many programs and announcements that are targeting marginal seats—certainly not as severe as the pork barreling and 'sportsrorts' that occurred in the lead up to the 2019 election—but a shameless targeting, nevertheless. Almost 40 per cent of the infrastructure funding for New South Wales is allocated to the seat of Dobell—$1.3 billion—and in South Australia, $2.2 billion has been allocated in the seat of Boothby, also for additional infrastructure. Both are marginal seats held by the Liberal Party and seats they need to hold if they are to win the next election. Two marginal seats: $3.5 billion in funding. That's a massive amount of funding and, based on the ability for the Coalition to throw money at low-value projects, such as the multitude of public carparks that were allocated in areas that weren't located near public transport hubs—it's unlikely that these represent value for money.

This is a government that has a history of pork barreling and doesn't consider this to be a problem; simply a process of providing government support directly to those parts of the electorate that support the government. While a specific funding for the people living in the seats of Dobell and Boothby is excellent news for those communities, it's also a question of whether that funding will be delivered, should the Coalition win the election. There was an earlier announcement in January by the government to provide a one-off $800 payment to aged care workers—which seemed like excellent news for those workers—until it was revealed the eligibility for the full payment was restrictive, it was also a pro-rata payment and by the end of March, 97 per cent of age care workers had not yet received the payment.

Budgets do have to consider several different issues—political and financial considerations, of course—but there are personal aspirations as well. It's evident that there's a three-fold effect for Frydenberg—secure his own seat of Kooyong, which is under serious threat from the independent candidate, Monique Ryan—shore up his own leadership credentials and, finally, try to win the election for the Liberal Party.

Frydenberg has been very open about the influences of Margaret Thatcher and Ronald Reagan in his political and economic thinking, so having large budget deficits and spending large amounts of money on government programs must be an affront to his Thatcherite-Reaganite ideology. Frydenberg also speaks openly about his leadership ambitions, and this budget is about positioning himself for the leadership of the Liberal Party after the election.

Morrison is unlikely to hold onto the position of prime minister if the Coalition finds itself somehow winning the 2022 election. If Morrison loses the election—the most likely outcome—he's unlikely to hold onto the leadership of the Liberal Party, and may even leave parliament altogether, following on from the pattern of leaders losing an election. The last prime minister to lead their party after losing an election was Gough Whitlam in 1975. Malcolm Fraser, Paul Keating, Kevin Rudd: all resigned the leadership and resigned from parliament after they lost their respective elections in 1983, 1996 and 2013.

Of course, whenever there's a budget, there's also a budget reply speech and the leader of the opposition, Anthony Albanese outlined some of areas Labor will focus upon if it's able to form government at the next election—including a major reform of the aged care sector, promising to invest $2.5 billion; cheaper child care; boosting wages; greater investment in infrastructure, training and education—with all these issues dovetailing into easing cost of living pressures. The responsibilities for the leader of the opposition are different to those of the treasurer—most of the effort goes into painting a picture of what they'll implement if they manage to get into government. Oppositions don't have access to treasury resources, they're not even required to produce detailed figures—it's just the broad brushstrokes and 'feelings' of what their government will look like, if they can get there—but, essentially, Albanese has ticked all the boxes expected from a leader of the opposition.

> Anthony Albanese: My fellow Australians, I have unlimited faith in our country's potential. And if I have the honour of serving as your prime minister, I can promise you this: I will work as hard as I can, every day to see that potential realised, I will act with integrity, I will lead with responsibility. And I will treat you with respect. We have been through a tough couple of years. But I know our best days can be ahead of us, I will work with you to build a better future. And I say to this prime minister, who himself declared months ago, he was campaigning and not governing: call the election, call it now and let the people of Australia decide.

And the end of the budget reply speech, it was felt like the beginning of an election campaign launch and Albanese pleaded for the prime minister to call the election. There's not much left to do in this term of parliament: it's just a waiting game to see when the election is going to be called.

THE ONCE IN A LIFETIME FLOODS KEEP COMING

The flooding that affected eastern Australia earlier in the year has started up again in northern New South Wales and in Lismore. Several weeks ago, the National Party leader Barnaby Joyce downplayed the first round of flooding in February, when he suggested that it was a "once-in-3500-year-event" and just the natural cycle of weather: no need to be alarmed, and climate change issues were not responsible. A second "once-in-3500-year-event" has just arrived, which suggests Joyce is very poor at mathematics, or playing climate change politics yet again.

Climate change is due to be a key issue during the election campaign, and it's an issue the Coalition government will have great difficulty trying to downplay with the electorate. Scott Morrison has tried to change the perception of his government's antithetical approach to climate change, by indicating that he is the champion of emergency funding in the face of criticism:

> Scott Morrison: I know I've got critics who say you shouldn't be spending money on helping people during these crises.
> But we do, because we know Australians need it, because we know the need is real.

It was an unusual comment by Morrison: his critics were saying the opposite—that his government was not acting quickly enough, and it was allocating funding too slowly and directing the funding towards Coalition-held seats. This followed on from the criticisms of funding for the bushfire victims during 2019/20, where $4 billion was allocated to bushfire emergency funding and recovery, yet two years later, less than 0.1 per cent of these funds had been spent, and there was a negligible response to the floods in Queensland and northern New South Wales from the federal government.

It's unlikely for anyone to begrudge the spending of government funds on people who have had their livelihoods destroyed and their homes lost because of natural disasters, and it's obvious Morrison was creating an image of him fighting back imaginary critics to arrive as the saviour to the regions of northern New South Wales and Queensland, even though he arrived empty handed. It was one of the more bizarre statements from Morrison but while it may have seemed unusual to many people, it fitted into his ideological persuasions: government is not there to help, it's up to communities and individuals to resolve these problems and rely on market solutions wherever possible.

However, markets and private interests cannot resolve the events in Lismore or in south-east Queensland. There is no market-based solution that can resolve the bushfires that have occurred in Victoria, New South Wales and Western Australia. Of course, communities have been involved in local action in the absence of government support but, in times of crisis, governments need to provide support to the community. These natural disasters will provide a backdrop during the forthcoming election campaign, and a reminder of how little this government has acted on climate change mitigation.

Aside from these natural disasters, there are other issues that are also developing in the background, and one is the issue of preselection of candidates, which seem to be creating challenges for both sides of politics. The Labor Party has finalised its candidates in all its winnable seats, but one preselection in the seat of Parramatta has raised a few eyebrows. Andrew Charlton is a prominent economist: an advisor in the Rudd government and was instrumental in Labor's response to the global financial crisis in 2008, and he's now the Labor candidate in Parramatta. Charlton is a good choice for parliament, but the politics of this is terrible: he lives in the eastern suburbs of Sydney, over thirty kilometres away from Parramatta, in the heart of western

Sydney. Charlton has indicated that he will move to Parramatta if he does win the seat, but this is what candidates always say before an election and, if they win the seat, fail to move to the seat after the election.

He's white, he's male and he's from an Anglo–Celtic background. Parramatta is a far more diverse area than Bellevue Hill in the eastern suburbs and it is a vexed question—like the issues that have arisen in the seat of Fowler, where Senator Kristina Keneally was parachuted as the Labor Party candidate, despite not living in the predominantly south-east Asian migrant area. Politics is about getting the best people involved, but surely it would be wiser to include the candidates who are more reflective of those communities that they hope to represent in parliament?

Good candidates need to be parliament: Peter Garrett was parachuted into the seat of Kingston Smith in 2004: he was an effective parliamentarian and become minister for the environment and minister for school education. Malcolm Turnbull—although he wasn't parachuted into the seat of Wentworth; engaged in a nasty preselection battle against a sitting Liberal Party member—made a valuable contribution to Australian politics and became prime minister.

Are these people more credible than the branch stacker who carefully manipulates the numbers to become the local member, and sits in parliament for twenty years or so, and achieves very little for their community? There needs to be a balance between the two scenarios but getting good people into politics outside of normal selection processes is essential to the good workings of parliament.

These preselection issues in the Labor Party, however, seemed to pale in significance when compared to the final speech made by the outgoing Liberal Party Senator Concetta Fierravanti-Wells who, through a factional deal within the New South Wales branch of the party, was forced into third position on the Senate ticket, effectively ending her political career. It's safe to assume she isn't fan of Morrison:

> Concetta Fierravanti-Wells: He [Morrison] is adept at running with the foxes and hunting with the hounds, lacking the moral compass and having no conscience... whose actions conflict with his portrayal as a man of faith. He has used his so-called 'faith' as a marketing advantage.
>
> By now, you might be getting the picture that Morrison is not interested in the rules-based order. It is his way or the highway—an autocrat, a bully who has no moral compass. In my public life, I have met ruthless people—Morrison tops the list, followed closely by [Alex] Hawke—Morrison is not fit to be prime minister, and Hawke certainly is not fit to be a minister.

This factional deal pushed Jim Molan into the winnable second position on the Liberal Party Senate ticket—known as the 'Butcher of Fallujah' for his role in Iraq as an Australian military commander and, at the age of 71, would not been as the future of the Liberal Party in New South Wales. The Senate career of Fierravanti-Wells was to end after seventeen years, but it's also a question of whether she would have come to mention her opinions of Morrison in the Senate if she hadn't lost her winnable position on the ballot paper.

Labor's Senator Lisa Singh—a good quality candidate—was also demoted in the Senate ticket for the 2019 federal election, and she made public criticisms of the backroom deals of the Labor Party at the time, but nothing compared to the personal criticism aired by Fierravanti-Wells.

Fierravanti-Wells accused Morrison and Alex Hawke of corruption, destroying the Liberal Party, and it's not often for a member of the government to suggest the prime minister is not fit for office. In return, Morrison dismissed Fierravanti-Wells' speech as 'disappointment' after losing her political career. But this seems to be a pattern with Morrison—to the many Liberal Party women who have made negative character assessments of Morrison—he condescends, mansplains, and dismisses their talents. The speech by Fierravanti-Wells almost drowned out the release of the budget this week and has the potential to derail the entire Liberal Party election campaign.

Perhaps parliament has not lost a great candidate in Fierravanti-Wells. Although Morrison and Fierravanti-Wells are conservative and right-wing, they are not members of the same Liberal Party faction: Fierravanti-Wells is part of the National Right; Morrison is in a Centre-Right grouping, also known as the 'Morrison Club'. Although her comments may have been swayed by a factional deal that ended her political career, it doesn't invalidate what she said. Her comments have been supported by other people associated with the Coalition: Julia Banks, Brittany Higgins, Barnaby Joyce, Gladys Berejiklian. Michael Keenan, a former Liberal Party minister, complained that Morrison was an "absolute arsehole".

It's well documented that Morrison cheated his way into the seat of Cook by using his contacts at News Corporation—to whom he funneled large amounts of advertising revenue when he was the head of Tourism Australia—to destroy the preselected Liberal Party candidate, Michael Towke in 2007, who had won the preselection vote by eighty-two to eight. There have been suggestions that Towke will break his silence on this preselection saga, and while it may not cause Morrison to lose the seat of Cook—he currently holds it by 19 per cent—it will create yet another headache in the lead-up to the election campaign.

Two of the most senior members of the Liberal Party—Morrison and Frydenberg—are facing immense problems: Morrison is trying to win the election; Frydenberg is struggling to win his own seat of Kooyong. Fydenberg's solution: pay for larger signage, with the streets of Kooyong littered with the large-format posters and electronic billboards displaying Frydenberg's magnified face and the Liberal Party blue. Aside from published opinion polls—and seat-by-seat polls are rarely accurate—this is clearest sign that Frydenberg will have great difficulty winning the seat.

Morrison has been asked by Liberal Party candidates in marginal seats to refrain from appearing in any campaign material, or even come to these electorates, and a prime minister restricted on where they can appear during a campaign is going to present many logistical problems. And in a sign of how difficult it will be for the Liberal Party to win the election, Frydenberg is being asked by candidates in marginal seats to appear in their campaigns, rather than Morrison. This presents a logistical problem for Frydenberg: he can't be in two locations at the same time and needs to spend more time in his local seat than he otherwise would need to.

Many other Liberal Party candidates, such as Dave Sharma in the seat of Wentworth, have removed all party paraphernalia from their advertising material, and adopted teal colours, rather than the traditional Liberal Party blue. It won't be enough to ward off the threats coming the Voices Of candidates—also known as the 'teals'—the electorate is attracted to authenticity in their candidates, and it's unlikely that a last-minute switch to the colour of their opponents is going to help the Liberal Party. Morrison recently claimed that he's not trying to 'be someone else' but he is the master of behaving like a political chameleon and presenting to the public as someone who he is not.

Other Liberal Party candidates are trying this same approach, but the strategy is one dimensional and has been found out by the public: it may have worked in 2019, but it's unlikely to work again in 2022.

There was a Roy Morgan opinion poll released during the week and showed a decrease in support for the Labor Party in two-party preferred voting intentions: 55.5 per cent—a drop of 2.5 per cent—while the Coalition registered 44.5 per cent. The pollster suggested that it was caused by allegations of the bullying of Senator Kimberley Kitching—widely alleged by the Liberal Party and the media, without any substantiation—this drop could be within the margin of error in opinion polls, but it could also relate to other issues.

Of course, speculation is running rife of an election being announced for 7 May, but there are still many seats which do not have a Liberal Party candidate, especially in the key state of New South Wales. The Morgan poll may have created a fillip in Morrison's mind, but it's hardly an election-winning position, and he may wait longer to see if there's any kind of boost from the release of the budget. But this is also unlikely: the comments made by Fierravanti-Wells were designed to damage Morrison, and the effect of her narrative is likely to linger for some time to come.

***

TROUBLES WITHIN THE RANKS

8 April 2022

The Liberal–National Coalition is entering the federal election campaign period in the worst possible shape and just when Scott Morrison feels he might be on the verge of getting clear pathways, along comes another Liberal Party member of parliament providing a free character assessment:

> Catherine Cusack: …my way or the highway. It's one thing to say to your own members in the Liberal Party, but for that attitude to spill out and impact funding decisions, public funding decisions that flood victims are depending on, is outrageous.
> But no, I can't bring myself to vote for this government after what occurred here.

Catherine Cusack, a Liberal Party member in the New South Wales parliament, announcing to the world she's not going to vote for the Liberal Party. The logical progression from here is that if the prime minister has difficulty convincing his own party members to vote for the Liberal Party, he's going to have far greater difficulties convincing the Australian electorate. The budget recently released by treasurer Josh Frydenberg didn't have the effect the Coalition was hoping for within the electorate; every opinion poll is stubbornly stuck at low levels of support for both Morrison and the Liberal Party. With just over a month to go before the federal election, all the signs are suggesting it will be very difficult for Morrison to turn perceptions of his government around in time to secure an election victory.

Despite what many of his supporters in the media are suggesting—and despite the remarkable achievement of winning the 2019 federal election—Morrison is not very skilled as a political operator, or 'a formidable campaigner'. While Morrison does bring considerable energy to a campaign, it's an energy that's misplaced on spin, marketing and perceptions. The Liberal Party is also amid an extremely bitter, brutal and expensive civil war between its various factional groups, culminating in a Supreme Court case in New South Wales which essentially is a battle between Morrison and the rank-and-file membership of the Liberal Party over preselection issues.

While the official campaign is yet to be announced, all sides of politics were behaving as though it had. Morrison was in Newcastle at the Edgeworth Hotel, when he was confronted by Ray Drury, a disability pensioner:

> Ray Drury: I've been fighting for twelve years, mate—you treat a disability pensioner that worked all his life … he paid his taxes, now he's getting taxed again. This is what you said when you got elected last time, 'we're going to help all those people that worked all their lives, paid their taxes and those that have a go, we'll look after you'.
> Well, I've had a go, mate, I've worked all my life and paid my taxes—you better fucking do something, I'm sick of your bullshit.

Morrison listened patiently before Liberal Party minders escorted Drury away from the media cameras, but the damage had already been done. The exchange was broadcast on national television and shared widely on social media for several days.

Michael Towke delivered on his promise to explain the events from 2007, when he was defamed by Morrison during a Liberal Party preselection battle and he fired away with his controlled invective on *The Project*. The Liberal Party has been loose and disorganised, and the Labor Party had been tight, professional, and disciplined. However, this is a replica of the pre-election phase in 2019, where most people assumed the Labor leader at the time, Bill Shorten, had done enough to become Australia's next prime minister, only to fall short by a considerable margin. Of course, that could also be the case for Anthony Albanese in 2022, although it's looking less likely: there are far too many problems for the Coalition government, and they are all occurring at the same time.

Historically, this is one of the worst positions for a federal government entering an election campaign in history. The position for the Morrison government is worse than Labor's position in the lead up to the 2013 election, the Liberal–National Coalition in 2007, or the Labor government in 1996. In each of those elections, it didn't really matter what the government did to try and change its fortunes, nothing worked: the electorate had already made up its mind way before those election dates and the government of the day couldn't make up enough ground to get even close to winning.

Of course, there are the caveats that every election is different, and events can change the direction of the election result. There's also the unpredictable nature of the COVID pandemic that needs to be considered—the Labor campaign director, Paul Erikson, is currently afflicted with COVID, and it's highly possible that other key members of the campaigns of both sides, or even the leaders, could contract COVID as well.

One election does stand out for Morrison as a beacon of hope, and that's the 'GST election' of 1993, where Paul Keating was in a similar position to Morrison—not as severe—one month out from the election but went on to win that election. But there was a signature issue in that election—Keating made the campaign all about the goods and services tax and his opponent, John Hewson, primarily because he didn't have much else to offer. Morrison has already had his 'miracle victory', and that was where he made the 2019 election all about Shorten and franking credits: history rarely repeats, especially in consecutive elections.

Morrison is now in a far worse position than anyone before in modern Australian history; he needs everything to go right for him, but everything is going wrong. Again, history may provide some relief: John Howard was in great political trouble in the lead up to the 2004 election against Labor's Mark Latham, but once he commenced the election campaign by asking: "who do you trust on the economy"—every political problem that he had dissipated, and the electorate focused on those issues that mattered to them the most. Morrison doesn't have this luxury of asking "who do you trust on the economy" because he's racked up almost a billion dollars in national government debt, wages have stagnated, and he presided over the first recession in thirty years. He can try running a campaign on the economic management, but it's not going to work in 2022, in the same way as it did for Howard in 2004.

Perceptions are also relevant here, even if they are sometimes misguided. Howard frequently pointed to Gough Whitlam and economic mismanagement, even though the figures don't justify this characterisation: global issues arrived at the time when Whitlam has started opening the economy in a more *laissez faire* manner—cutting tariffs, for example, which had a short-term impact on jobs. Whitlam also implemented large spending programs in the public service, education, health, and on a wide range of reforms that increased government debt but benefitted the community. Neoliberal economists attack this approach of debt-funded reforms—ignoring the fact that the Menzies implemented large budget deficits from the mid-1950s through to the mid-1960s—but Whitlam was a very good user of debt, especially in implementing free education and health.

The Murdoch media—even at that stage in the early 1970s—pushed the memory of Whitlam as a bad economic manager, and Labor as being untrustworthy with public finances. Again, this flies in the face of publicly available economic data: the thirteen years of the Hawke–Keating governments provided economic stability, although this was hampered by the recession in the early 1990s. The economic conditions created by Labor at the time also lead to economic growth and a recession-free period for twenty-nine years, broken by the recession in 2020. With Morrison, there's nothing really to show for: it's mainly been a litany of wastage, although it could be argued that the COVID pandemic created a wide range of conditions that can't be blamed on the government. However, there's no major infrastructure, which has been at record low spending levels over the past nine years. No amount of spin or 'photo opps' can mask over these issues.

For all the problems Morrison has been dealing with, there have been questions about whether the opinion polls can be trusted, especially when comparing the difficulties the Coalition faced in 2019, including poor opinion poll ratings, yet managing to win the election, despite every opinion poll predicting an easy victory for Labor.

As is usually the case in the lead up to an election campaign, opinion polls are released more frequently, and there were another four polls released during the week. The Morgan poll reported 57 per cent for Labor, to 43 per cent for the Coalition in two-party preferred voting; Newspoll showed 54 per cent to 46 per cent, Ipsos was 55 per cent to 45 per cent, and the Essential poll was effectively 53 per cent to 47 per cent—all in Labor's favour—with an average aggregate vote of 55 per cent for Labor and 45 per cent for the Coalition. Even with an astronomical margin of error, these opinions polls all point to election losing positions for the Coalition.

The budget was released just last week to great praise from the usual supporters in the media and was seen as Morrison's last chance to impress the electorate, but it sunk like a lead balloon and was overshadowed by the other difficult events and bad news for the Liberal Party.

Last week, Senator Fierravanti-Wells accused Morrison of being "a bully", lacking a moral compass and not fit to be prime minister. This week, another Liberal Party member has announced she won't vote for the party at the federal election. Typically, the budget was well received and promoted by the mainstream media, but leading economists said that it was poor, and the public seemed to agree with these sentiments.

The Coalition cheer squad at News Corporation, Nine Media and the ABC, promoted the budget at every opportunity, explaining to the public that it was precisely the economic remedy Australia needed, and then going on to question Albanese about his big-ticket items: how was a Labor government going to pay for the $2.5 billion to reform the aged care sector? Education, improvements in health—where is the money coming from? Higher taxes? Cutbacks?

In the process of berating Albanese over funding promises, the media forgot to ask how the Liberal–National government was going to pay for the $5.5 billion fee for canceling the French submarines contract. And the answer in both cases is by issuing Australian government securities bond, but the media behaves as though Coalition governments have access to a magic money tree from somewhere near the back of Bourke—no questions asked—but Labor governments must find money from elsewhere, usually through nefarious activity or raising dreaded taxes. But this is all moot: at this stage, it doesn't really matter how much the mainstream media wants to push the case for the re-election of the Morrison government, it's falling on deaf ears.

There is a change in the air, but there was also a change in the air in 2019, before that evaporated and became a mirage. Opinion polling companies have changed their methodologies—they had to, as it's not in their financial interests to be consistently wrong—and in recent times, they have become more reliable. Perhaps their only recent mistake was to underestimate the magnitude of the Labor landslide victory in the 2021 Western Australia election which, in some sense was understandable: polling which suggested the Liberal Party would be reduced to just two seats in a parliament of 59 would scarcely be believable and would have to be re-weighted to have a level of credibility.

Polls are inherently unpredictable: an opinion poll may reflect values in the electorate today, but that could be different in the following week. They are a valuable guide at assessing future events, but that's where it ends—there's a reason why the cliché of 'the-only-poll-that-counts-is-the-one-on-election-day' is used, because it's true: an opinion poll is worthless, compared to the real value of ballot papers cast on election day. Labor is still heading towards a small majority, but nothing in politics is certain, even at this late stage.

Politics can change very quickly, and the events of this week have underlined this. A few weeks ago, there was much concocted pressure on Albanese surrounding the death of Senator Kimberley Kitching and the 'Labor mean girls' narrative pushed through by the media. A short time later, all the pressure is now back on Morrison.

It also must be pointed out that the pressure on Morrison is not fueled by the Labor Party, it's the negativity coming from the Liberal Party. It's not often that party members and Senators dump on their own party but when it does happen, it tends to happen in the middle of a term, not towards the end of the term and so close to an election, where party discipline is enforced by key party whips. This hasn't occurred on this occasion. Following on from the character assassinations provided by Senator Fierravanti-Wells last week, the media finally latched onto Morrison's preselection saga in the seat of Cook in 2007.

This information had been publicly available since at least 2009 but his opponent in that preselection battle, Michael Towke, seemed like a relieved man to finally get something off his chest after fifteen years, when he revealed his side of the story to *The Project*.

> Michael Towke: At the time, as he [Morrison] was desperate and it suited him to play the race card. I guess when you get to parliament and become the prime minister, you're not an operative anymore. You've got the seat you want. You may not have to sort of lower yourself down to those tactics.
> And I'd like to think... I'm not saying he's a racist, I don't know him well enough, but he certainly used racism, Islamophobia, bigotry, with refugees, with dead families of dead refugees, with migration policies, and he's been dumped on by his own side.

There are other issues from the period before Morrison entered parliament: sacked from the Office of Tourism in New Zealand in the early 2000s; sacked from Tourism Australia by the minister of tourism in 2006. The sackings were made public but the details and reasons for the sacking have remained confidential: few people in mainstream media were curious enough to investigate these details—that was left to independent media journalists—but the curiosity has become more heightened since Fierravanti-Well made her speech in parliament and Towke appeared on national television.

It was also revealed that in 2007 during the preselection contest in Cook, Morrison denigrated Towke's Lebanese heritage and claimed he was a 'secret Muslim'. There are several people from an Islamic background in Australia parliaments: Ed Husic, Anne Aly, Jihad Dibb, all fine community representatives but in an unsophisticated and predominantly white Christian community in the Sutherland shire, Morrison weaponised Towke's background against him, made assertions that were simply untrue, and played the hard right-wing racist card to achieve his goal to become the member of Cook and, ultimately, the prime minister.

It's hard to know what Towke's political career would have been like if he became the member Cook, instead of Morrison: certainly, on paper, he seemed to be a highly credentialled candidate, and this may have carried on through his parliamentary career. Or he may have been swallowed by the internecine warfare that usually afflicts the New South Wales Liberal Party and become one of the major factional players. It's a question which will never be answered.

If the media had done their job that the public expects of them and reported these matters with greater detail and more scrutiny, the person who is perhaps one of the worst people to have entered parliament, would have been blocked and would never have made it to the position of prime minister. As it stands, a compliant media which has largely downplayed anything too negative about Morrison over the past fifteen years, has facilitated and promoted the worst prime minister in Australia's federation.

There are many people at News Corporation, Seven West, Nine Media, Ten Network and the ABC who need to think about why they are political journalists and what keeps them in the profession: is it just the viewpoint of their proprietors and their editors, who in most cases seem to be compromised? Is it to slant the news towards conservative interests? Is it the regular pay packet? Ego? Or is to inform the public with balanced material and hold power to account?

There are some very good political journalists in Australia—Paul Bongiorno, Katharine Murphy, Laura Tingle, Malcolm Farr, Amy Remeikis—and there are many former mainstream media journalists who work in independent media outlets such as *The Saturday Paper*, *Independent Australia*, Michael West Media, Anthony Klan and new wave journalists such Jordan Shanks-Markovina or Serkan Öztürk at *True Crime News Weekly* working in digital media. But their work has an unfair counterbalance in legacy media. Sky News and News Corporation dominates Australian news coverage; the ABC is littered with former News Corporation journalists who appear on programs such as *Insiders* and *Q+A*, with a sole purpose of disrupting political conversations and steering it away from good sensible debate.

It's an unusual business model which seems to be targeting an aging demographic at the expense of the new, and promoting extremist agendas such as the anti-vaccination/anti-lockdown groups, the radicalised QAnon crowd, and the sovereign citizen movement. Perhaps these are the only groups left with an interest in legacy media, and it's a battle amongst the traditional free-to-air channels to appeal to this dwindling audience.

Despite the one-sided coverage displayed by legacy media, the Labor Party is still polling well and expected to win the 2022 election—with the usual caveat that this is the same position it was in 2019, only to go on and lose that election. If Labor does win the 2022 election, it will show that it can win elections without the support of the mainstream media, and possibly place the need for media reform on the backburner: legacy media is pushing itself into a sea of irrelevance by itself, so why expend political energy and capital on a hobbling media edifice that is sowing the seeds of its own destruction?

A better mainstream media might have prevented Morrison's preselection in the seat of Cook in 2007 but political characters of that nature usually move elsewhere to pursue their personal and political agendas. It's quite possible Morrison might have resurfaced in a range of Liberal Party-held seats on the North Shore of Sydney in 2010, or the eastern suburbs in 2013. Or the outskirts of Melbourne in 2016; and then the public would be dealing with this troubling political character now and into the future, instead of seeing the backend and final days of his career. Sometimes, it is a case of being careful of what to wish for in politics.

THE BATTLE OVER THE FUTURE OF THE LIBERAL PARTY

Not everything has gone wrong for the prime minister, with the New South Wales Court of Appeal adjudicating that the three-person *junta*—Scott Morrison, Dominic Perrottet and Christine McDiven—that intervened and took control of the New South Wales branch of the Liberal Party, was legally valid. In case anyone missed it, *Christine McDiven is a woman*: Morrison endlessly pointed to McDiven's gender, just to remind the public that the Liberal Party is doing something about its diabolical gender equity issues. The Court's decision provided Morrison with the right to preselect candidates in twelve seats in New South Wales: a quarter of the seats in the entire state.

Critics of this verdict pointed out that this was reminiscent of Russian President Vladimir Putin in Russia's elections, but Putin chooses *all* his candidates and then goes on to invade Ukraine, so the public should be thankful that it hasn't reached those levels in New South Wales. It is an outrageous situation but, once again, the media reported this as a victory for Morrison, rather than usurping of the rights of Liberal Party rank-and-file members and bad news for democracy.

This is a situation that has never happened before on such a scale, and so close to an election date. If the Labor Party parachuted that many candidates in New South Wales—and to be fair, those parachutes have been getting quite a bit of a workout recently—there would be an absolute outcry from the media.

Perhaps one, two or three seats, but twelve? Preselecting candidates a month away from an election doesn't give them too much time to prepare but it worked in the inner west Sydney seat of Reid, where Fiona Martin was preselected by the Liberal Party one week before the election was announced in 2019, and then went on to win that seat. Late notification might be a minor irritant, but the removal of rank-and-file members of the Liberal Party in the choice of candidate is the real issue and could further derail Morrison's election campaign.

The occasional parachuting of a candidate from outside may not be appropriate, and the first point always must be choosing the best local person possible to represent the local area. But sometimes it's better to choose a high-profile candidate that fits into that community. Labor's Kristina Keneally was parachuted into the seat of Bennelong to face John Alexander during the 2017 by-election, and many people expected her to win. She didn't but at least it was in a seat that matched the candidate up with the community. In 2022, Keneally was preselected for the seat of Fowler, and that appears to be the wrong choice.

In the case of the Liberal Party, the courts have adjudicated that there is nothing illegal in the federal intervention of the New South Wales branch of the Liberal Party: it's not the role of courts to judge on morality, ethics or democracy, its sole role to adjudicate on the law. In this case, the court was legally correct, but wrong on the principle of democracy.

Morrison claimed his intervention was necessary to rescue the political careers of Sussan Ley and Fiona Martin, the only part missing here was the motif of the man in shining armour riding in on a white horse to save the women of the Liberal Party. Although Ley and Martin were having issues with their local party branches, Morrison's agenda was purely about getting his type of people into the preselection ring, hopefully into parliament, and expanding his personal sphere of influence.

This case was more about the future direction of the Liberal Party, certainly in the state of New South Wales, Morrison's home turf. Morrison's Centre-Right faction is a true right-wing reactionary group, inclusive of extremists from One Nation, QAnon and assorted Christian and Pentecostal conservatives. However, Australia is neither extreme left or extreme right, as far as the political spectrum is concerned: it hovers somewhere moderately in between, and political parties which stray too far away from the centre will find themselves out of office for a long period of time. The warning signs for the Liberal Party have been there for some time, and Morrison is possibly sowing even more seeds for a heavy defeat by choosing candidates who are out of step with mainstream national values.

During her attacks on Morrison, Cusack—who has been a long-term member of the Liberal Party—said that the party of forty years ago, had been replaced by a new guard of conservative people with no interest in democracy, no interest in community, no interest in anybody else, except for their narrow minded bigoted ideological and religiously-based agendas, which appeal to few people within the community.

There's no question Morrison is reforming the Liberal Party in his own image, but this is usually performed by political parties when they're in opposition—it's easier to redefine themselves and implement these reforms when there's less exposure on them and more time available to them. But Morrison's reforms are being played out in the public, one month before an election.

It's not clear whether this is ideological overreach or arrogance, or just a belief that whatever the Liberal Party does, it doesn't really matter: the party has managed to win re-election over the past two federal campaigns without doing much to deserve it, and Morrison is probably expecting that the same will occur in 2022: *people don't care enough about democracy, so the Liberal Party will do as it pleases.*

It's becoming more apparent that the Labor Party won't have to campaign negatively during the 2022 election, because the Liberal Party is more than adequately doing the work on its behalf. Morrison brushes away the Liberal Party attacks on his leadership and on his government by suggesting some people in the party are disappointed because they haven't got what they want, or they've got an "axe to grind" for undefined reasons. But it seems there are too many disappointed people within the Liberal Party and too many holding their axes to grind, and it doesn't seem to be a recipe for success at present.

All political parties go through these ideological divisions—the Labor Party has split three times in its history, through lifelong feuding splits that sometimes lead to violence and bitterness. The Liberal Party tends to implement these splits underneath the surface, where there are more subtle takeovers by the party, although the open ideological splits between John Howard and Andrew Peacock caused many problems for the Liberal Party in the 1980s and made the party unelectable for almost a generation.

Morrison's attempted takeover of the Liberal Party is not so much an ideological dispute, but a dispute over personalities, with the introduction of spiteful culture war warriors and religious fanatics. The Liberal Party is currently in a mess and a party ignores the values and wishes of its grassroots membership at its peril.

If Morrison was the brilliant political operator that many of his supporters claim he is, he would have commenced this *coup* of the party years ago. But attempting to take control of the party in the sunset period of this parliamentary term and on the cusp of an election is foolish. It's Morrison choice, but he has decided that he doesn't need the grassroots Liberal Party membership, certainly not in New South Wales.

There have been some themes that Morrison has been pushing in the lead-up to the election campaign, the primary one being that the past few years since the coronavirus arrived in early 2020 have placed a great strain on the community but despite this, the government has managed to pull Australia through this pandemic. Of course, it has been difficult for the community and for government, but the pandemic is continuing into its third year, and there's no sign of it ending any time soon.

Compared to many countries around the world, Australia has managed the pandemic very well. But it could have been so much better, with so many problems in the vaccination rollout and quarantine issues. One other factor Morrison is overlooking now is that the electorate doesn't tend to reward politicians if they consider they were simply doing the job expected of them. This was the experience of the Labor government when they successfully managed the global financial crisis in 2008, but virtually received no reward at the 2010 election, although there were many other peripheral issues that influenced that election campaign, especially the removal of Kevin Rudd as prime minister and other issues related to mining taxes and carbon emission management.

In politics, there is far more pressure placed upon a prime minister, when compared to a leader of the opposition, especially when they are so far behind in opinion polling. In most of his recent media appearances, Morrison has appeared angry, ruffled, and trying to spin his way out of every political problem. In contrast, Albanese appears far more relaxed and seemingly confident, and in a choice between the two, it would be preferable to be in Albanese's position than Morrison's.

Despite the problems Morrison is facing, most of the commentariat continue to refer to 2019, when the Coalition, littered with division and incompetence, managed to eke a narrow election victory. This is the whispering in the heart that troubles every commentator and makes it difficult to rule out another election victory by the Coalition, with most people waiting for a flick of the switch or a 'who-do-you-trust-on-the-economy' moment which summons the nation to start focusing on the issues that matter.

But it's the new issues—or the revelations of issues from the past—that keep creating problems for Morrison. Jordan Shanks-Markovina—a.k.a. Friendly Jordies—released another video during the week and it focused upon the infamous prayer room at Australian parliament house. This time around, it wasn't an allegation, but a leaked report produced for the Department of Finance by a Sparke Helmore Lawyers: information about sexual acts performed in the prayer room; there is a reference to Tim Wilson and James Newberry, a politician from the Victoria parliament—what he was doing at parliament house in Canberra is unclear, although the leaked report may have provided the real reasons for his presence.

Former Liberal Party member, Christopher Pyne, is also mentioned in this report, there's also a reference to male escorts arriving at the parliamentary prayer room. There's no evidence to suggest any of these sexual acts mentioned in the report occurred; it's from a summary of the information contained in the report "Independent investigation into alleged inappropriate workplace behaviours".

There's also information in Shanks-Markovina's video about the behaviour of the Australian Federal Police in trying to cover up these issues. Nobody has come out to refute the material from this report, but whatever the substance of the material, it was yet another issue for Morrison to deal with.

Some of this commentary about this report did devolve down to the level of homophobia, rather than looking at the lack of character shown by the people that were mentioned in the report. People are adults and can make their own choices about what they do in their private lives and personal time. But parliament house is a workplace, and the alleged actions took place in a dedicated prayer room used for quiet reflection and peaceful religious meditation. Calling in sex workers into the workplace—allegedly—is an abuse of the position of parliamentarians. This is not to moralise or pass social judgement, but parliament house is a workplace and the venue where important national legislation is formed.

It's also the sign of the last days of a government, where they've given up on governing and just don't care what the political consequences are: it was reminiscent of the final months of the New South Wales Labor Party when they were in government in 2011, where the activities behind the scenes at New South Wales parliament house involved members of parliament dancing on table tops in their underwear, drunken alcohol fueled parties, allegations of rape. After sixteen years in office and headed for election defeat, the New South Wales Labor government just didn't care anymore.

Eleven years on, it's a different location, a different administration and a different parliament, but the sentiment and feelings are the same. A government that has given up governing and using up whatever privileges it has, before it's all taken away from them.

***

WEEK 1: MEDIA BEHAVING BADLY

15 April 2022

The election date has been set for 21 May after Scott Morrison visited the governor-general at Yarralumla and requested the dissolution of parliament, and the issue of election writs. Morrison entered the campaign in the worst possible shape, with a wide range of political problems that remained unresolved, including several Liberal Party backbenchers giving character assessments and listing the reasons why he should not be prime minister.

There's no question Morrison is facing many difficulties, but it was the Labor leader who started off the campaign in the worst possible way. Anthony Albanese provided his first media conference of the campaign in the marginal seat of Bass in Tasmania—a hostile reception was provided by media pack—and he couldn't answer two questions from a journalist: what is the reserve bank's cash rate and what is the official unemployment rate.

It was a classic 'gotcha' strategy employed by the media and it seemed like a coordinated questioning tactic from the journalists in attendance. And they ended up getting the headlines they were after, it guaranteed negative headlines for Albanese for the next few days, and it's likely to be something that comes up frequently in the election campaign over the next six weeks. It's primarily a mainstream media strategy to derail Labor's agenda:

they've done it before, and they'll do it again. Albanese should have known those figures or at least had a strategy in place to deal with the question if he didn't know the answer. But was it fair questioning from media or just a part of the political process that all leaders need to be prepared for, especially during an election campaign?

The prime minister was also castigated several weeks ago for not knowing the price of a litre of milk, so it's not just the leader of the opposition who is receiving these inane questions, but it's probably fair to assume that few of the journalists asking the question knew what the cash rate is and probably don't even know what it refers to.

The 'gotcha' questions in modern politics are predictable and add little to the public discourse. But it's part of the game of politics and politicians need to be prepared, irrespective of how inane the questions might be. Journalists want to keep showing that they lack the intellect to ask the deeper questions and they just look for the trick question to catch a leader out: Morrison is asked about the price of milk; Albanese is asked a similar question:

> News Corporation journalist: What's the national unemployment rate?
> Anthony Albanese: National unemployment rate at the moment, is… I think it's 5.4… sorry, I'm not sure what it is.

Albanese fumbled, but if he was more adept in this situation, he would have given the response the leader of the Australian Greens, Adam Bandt gave when he was asked a similar question at the National Press Club:

> Australian Financial Review journalist: Talking about the fact checking exercises, you said in the speech that wages growth wasn't going particularly well. What's the current WPI?

Adam Bandt: ... [exasperated pause] ...*Google it, mate!* ...if you want to know why people are turning off politics, it's because what happens when you have an election that increasingly becomes this basic fact checking exercise between a government that deserves to be turfed out and an opposition that's got no vision. This is what happens. Elections should be about a contest of ideas, politics should be about reaching for the stars and offering a better society. And instead, there's these questions that are asked about, can you tell us this particular stat, or can you tell us that particular stat...

And those questions are designed to show that politicians are somehow out of touch, and not representative of everyday people. Well—*news flash!* Most of the people in Canberra are on six figure salaries just passing time until they go out and work for their coal and gas corporations and get a six or seven figure lobbying job.

Do you know what would be a better way of showing that politicians are in touch with the need of everyday peoples? It would be passing laws that lift the minimum wage; it would be making dental and mental into Medicare; it would be making sure that we wipe student debt and build affordable houses. And when you've got wages growing at about two and a half percent and inflation growing at about three and a half percent, that is part of the problem. And I would hope that at this election, we can lift the standard and turn it into a genuine contest of ideas.

There's no question Albanese should have been able to recall those numbers—he probably did know, but under the pressure of the first media conference, couldn't get those numbers out. Regardless of this, there should have been a strategy to deal with this incident, which is inevitably going to happen during a campaign. When Morrison is asked these questions, if he doesn't know the answer—which is usually the case—he will have a quick-fire response: 'whatever the number is, it's going to be much lower under the Liberal Party'. Then he ends the questioning and moves on: Morrison has greater agility in these situations.

Albanese could have suggested: 'hang on a minute, I want to make sure I'm providing the correct answer'. Then looked it up on his phone, or he could have asked Senator Katy Gallagher—who was standing right next to him—to provide those figures. It would have looked awkward and clumsy, but it would have avoided two days of media drama. It was a surprising turn of events: politicians of all persuasions are media trained to the last inch of life; war gaming and simulation training; where staffers or fellow politicians take the place of journalists and fire away the trick questions to catch their leader off guard. Perhaps Albanese didn't do enough of that, or perhaps it was first day election campaign nerves.

One other factor is that the incident might humanise Albanese—of course, many people who heard about this mistake would have understood that these are figures that a senior politician, especially one who is aspiring to become the prime minister, should be able to recite. But it's difficult to accept that a blunder on day one of a campaign—as much as the Liberal Party and parts of the mainstream media wants to keep promoting it—will sway enough people who were thinking of moving their vote from Labor, back to the Liberal Party. John Howard provided the wrong official interest rate at the beginning of the 2007 federal election campaign, and it would be foolish to suggest he lost that election based on one mistake.

Former treasurer John Kerrin couldn't recall the meaning of gross operating surplus in 1991, and it fed into a feeling of general incompetence of a treasurer who had just replaced Paul Keating and fast-tracked the end of Bob Hawke's tenure as prime minister. But it wasn't the *only* reason. While mistakes such as this can cause many difficulties for a politician, it's the media that tends to focus on these issues more than the electorate ever will.

An election is always far greater than a leader forgetting two critical numbers to start off their campaign, but it does call into question Labor's media management. Although it was held outdoors, Albanese's media conference was in an enclosed area where there were over twenty journalists—and their respective camera crews and boom microphones—shouting out questions and demanding answers from Albanese and Gallagher, who looked flummoxed by this seemingly endless mayhem. Media management plays a critical part within election campaigns, and when compared to Morrison's streamlined and controlled media conferences—where hand-picked journalists ask soft and massaged questions—Albanese's conference was out of control, and it's no wonder that the sheer persistence of a maniacal media scrum extracted an incorrect answer from him.

Albanese should replicate Morrison's media strategies—deflect, belittle journalists, and put them in their place. It might not be in Albanese's character to behave in this way, but he has provided too much respect to journalists who have done little to deserve it and this might not be the best way to win an election campaign. Labor has had three years of looking at the behaviour of Morrison: they should learn from his strategies, even if it is to only negate one advantage that Morrison might have.

However, negating this advantage might not be worth the effort: with the indomitable media forces of News Corporation, Seven West and Nine Media lined up against Labor Party interests, it doesn't really matter what Albanese does, faults will be found that will be used against him. The power of these forces can never be underestimated, but it's not as though these forces have only aligned in recent times: commercial media interests usually contrive material that works to keep Labor out of office; it has been like this since the Labor Party was formed in 1893 and their current team should have worked out the correct strategies to deal with this problem.

In a sign of this symbiotic link between the mainstream media and the Liberal Party, Morrison hosted a private drinks function for the traveling media at the Nepean Rowing Club in western Sydney, on the edge of the Hawkesbury River, which, unfortunately for Morrison, was gatecrashed by the Blue Mountains Young Citizen of the Year and climate change activist, Adisen Wright, who was keen to ask the prime minister a few questions:

> Adisen Wright: Scomo... I just wanted to say I'm pretty astounded, as a young bloke here. Good to see you ... Can I get a photo? Is that alright?
>
> Morrison: Are you in the press pack?
>
> Wright: No, I'm a local, I live up in the mountains. So, can I ask one question?
>
> Morrison: Yeah, sure...
>
> Wright: I'm just up the mountains, so I came down today—my mate works behind the bar...
>
> Morrison [bemused]: Oh, okay...
>
> Wright: I just want to ask one question Scomo, look um across... I hope you don't mind, I'm just recording...
>
> Morrison [angry]: ...no, why is it recording?
>
> Wright: Because I just want to ask you a question.
>
> Morrison: Mate, sorry, this is a private event.
>
> Wright: Oh, sorry about that.
>
> Morrison: This is a media... this is drinks for the media.
>
> Wright: I just want to ask a question...
>
> Liberal Party minder: Sorry, what's going on?
>
> Wright [shouting while escorted from the premises]: Scomo! Scomo! Across the river here, across the river, people lost their houses, people lost their houses. And they were burnt ... what are you going to do, detain me?

Morrison was furious with Wright's intervention, and it was a level of anger very well hidden from the public view. During the 2019 election campaign, Morrison held a private screening of *Game of Thrones*, and offered free drinks and food to journalists. Albanese also hosted free drinks for the media during this week, but from all reports, didn't abuse anyone or call for anyone to be ejected.

Journalists were criticised for attending these events but were quick to defend themselves by suggesting that private drinks and social events have always been offered to them by political leaders and doesn't influence their reporting and commentary but it's difficult to accept that receiving any kind of largesse from a politician wouldn't lead to more favourable media coverage. It's an unprofessional arrangement: the public wouldn't accept doctors socialising with their patients; teachers drinking with students; psychiatrists lunching with their clients. Professional standards suggest journalists shouldn't be socialising with the politicians they are meant to be holding to account and reporting on without fear or favour.

Journalists should be neutral, analytic and separate from politics, and there needs a professional distance. Otherwise, it's easy for a journalist to become a government courtier—which there seems to be too much of—rather than being engaged in constructive and professional journalism.

The standards of political reporting and journalism are not high in Australia, and it was clearly on display during the first week of the election campaign. All sides of politics should be scrutinised, and there should be an expectation that there's fair treatment of the government and opposition. But in Australia, this is an unrealistic expectation. The Morrison government has been inept, corrupt, divisive and incompetent, but most of the focus has been on Albanese and whether the Labor Party is ready for government. Of course, aspirants need to be carefully scrutinised but not at the expense of allowing the behaviour of conservative politicians to slip through the cracks and not be highlighted at all. This scrutiny should be welcomed and focused on policy matters, not ludicrous 'gotcha' questions that are purely designed for a propaganda-inducing headline.

Media interests are aligned with the interests of the Liberal Party, and this is not going to change unless there are fundamental changes in the way the media operates in Australia. And this applies to the entire media eco-system: News Corporation, Nine Media, Network Ten, Seven West, and increasingly, the ABC. It's a mediocre alignment and the performances this week are, unfortunately, a taste of what the public can expect over the next five weeks of this election campaign.

While there have been exceptional political journalists since federation, there has never really been a 'golden age' of journalism in Australia. The contemporary journalist waits for leaks or government media releases and, generally, provides a running commentary about the government which, essentially, is provided by government. The veterans and more experienced members of the press gallery are appalled by the laziness of the new breed of political journalists within the mainstream media who lack the knowledge and the history of Australia's political system and are more consumed with the breakthrough story that will somehow land them a promotion, or a better job at a different media company.

Good quality journalism does exist in Australia, mainly within the independent sector, but good quality reporting within the mainstream is few and far between. To focus on a mistake made by Albanese on day one of an election campaign and let it run for the rest of the week—and, more than likely, let it run every day during a thirty-five-day campaign—just indicates how bereft of ideas these political journalists really are. Certainly, highlight numbers that should have been known by Albanese, but the management of the country, and the capabilities of a potential prime minister, can't be defined by a two-second incident, despite what the media wants the electorate to believe.

NO CHANGE IN OPINION POLLS

Elections are not won or lost on the first day of the campaign, despite what many people in the mainstream media are suggesting. The first week of the campaign is almost over—the Easter and school holidays have commenced—and there's still a long way to go. New opinion polls created just before the campaign started, haven't shifted: Newspoll was similar to its previous survey, showing a slight dip in Labor support, and the Morgan poll showed no change: 57 per cent for Labor and 43 per cent for the Coalition in two-party preferred voting.

The Labor Party needs to make a net gain of seven seats to form government; conversely, the Coalition needs to make sure it doesn't have any net losses to hold on to government.

Opinion polls still strongly suggest a change of government will occur, but an inspection of the seat-by-seat analysis suggests it's still a difficult election for Labor to win, despite all the mayhem and division within the Coalition over the past three years.

While most media attention was still highlighting Albanese's mistakes from the first day of the campaign, it will be interesting to see the errors made by Morrison, which are sure to follow. It's easy to assume that, based on the election reportage from the media so far, the election is already over, but a drastic act or event that occurs on day one of the campaign must be put aside by that political leader, reset, move on, and focus back onto the issues that they want to talk about and those issues that resonate with the community.

There are many issues that are resonating: climate change; cost of living pressures, wage stagnation; lack of action for bushfire and flood victims; protection of Medicare; women's safety; failures in vaccination rollout.

Those issues remain, irrespective of whether a political leader remembers or forgets a key statistic during an election campaign. Albanese and Labor have to keep hammering away at these issues, and remember that it's not just the Liberal–National Coalition that they're up against: they're also up against the conservative mainstream media, who will do them no favours at all, and will work against their interests at every opportunity. This is the nature of election campaigns: pushing the key messages every single day for six weeks until the close of the polls on election day.

An election campaign is a game of the little victories: a political party is not going to win all of them, with the obvious objective to have more of those victories than losses. It's a similar method to sports psychology: learn from the loss, gain whatever can be gained from the loss, put the loss behind and move onto the next issue and aim to win that contest. It's the accumulation of these smaller victories that determine the success—or otherwise—of the campaign.

Sometimes, the issues that appear can arise out of nowhere and can derail an entire campaign. During the week, it was revealed that a $500,000 payment has been made to Rachelle Miller, a former Liberal Party staffer to former minister for education, Alan Tudge. Miller and Tudge were involved in a consensual affair, but Miller alleged that she had been bullied in the parliamentary offices of Tudge and attorney-general, Senator Michaelia Cash, and also alleged she was emotionally and physically abused by Tudge towards the end of this relationship.

Questions were asked of Morrison about this payment, but he asserted that it was a private matter and not worthy of public discussion, and most of the media acceded to this request and stopped asking further questions. The media was incurious of this $500,000 use of taxpayers money that had been paid to a former

Liberal Party staffer: was it hush money; was it a confidential payment to remove an issue during an election campaign? It was an unacceptable—and unexplained—use of public monies, and it was also unacceptable that the media decided not to further interrogate the issue with Morrison or Tudge.

The parliamentary status of Tudge was also unclear. Tudge had been relieved of his duties as minister of education—due to the allegations Miller had made against him—but Morrison couldn't explain whether Tudge was still the minister for education, although he outlined that he was still a member of the Cabinet. Which of course, brought up the question of whether Tudge was still receiving a Cabinet member's salary, and what his actual role was if he was no longer the minister.

Of course, a prime minister wants to reduce and remove problems during an election campaign but by doing the minimal amount possible—a *de facto* sacking of a minister, removing all the duties and powers, while not *actually* sacking the minister. This resulted in another pertinent question: after all the allegations made against Tudge, what does a minister in the Liberal–National Coalition need to do to be fired?

The Westminster system has existed for centuries, but the Liberal–National Coalition seems keen to ignore conventions and trash the system. Ministers need to be held to a high standard for the public to have confidence in the political system and it's a standard that has deteriorated in recent times. Sussan Ley was stood down for misusing her travel expenses in the previous parliament, but after the 2019 federal election, was reinstated. National Party Senator Bridget McKenzie was sacked during this parliamentary term for her role in the 'sportsrorts' affair in the lead-up to the 2019 election but was reinstated twelve months' later. In most other worlds, professional misdemeanours have consequences: in the modern Liberal Party, it's a pathway for promotion.

Towards the end of the first week, the leaders were following different trajectories: Albanese attended a rally for the Australian Nursery and Midwifery Federation in Melbourne, and sharpened his media appearances, reducing his conferences to just eight minutes. Of course, this reduction of media conference time became an issue, with journalists complaining that Albanese had 'broken a promise' to 'answer every question', and this was somehow an indication of how he'd behave if he ever became prime minister. It might come as a surprise to many political journalists, but elections are not about them: it's about the electorate and the political leaders. But this episode should have indicated clearly to Albanese: no political journalist in the mainstream media is a friend to the Labor Party—and nor should they be—but they display a hostility that is never provided to Liberal Party leaders and, irrespective of how minute an issue might be, they will magnify it, even if it is to equate Albanese reducing his media conference schedules into somehow not being fit to be prime minister.

Morrison appeared on a different part of the campaign trail—a standard conservative politician's announcement of a $250 million dollar cash injection for oil refineries, for reasons which were not entirely clear, although oil companies are the largest donors to the Liberal Party. He also announced that he was dumping his plans to introduce a federal anti-corruption commission—a commission that was promised all the way back in December 2018—and, as to be expected, very few questions were asked about this by the media pack and the ones that were, were easily batted away when Morrison went on to blame Labor for not being able to implement this commission. Again, no questions asked about how an opposition could have stymied the anti-corruption commission if no legislation to introduce it had been tabled in parliament.

After these announcements, Morrison visited a factory in western Sydney with the Liberal Party candidate for the seat of

Lindsay, Melissa McIntosh, which provided him with further photo opportunities, this time, working on a sewing machine. Again, no complaints from the media throng: a lack of curiosity about stamping out corruption but securing the video and photographic footage of the Prime Minister operating a sewing machine: the important issues. Who's got time to worry about corruption or ask how all of this will improve the reserve bank cash rate or the official unemployment rate?

The interactions between politicians and the media are critical during an election campaign, but a new dynamic between legacy and new independent media has developed, where journalists have commenced attacking each other. Experienced journalists such as Paul Bongiorno, Barrie Cassidy and Bernard Keane attacked ABC political editor, Andrew Probyn, claiming that the ABC has been cowered by the Coalition government, was not upholding journalistic ethics and standards, and essentially pushing through government talking points.

The quality of mainstream political journalism in Australia is abysmal and largely pointless, more intent on protecting vested interests in this country, instead of holding those vested interests—and government—to account. The claims that the ABC is effectively being controlled by the Coalition government to suit its narrative and its political agenda have been easily dismissed in the past as social media trolling and a motley collection of disaffected radicals and keyboard warriors on the internet with nothing better to do with their time. But when experienced journalists are pointing out the errors of the mainstream media and making the claim that they're effectively running a protection racket for the government and have lost their way, it's time for more people to start taking notice.

***

WEEK 2: THE FINE ART OF THE SCARE CAMPAIGN

22 April 2022

Every week in an election campaign is like a long chapter in a book and so it was when the campaign entered its second week. And for all the aficionados of Australian politics, there's another four weeks to go: the mainstream media prefers to downplay the significance of elections and feels it's something to be endured rather than enjoyed—an attitude that is difficult to understand, considering elections are meant to be pinnacle for political journalists—elections in democracies should be cherished and championed, not dismissed with a sense of dread and frivolity.

The second week of a campaign—not dissimilar to the second chapter of a horror thriller novel—where 'scare tactics' start to feature prominently and each side of politics chooses an issue that will alarm the sections of the community that they believe is vulnerable to and hope enough people will listen closely enough and vote for that party, based on the merits of that issue. Scott Morrison commenced the week by magnifying carbon taxes, mining taxes and retiree taxes—even though Anthony Albanese has definitively ruled these out.

Not to be outdone, Labor is focusing on the introduction of the cashless debit card for all pensioners which, based on what the Coalition has said in the past, and the fact that they already have the cashless debit card in place in testing sites in several parts of Australia, is much closer to the truth. Scare campaigns can't be manufactured from thin air; there must be a semblance of truth to support them. Labor did implement a mining tax in 2011, before it was repealed by the Coalition in 2014, but it never implemented a carbon tax, nor did it ever pledge a 'retiree tax'—these are the words of the Coalition—but, in politics, perceptions are what matters, even if it's not correct.

Perceptions are what the Liberal Party has focused on, particularly since 2013, but even before that, when it claims it is the party of lower government expenditure. Former prime minister Malcolm Fraser had his infamous 'razor gang' in the 1970s that reduced funding for the ABC, pensions, unemployment benefits, and the Medibank system that had been introduced by the Whitlam government. It's one of the tools of the Coalition to remove or reduce the programs they are ideologically opposed to: Medicare, the ABC (again), the National Disability Insurance Scheme. Labor is perceived to the party of higher taxes, even though the evidence suggests it's the Coalition that has collected the highest proportion of taxes to gross domestic product over the past 50 years. Higher taxes, in themselves, are not the issue: how these taxes are applied within the economy and how that revenue is spent is the fundamental issue.

While the issue of tax can be easily whipped up into a frenetic frenzy during an election campaign, it's best to look through the fog created by these frenzies and inspect specific targeted programs that may cause difficulties for the more vulnerable members of the community, and the cashless debit card seems to be one of those programs. This program is known by many names—cashless debit card, the basics card, the Indue card—but it's a system that has been trialed across Australia over the past seven years; Ceduna in South Australia, the east Kimberley and Goldfields regions in Western Australia, and Bundaberg and Hervey Bay in Queensland. Labor's attacks on the cashless debit card and the belief the Coalition will extend this program to other people receiving government pensions and social security payments had more credibility, because these attacks are reiterating the words already made by senior Coalition ministers such as Senator Anne Ruston and Paul Fletcher:

> Paul Fletcher: Our Liberal–National government is committed to the cashless debit card.
> Anne Ruston: I think the conversation that we need to have is about the value of the card, the advantages of the card. The new technology has been a real game changer in the ability for the card to actually provide additional value to participants. There is a broader application for the whole community and something that we would like to have a conversation with them about.
> ABC journalist: Do you plan to make it compulsory at some point?
> Anne Ruston: I'm not going to preempt that: I think this is the start of a consultation. We've run a number of trial sites. We're seeking to put all income management onto the universal platform, which is the cashless debit card. And I think then the conversation needs to be had about what are the advantages of this card. And it's up to us as a government to go and sell those advantages in the hope that the Australian community will see the value of it.

There's the record of at least two ministers suggesting the government would consider extending the cashless debit card to pensioners—that doesn't mean that the government will definitely extend the program—but two ministers advocating for the extension of a cashless debit card, as well as a prime minister who first proposed this plan when he was minister for social services in 2015, suggests that the proposal to extend this scheme is far more advanced than the government is wishing to reveal.

There's also the consideration of key legislation that arose from the Social Security Amendment Bill, which clearly states a continuation of cashless welfare and the option to apply the scheme to age pensions. This is an amendment which came into effect in 2020, so the government can already extend the scheme to age pensions, if that's what they wish to do, and if they do manage to win the 2022 federal election. There are also other draconian measures within this legislation: recipients of the Newstart allowance will be subjected to random drug tests, and a failed test will automatically place the recipient onto the cashless debit card scheme.

The Coalition government also has form with these matters: Morrison was the instigator of the failed Robodebt system, a scheme which ended up costing taxpayers $1.2 billion. While it can be argued that the government might not extend the cashless debit card across age pensions if it does win the 2022 election, it's easier for the Labor Party to mount a scare campaign, because the legislation for an extension is already in place, and the Coalition has put in place many draconian social services measures in place in the past.

Of course, the Coalition will complain about 'scare campaigns' but it's difficult for them to argue the case, especially after one of most effective and deceptive scare campaigns ever during the 2019 election campaign, when they claimed the Labor Party was proposing a 'retiree tax', which then morphed into a 'death tax', with both terminologies picked up and used by journalists to attack the leader of the opposition at the time, Bill Shorten.

Labor never had any plans for a retiree tax, but the Liberal Party was able to weaponise pledged changes to capital gains tax on negative gearing and franking credits on shareholdings—changes to the tax system that were welcomed by many leading economists—and convinced enough people in the electorate that the changes were going to affect them directly, even if they didn't own shares or a property investment.

In the 2022 campaign, Morrison is again claiming that Labor will introduce a retiree tax on the basis that they haven't rescinded their proposal from 2019: a false premise on two counts—it never existed in the first place, although it's clearly difficult to rescind a policy if it doesn't exist. Clever politics, perhaps, but a disaster for good public policy.

Morrison was also campaigning in Perth, prominently announcing he was "never ever" going to introduce a mining tax or a carbon tax, although political leaders do need to be careful when they say "never ever", in context of the political problems it created for John Howard when he claimed he would "never ever" introduce a goods and services tax, before going on to introduce it at the next election.

These key messages play out well in the mining state of Western Australia, and the issue of carbon and mining taxes were whipped up into a vicious frenzy back in 2012 after the Labor government introduced carbon pricing and a watered-down mining tax. This vociferous campaign was led by the mining magnates Gina Rinehart and Andrew Forrest—who, collectively, increased their net worth increased by $58 billion during the first year of the pandemic in 2020—and they managed to enroll their mineworkers as a part of these anti-Labor protests, but then going on to retrench most of these workers after these pricing mechanisms and taxes were repealed by the Coalition government in 2014. So much for company loyalty.

However, a 2022-style scare campaign on mining and carbon taxes might not have the same resonance a decade later. There is more public awareness and a better understanding of the relationship between taxation and mineral extraction. For example, Qatar and Australia, have similar export outputs of liquid natural gas: the Qatari government receives $26 billion a year through royalties, the Australian government received only $0.8 billion through the petroleum resource rent tax, and that's a sizable difference. That additional revenue could fund universities, schools, hospitals, a more effective and better police force, defence, key infrastructure. It also suggests that if Morrison is relying on revisiting and rebooting scare campaigns from yesteryear, he might not have too much to offer for the future.

The other consideration is Morrison's propensity to mislead, fabricate and lie, for political benefit. Of course, to accuse a politician of lying doesn't have much resonance with the public, because the public expects that this is what all politicians do. But Morrison lies and misrepresents too many times for his own good, even when he doesn't need to and that's an issue that he does have to contend with. He has a propensity to deny comments he has made, even though he's on the record of having made those comments, and there's clear video evidence of those comments. And just like the 'boy who cried wolf', the more a leader lies, the less credible and believable they become.

Former prime minister Tony Abbott also had this propensity to say one thing to the public before an election and then act differently afterwards, as was evident on the eve of the 2013 federal election:

> Tony Abbott: I trust everyone actually listened to what Joe Hockey has said last week and again this week:
> no cuts to education, no cuts to health, no change to pensions, no change to the GST, and no cuts to the ABC or SBS.

The Abbott government then went on to reduce funding for Medicare, cut funding from the SBS and then the ABC to the tune of $783 million. The issue for Abbott was different to Morrison: while Morrison denies a statement he has clearly made, Abbott made a promise he didn't need to make—the Liberal–National Coalition was clearly going to win the 2013 election—

but he made the promise anyway, and then immediately did the opposite once he was in government. Morrison and the Liberal Party don't have too much credibility on their promises and announcements; and in the court of public opinion, it's the level of credibility that matters the most.

It was also apparent that are two campaigns running: the real-world campaign, and the more unreal one that is fluctuating within the mainstream media. The edifice of Murdoch–Nine Media–Seven West Media is supporting the Liberal Party, even though they probably realise that it's unlikely for the government to be returned at this election. However, old habits die hard: it's the reason why Morrison's distortions and lies are magnified by the media; it's also the reason why the media keeps telling the public that nobody knows who Albanese is; and their continuous complaint that there is no vision and policy in the election campaign.

These tactics, of course, are to convince the electorate not to make a change of government and to diminish their interest in politics and the campaign. Every election offers policy, vision and a level of dynamism and excitement on the ground, especially if there is a sense that a change of government is on the cards. There is also a renewed interest in independent candidates, especially those candidates making a push for a more environmentally friendly government, such as the member for Warringah, Zali Steggall. This is resonating in other parts of northern Sydney and in key Liberal-held areas within inner Melbourne and could result in surprising results in these areas that are dominated with independent candidates associated with the teal movement and the Climate 200 group.

These environmental issues are feeding into other aspects of the campaign. Labor pushed the message of the merits of renewable energy and electric vehicles, which was based on the more tangible changes already occurring within the electorate—since the last federal election, although coming from a low base, there has been a dramatic increase in the purchase of electric vehicles, from 0.2 per cent of the market in 2019, to 3.4 per cent in 2022. Charging stations have also become more visible in inner city parts of Sydney and Melbourne. Morrison derided electric vehicles in 2019, claiming electric utes "couldn't tow a boat" and would see the "end of the weekend" but this tactic is unlikely to be repeated in this year's campaign because—obviously—weekends haven't ended, and there is a wide range of electric utes on the market that have demonstrably been shown to be able to easily 'tow a boat'.

In the absence of substantial policies, Morrison decided to return to traditional conservative 'culture wars', and introduced transgender issues into campaign, using the newly preselected Liberal Party candidate in the seat of Warringah, Katherine Deves, as a conduit.

Since her preselection, Deves has made offensive comments about the transgender community, including incorrectly claiming that gender reassignment surgery was available to school-aged teenagers—it's not—that transgender children were "surgically mutilated and sterilised", and anti-transgender activism was equivalent to "standing up against the Holocaust".

There was much confusion about why the Liberal Party had preselected a candidate with such offensive beliefs in an area of north Sydney that while not regarded as socially progressive, is not a hot-bed of bigotry and religious conservatism. However, it became obvious that Deves' candidacy was not about winning the seat of Warringah for the Liberal Party, but telegraphing these messages to other marginal seats in the region that would be more receptive to these beliefs, possibly in the seat of Parramatta and Lindsay in western Sydney, with the hope that it would filter through to other parts of the country.

It's a despicable tactic, but it shows that there is no base level that Morrison won't stoop to, if there is a vote to be gained.

Transgender issues had been magnified in this part of the campaign and ramped up through the issue of transgender people participating in women's sport, even though there was no evidence that it's an issue in any sport in Australia but, somehow, this was narrowed down to a message that in community sports, young girls shouldn't have to participate against boys.

There's a reason why former Liberal Party Minister Michael Keenan suggested Morrison is an "absolute asshole" in 2018, because that's exactly how he behaves. Morrison sought a divisive issue to create a political opportunity, not so much to win the seat of Warringah, but to create conflict in other areas within New South Wales, find a receptive audience and win seats elsewhere. It was a despicable tactic but showed that if there's a vote to be gained, irrespective of how low the behaviour needs to go, Morrison is never too far behind there.

The transgender and "men in women's sport" issues seemed to navigate between Olympic sports, China and Russia—or whichever negative issue Morrison decided to bring up—and selecting Deves as the candidate in Warringah seemed to be a classic diversionary tactic and, if the electorate was arguing about "men in women's sport", it meant that they weren't discussing the important issues of climate change, corruption, the state of the economy, and the cost of living. It was also another example of the Liberal Party being able to choose a niche issue that doesn't directly affect many people within the community but magnify it with such intensity that it encompasses the entire debate and drowns out every other single issue.

A recurring theme that appeared again from many political journalists covering the election was to claim that the campaign was "boring", "dull", "dismal" and lacking the "fizzle and pop"—without ever articulating what could make it interesting to them, or ever accepting that they have a public interest responsibility to find the parts of the election that can be made more relevant to the community. It's quite a stunning admission: it's hard to imagine journalists from the *Washington Post* or *New York Times* filing stories complaining about a United States presidential campaign being too boring or not very exciting and, if they did, they be shown the door and fired by their editor-in-chief immediately.

Federal election campaigns occur every three years and are the climax of a parliamentary term. If political journalists can't be bothered to show enthusiasm for an election campaign, perhaps it's time for them to seek professional opportunities in other fields: politics might not be right for them. Australia is not replete with fine political journalism, and it seems to be a commitment to holding up the power for conservative media interests, rather than holding power to account. Journalists focus on the 'gotcha' question, rather than a focus on policy: they probably don't even know what policy is and, seemingly, what the role of their jobs are.

A focus on the "fizzle and pop"—the questions and answers on official cash rates or unemployment figures; still enthusing about the fact that Albanese was caught out on a critical number on day one of the campaign and dragging it out through to the end of the second week, hoping it would finish off the leader of the opposition. The travelling media pack was the one that was becoming more insignificant and "boring", "dull", "dismal", not the campaign itself, and the more they harped on about these minor matters, the more ridiculous and out of touch they look.

THE OPINION POLL FLURRY

During election campaigns, opinion polls are published more frequently, and they're used in different ways to justify the events of the campaign, which then directs the news for the rest of the week, irrespective of how minute a change in the polls might be. There was a big fuss about the Resolve poll during the week, which showed a decrease in electoral support for Anthony Albanese, although they didn't publish their usual two-party preferred figure, which suggests it was either unchanged, or not favourable for the Liberal–National Coalition. Newspoll was also released during the week, as was the Essential poll, and neither showed any change from their previous poll reporting.

A Morgan poll released towards the end of the week showed a slight drop for the Labor Party, but it still revealed a large gap, recording 55 per cent for Labor and 45 per cent for the National–Liberal Coalition in two-party preferred voting terms. This suggested that either the electorate had not fully switched on after two weeks of the campaign, or the perception of both leaders and parties is set and unlikely to change very much during the campaign.

The aggregate of polls suggests an election winning position, with the proviso that the poll readings were very similar for the Labor Party during the 2019 federal election—and shown to be wrong—and the polls could be also wrong in 2022. However, much of the media commentary during the week suggested a minority parliament was the most likely outcome—even though none of the polls have been suggesting this—and went on to claim that this would be a disastrous outcome and a reflection of the Labor turmoil that existed during 2010–13, after which the Coalition was voted into office.

But this commentary ignores that fact that the minority Gillard government during 2010–13 was one of the most productive periods of Australian federal political history, with a higher level of legislation passed than many other governments, and more major reforms and innovations than many previous governments. Former prime minister Julia Gillard was an excellent negotiator and the turmoil that existed at the time was a creation of underhanded campaign by Kevin Rudd to undermine Gillard,

WEEK 2: THE FINE ART OF THE SCARE CAMPAIGN

as well as the toxicity of the leader of the opposition at the time, Tony Abbott, and the ruthless campaign of the media and mining industries against carbon emission pricing and mining taxes. The minority government wasn't the problem: many state governments around Australia have managed minority positions successfully, without the turmoil that was evident during the time of the Gillard government, which was caused by many other factors.

Who would be the better negotiator in the event of the minority parliament? In the parliamentary term just completed, there were eight members of parliament sitting on the crossbench, and it's likely that six of these will be returned after the election: Adam Bandt, Zali Steggall, Helen Haines, Bob Katter, Andrew Wilkie and Rebekha Sharkie. In addition, independent candidates are strongly favoured to acquire the seats of Wentworth, Goldstein and North Sydney. The seat of Kooyong—currently held by treasurer Josh Frydenberg—is also in play, as is the seat of Hughes. The safe Liberal Party seat of Curtin in Western Australia is also facing a strong challenge from an independent candidate—Kate Chaney—and there are several other serious challenges in Liberal Party held seats in the North Shore of Sydney, and inner Melbourne.

If all these seats fall to independent or smaller party candidates, there's a possibility of a large crossbench of fourteen, which would be the largest crossbench in Australia's history. It also must be remembered is that these seats would be coming off the Liberal Party, so in the case of a minority parliament, the Coalition may not hold enough seats to form any type of government, leaving Labor as the only viable party of government. Even so, if the Liberal–National Coalition was able to form a patchwork 'coalition of coalitions', it's unlikely to see how this could work, given that many of these independent candidates have consistently spoken of climate change, corruption and integrity, women's safety, government incompetence and mismanagement as the key issues they'll be campaigning on during this election. Could the potential bloc of independents also request a change to the Liberal Party leadership as a condition for their political support? Who could this leader be? It's hardly likely they would support a change to Peter Dutton, and there's no guarantee that the other potential leader, Frydenberg, will be sitting in Parliament after the election. There are too many hypothetical permutations to consider, and they might be moot, considering Labor is still highly favoured to win the election outright—at least, according to opinion polls.

Another theme consistently appearing during the campaign—at least for the Labor Party—is the question of how election pledges are going to be paid for, and where the funding is going to come from. It doesn't matter what the policy is, it's the first question on the lips of the political journalist: "how are you going to pay for it?". Whether it's Bill Shorten announcing a reform of the National Disability Insurance Scheme, Albanese announcing $2.5 billion package for aged care, Tanya Plibersek announcing a schools funding package, or Jim Chalmers announcing a renewable energy fund: it's coming from a different mouth, but always the same question. And whenever the question arises, it's the giveaway that a political journalist isn't interested in policy; they're happy to show to the world they have a paucity of intellect and have no imagination at all. It's rarely about the merits of the policy, or how a policy could add value to the Australian economy, it's the same 'show us the money' charade.

And, of course, the answer to "where is the money coming from" is the same at is has always been and is the same location the Liberal–National Coalition always seems to find money: the reserve bank of Australia. Journalists never ask leaders of the Liberal Party "where is the money is coming from". No journalist has asked Morrison or Frydenberg how they will pay for the $5.5 billion cancellation fee for terminating the contract with French submarines manufacturer, Naval Group; or the $21 billion that was wasted on JobKeeper payments on companies that didn't need it; or the $30 million land purchase in western Sydney for land that was worth only $3 million; or the $500,000 hush money paid to former Liberal Party staffer Rachelle Miller after workplace harassment from two government ministers. But if the Labor Party is going to be interrogated over where money is coming from—and it should—so should the government, especially when the figures are far greater and have been spent on wasteful purposes.

THE FESTIVAL BLUES AND THE FIRST DEBATE

Anthony Albanese is not a musician, although he's passionate about music. He is a practicing deejay though, and he does like the legendary punk rock band, The Ramones, and the enigmatic Australian band, Radio Birdman. While he might not have the opportunity to see as much live music as he'd like to, it's not hard to imagine Albanese in the 1980s watching an obscure American indie-band at the Trade Union Club in Surry Hills, part of a heaving crowd at the Gaelic Club on Devonshire Street, or catching a glimpse of the Laughing Clowns at the Annandale Hotel in Sydney's inner west.

Albanese appeared on stage at the Byron Bay Bluesfest, at the invitation of Jimmy Barnes, a lifelong supporter of the Labor Party. It might not be the most appealing part of the gig for a politician to appear on stage but Albanese only spoke for twenty seconds to talk about how Labor is the party that supports the arts and music industries, and then went on to introduce Barnes onto the stage.

It was not a big deal, but the media let loose and had a field day, or in the parlance of the music industry, 'a big day out'. Reports from people who were in the crowd suggest that the reception to Albanese was positive, with some heckling from parts of the audience but, generally, he was well received. The media reported events differently: Albanese had "gatecrashed"—even though he had been invited by Barnes—it was a "boo fest", an unimaginative pun on "Bluesfest", and he had received a poor or mixed reception. The ABC went to the extent of doctoring and amplifying the audio, using a small snippet from the audience to make it seem as though the entire audience reaction to Albanese was entirely negative and hostile.

The media reporting of Albanese during the campaign has been febrile and attempts to magnify every single issue of Labor wrongdoing—real or perceived—and in the absence of this, fabricates or manipulates a negative news story. In their eyes, Albanese cannot do anything right, even if it is an innocuous appearance at a regional music festival, whereas Morrison seems to be perfection personified, like a prime minister afflicted with the Messiah complex. But these constant media attacks on Albanese have just become too intense and too unsophisticated for them to work effectively in favour of the Liberal Party.

The first leaders' debate was also held during the week on the pay-television station Sky News—a sure guarantee that not many people would see it—and it resulted in a narrow victory for Albanese. Leaders' debates during election campaigns are of national significance, and they should be available on a free-to-air channel, preferably on the ABC, not on a restricted news channel on Foxtel, which only 10 per cent of the electorate has access to.

Aside from the issue of access, the event was a reasonable debate. There was a studio audience of 100 undecided voters: every question asked of Morrison and Albanese came from this studio audience, and most of these questions were far superior to the questions professional journalists have been asking the leaders over the past two weeks. Albanese was judged by the audience to have won the debate—forty to thirty-five—with twenty-five people undecided.

It's difficult to assess exactly what this means: Labor has won every election debate since the 2013 federal election, but it has lost every election in that time, in 2013, 2016 and 2019. It does suggest that the people who have attended all those debates over the past nine years, listened intently to those debates, and scrutinised what the respective leaders have had to say, and have decided that Labor offers better solutions. The issue is that not everyone in Australia is in that studio at the same time: not everyone in Australia takes too much notice of these debates or scrutinises the issues as closely as these studio audiences. These national debates do have some influence in the electorate but probably not enough to make a significant difference.

Televised election debates are a tradition in Australia—as they are in many democracies around the world—but it's reached the point where they are not so worthwhile anymore. It might be a leftover from the great televised debates from the Kennedy-versus-Nixon era in US politics, or televisual incidents such as John Hewson's 'candle-on-the-birthday-cake' interview with Mike Willesee in 1993 that almost destroyed his election chances. Former Labor Party leader, Mark Latham, outlines in the *Latham Diaries* that he and John Howard had an intense and productive debate during the 2004 election campaign, only for it to be outrated by a reality television show.

Once again, the mainstream media was keen to put the narrative back on track and suggested that even though Albanese was judged to have won the leaders debate by a public audience, commentators suggested that he should have won by a greater margin, some overrode the public vote to suggest it was Morrison who won the debate. It continued the narrative the media wants to present to the public: Albanese just cannot do anything right, even when he does something right. If he appears on stage at the

Bluesfest, that's obviously wrong. If Albanese wins the national leaders' debate, that's obviously wrong too, because Albanese is not a winner and, by extension, Labor is not a party of winners. If Albanese does well, he needs to be better, just like an ever-extending yardstick that has no end.

Morrison is not an impressive public speaker. While his voice holds the right modulation and has an authoritative tone, a read through of the transcript from the leaders' debate offers little coherence, a scatter-gun approach of ideas which are hard to connect: it's a lot of words and seemingly makes sense while listening in real time, but on reflection and closer inspection, it's a pastiche of ideas that seem dissonant. Albanese has a better level of connectedness, although some commentators suggest his voice has a harsher style that grates on some people.

The week ended with Albanese testing positive to COVID and, as it's a new situation for election campaigns in Australia, it's hard to know exactly how this will affect the third week of campaign, although the Labor Party has enacted its continency plans for exactly this kind of situation and will try to run this as smoothly as possible: it will either be a complete disaster, or after Albanese returns to the election campaign, people will wonder what the fuss has been all about. It's a high-risk process, but there is really no choice in the matter.

The third week of a campaign usually engages with the more substantive issues, and it's expected that Labor will navigate over to climate change, and integrity in politics. The Liberal Party also must navigate to the issues that it wants to talk about to the electorate, but it's hard to shake off the many negatives that have accumulated over the past three years, and the issues of incompetence, corruption and bad behaviour keep returning to the surface.

***

WEEK 3: COVID ARRIVES AND DUTTON'S WAR ON CHINA

30 April 2022

The third week of the election campaign commenced with an unusual development, where Anthony Albanese contracted COVID, and had to complete a seven-day isolation at his home in Marrickville. As was expected, the media drove a frenzy of reporting that Albanese sidelined through illness was a nightmare scenario for the Labor Party but, so far, his absence hasn't caused too many problems for his campaign. There are other ways to campaign during an election: during the United States presidential election in 2020, the Democrats' candidate, Joe Biden, rarely left his basement and still managed to win the election quite easily.

In Albanese's absence, other senior Labor figures have filled the gaps, including Jim Chalmers, Jason Clare, Penny Wong, Tanya Plibersek, Kristina Keneally, Tony Burke and Richard Marles, and it provided an opportunity for the Labor Party to highlight the credentials of other members from their team. While it was inadvertent, the contingency plans that were created if Albanese did contract COVID during the campaign, seemed to a blessing in disguise, and if it was ever going to occur during the campaign, it occurred at the right time for Labor.

Scott Morrison failed to take full advantage of Albanese's absence anyway: his activities were not dissimilar to the political strategies he'd used during the previous three years of his time as prime minister. There was a continuation of the photo opportunities and media stunts: cooking; pulling beers at a public bar; playing two-up on ANZAC Day; fishing; playing with furry animals and echidnas at a zoo; making macarons at a French bakery; more cooking; playing with dogs; and appearing with the attorney-general, Michaelia Cash at a children's racetrack.

Sometimes, more is less during a campaign, and the only campaign work that Morrison produced during the week was more media appearances without any substance and, perhaps, it was ramped up to avoid the diplomatic issues that were created when the Solomon Islands decided to create closer ties with the Chinese government, causing Australia to lose influence in the Pacific region.

The media did try to create a large story about Albanese's absence but, if anything, it highlighted the issue that election campaigns have followed a set and predictable formula for far too long and forced at least one side of politics to be innovative in their campaign strategies, even if it was a situation forced upon them by COVID.

All of a sudden, Albanese's day one mistakes that the media was obsessed with disappeared, although they occasionally returned to them during their moments of boredom: here was a bigger story that they could report on—Albanese was going to be away from the campaign, and surely this meant the chances of a Labor victory were doomed. But it created the opposite effect: Labor was able to show the depth of their team as a direct comparison to the members of the Liberal–National Coalition. Bill Shorten, Clare, Burke, Plibersek, Wong from the Labor side, compared with Josh Frydenberg, Peter Dutton, Sussan Ley, Melissa Price and Barnaby Joyce: it almost seemed like an unfair contest. The only highlight for the Liberal Party was Senator Simon Birmingham, who appeared to the best performer for the government, even though as a Senator, he wasn't contesting a seat in the House of Representatives.

There was a great chance that one of the leaders would contract COVID during the election campaign, and it's quite possible that with so many people afflicted with the virus, Albanese gained some sympathy with his forced isolation, as well as working on the campaign from home, which so many workers have been doing since the pandemic commenced.

The forced change to Labor's campaign could have provided an opportunity for the Liberal Party to campaign differently as well, but it was an opportunity they declined and seemed to continue with the strategy that was so successful during the 2019 election campaign: media stunts, photo opportunities and distractions to make the electorate focus on everything else except for the important issues.

Military generals have a tendency to fight the last successful war again, even if the next battle is quite different. Trying to win the 2022 election with the techniques and strategies from 2019—while this is tempting and logical on the surface—is not a winning formula. Every election is different: different themes, different characters, different issues, and different strategies need to be implemented to achieve success.

The media also proved—once again—how unimaginative they can be. Their immediate reaction to Albanese's absence from the campaign for the entire week was to describe it as the "nightmare scenario" and "a fatal blow" to Labor's campaign, instead of thinking through the different opportunities for a political party and how campaigns can be managed in a different manner. Essentially, this was a "nightmare scenario" and "a fatal blow" for the media because it disrupted the way that they want to play out election campaigns: having the chief protagonists from their pantomime off the circuit for a week meant that it was a nightmare for *them*, not for Albanese. Their daily schedules were ruined. They had to think up new clichés to run against Labor and Albanese—they couldn't go too hard on Albanese because he was unwell, and that might cause the public to offer more sympathy to him.

Both the Labor Party and the Liberal Party had contingency plans in place if either leader was afflicted with COVID, but it appears that the media didn't devise their own plans and, when the inevitable did occur, they were the ones who were left scrambling and bamboozled. And their inability to react to this change within the campaign brought up other questions of the media: how relevant is the traditional election campaign to the final electoral outcome? There hadn't been a discernable shift in opinion polls since the campaign commenced, and Albanese's absence hasn't made much of difference either.

However, one constant and predictable behaviour of the media didn't change during Albanese's absence: the ability to find flaws with the Labor Party and create an avenue of division, even when division doesn't exist. His absence fired up leadership speculation, and because other capable members of the Labor frontbench were being presented to the media, this would place pressure on Albanese's leadership position.

Jason Clare delivered an excellent first up media conference during Albanese's absence and, as a result, the media speculated whether Clare should be the leader of the Labor Party, rather Albanese, because Clare was more 'presentable' and 'photogenic', some even suggesting Clare was more well known in the electorate, even though outside of the group of people who closely follow politics, not many would be aware of who Clare is. This was primarily mischief making behaviour: a mainstream party is not going to change its leader halfway through an election campaign and if their leader is unwell, others stepping into the breach is hardly unexpected. But it didn't stop the media from pushing the 'Albanese-under-pressure' leadership angle.

As predicted, the issue of climate change did start to feature strongly in the campaign, but any suggestions that the Coalition would try to downplay the issue and hope it would go away were dampened when two National Party politicians, Colin Boyce and Senator Matt Canavan decided the middle of an election campaign is the best time to deride the net zero emissions target by 2050, even though most of the electorate seems to be in favour of the target:

> Senator Matt Canavan: The net zero thing is all sort of dead anyway, it's all over. It's all over, bar the shouting here.
> Colin Boyce: Zero net carbon emissions by 2050—Morrison's document is a flexible plan, it leaves us wiggle room.

It must be pointed out that Canavan's family members own substantial coal mining interests, an item the mainstream media rarely raises questions about. There is no actual plan of substance which details how the Coalition would achieve net zero emissions target by 2050. Morrison simply kept repeated the government would achieve the target, without outlining how it would achieve the target, and the comments by Canavan and Boyce underlined the lack of detail. Morrison will say whatever he needs to say at any given time—whether it's true or untrue is irrelevant. 2050 is almost thirty years away and whatever Morrison says—or whichever plan the Coalition adopts in 2022—could change the following day, as was the case with the canceled French submarines deal. The Coalition seems to have no problem changing or canceling long-term projects if it can see short-term political benefits.

Following on from his messages the previous week in Perth, Morrison ramped up his rhetoric on a carbon tax, revisiting culture war issues and flowing back into the debate about men playing women's sport and transgenderism. Again, it seemed to be more of a scatter-gun approach, feeding in from campaign talking points in other regions of Australia: if Canavan talks about net zero emissions targets, Morrison amplifies a message on carbon taxes. If Katherine Deves talks about transgender children in Warringah, Morrison says that it's unfair for men to be playing women's sport. If Peter Dutton talks about the national curriculum needing to get back to basics, Morrison talks about "political correctness gone mad". It's the behaviour of the gambler at the casino trying out their luck with their final chips: keep spinning and gambling away, hoping the lucky numbers appear of the face of the dice. But very little is working for Morrison, and with this scatter-gun approach, the election might be well and truly over for him and the Liberal Party.

Morrison became increasingly rattled; he looked confused, and he looked lost, and with each strategic tactic failing, wasn't sure about where to move to next. The strategies that worked so successfully during 2019, weren't gaining traction. In the background, senior Liberal Party figures were despairing that both the behaviour and messaging of Morrison during the campaign, coupled with the possible loss of many seats to independent candidates which would create a large buffer between the Liberal–National Coalition and the Labor Party, could result in the Coalition being out of office for at least a generation.

Campaigns and media reporting can, of course, hide what might be happening on the ground during an election, and it's still quite possible that there is a range of issues that could be floating under the radar that commentators are not aware of, or issues that are evident but not as prominently displayed to the media—as was the case during the 2019 federal election—but it's hard to detect this and the 2022 election feels so different to the past.

While Albanese might have been absent from the campaign, that didn't stop Morrison attacking some of his plans for government. Labor's announcement of a $2.5 billion injection into the age care sector was attacked by Morrison as being flimsy, uncosted and lacking an explanation of where the money was going to come from. Although this issue was amplified by the media, it was an attack that largely fell flat. After this attack failed, Morrison then attacked the proposal to employ an on-site nurse in every aged care facility across Australia—which, incidentally, was a key recommendation from the Royal Commission into Aged Care Quality and Safety that the Coalition had not acted on, twelve months after it was released. He then suggesting there was a severe shortage of nurses, and Labor would, therefore, need to recruit nurses from overseas, and possibly from countries which had lower nursing standards.

Every one of Morrison's claims then brought up other questions: why is there a nursing shortage in Australia if the Coalition has been in office since 2013? Why has the Coalition not acted on the recommendations from the Royal Commission into Aged Care Quality and Safety, twelve months after they were released? Why are there still so many issues within the aged care sector? The Coalition's past behaviour and inaction in government was finally catching up with it and Morrison could no longer hide behind excuses, because every excuse that he offered just reminded the electorate of another failure of his government. Of course, many of these issues could have been queried and highlighted in the past, but the need for good policy development has been sidetracked by bad politics and inadequate media reporting.

While it's hardly likely to arise from a Coalition government, irrespective of who wins the election, there needs to be a reform of the mainstream media in Australia. It was revealed during the week that the ABC news presenter, Fauziah Ibrahim, had compiled Twitter lists of 'Labor Trolls' and labeled Labor Party supporters as 'Lobotomised Shitheads', the lists including prominent progressive politicians and public figures. There had been criticisms of Ibrahim for her interviews of Labor politicians—which appeared to be far more aggressive and confrontational than those with Coalition politicians—and her support of anti-vaccination protests in Melbourne, on one occasion, announcing the demonstrations as "peaceful", while the live footage on screen displayed protestors violently attacking police and throwing objects at them. Ibrahim was stood down for a six-week period and did return, but it's hard to imagine that if an ABC presenter was found to have a similar social media list of Coalition politicians, they wouldn't have been sacked immediately for unprofessional behaviour.

Professional journalists are meant to behave objectively and represent the facts without bias. There has also been a tendency within the media to provide an unreal balance for the sake of it—for example, a medical professional outlining the benefits of COVID vaccines is balanced out with a radical anti-vaxxer with no medical training or experience, and the media then claims they've fulfilled their duty by providing "balanced perspectives", even though one side of the debate is spreading misinformation.

There are other ways this bias appears: the prime minister is gifted soft leading questions, whereas the leader of the opposition is presented with hypothetical scenarios that are impossible to answer. There needs to be a reform to media law and changing an industry that currently thrives on ignorance and misleading the public. This is not good journalism: there is too much laziness, too much poor thinking and not enough contextual critique. It's how bad players in politics remain in their positions: a media that fails to hold power to account. While it's not clear exactly what type of legislation is required—perhaps an investigation of Canada's *Broadcasting Distribution Regulations* could be suitable—there is no doubt that Australia needs a better fourth estate and the public and political system would greatly benefit from that.

WEEK 3: COVID ARRIVES AND DUTTON'S WAR ON CHINA

LEST WE FORGET

Anzac Day was commemorated during the week and it a day where the many Australian people who have died serving in wars are remembered, and that's exactly the way that it should be. But it should also be remembered that wars are caused by foolish political leaders, and are always a sign of political failure. To highlight this point—and of all days to announce it—the minister for defence, Peter Dutton, decided that it was a time to be prepared for war with China:

> Peter Dutton: The only way that you can preserve peace is to prepare for war and to be strong as a country—not to cower and not to be on bended knee or be weak.
> That's the reality.

Dutton should have been informed that Anzac Day isn't about him or the Liberal Party and if he was going to bring up this issue, his advisors should have suggested that he choose another day to do it.

In the regional Victoria town Drysdale—in the marginal seat of Corangamite—the Liberal Party drove a large mobile billboard truck with the face of their candidate Stephanie Asher on a street where another Anzac Day Service was being held. During a moment of peace and reflection, the party decided the best way to commemorate a solemn moment during a solemn day was to disturb it with a noisy truck driving around with partisan political advertising.

In Canberra, Scott Morrison was texting on his mobile phone during the main Anzac Day speech at the Australian War Memorial and, in his own speech, he inserted all his campaign talking points, including the 'Arc of Autocracy'—the meaning of which still remains unclear. While his supporters claimed that the prime minister texting on his phone during an Anzac Day speech is not such a big issue—Australia has more important issues to worry about—it was a sign of disrespect and indicated that for the Liberal Party, everything and anything is a political opportunity and available for political marketing, irrespective of what the circumstances might be.

Anzac Day has developed into a less solemn commemoration over the past decade or two: while it can't be expected that the entire day must be allocated to remembrance of fallen soldiers or the disastrous effects of war, it should be expected that official events can remain a politics-free zone. It should be a day where Australians acknowledge the futility of war—echoing the sentiments of Eric Bogle's anti-war song 'And the Band Played Waltzing Matilda' from 1971—rather than glorifying or sanctifying acts of war.

The Australian community could also ponder historical elements of Anzac Day: why was Australia involved in World War I? Why were Australian troops at Gallipoli? The disastrous events at Gallipoli were instigated by the prime minister at the time, Andrew Fisher, calling for Australia to provide a "blood sacrifice" for empire, and the foolishness of Winston Churchill, in his racist assumption a multi-nation army landing from empire could easily defeat a Turkish army, within a beach head that was impregnable. These are the issues that should be considered, because it's hardly likely that any Australian politician would be prepared to strap on a rifle and go to the frontline to support the troops. In this context, Morrison unable to refrain from texting on his mobile phone was a sign of high disrespect.

Ramping up the fear of China and suggesting that Australia needs to prepare for war—on Anzac Day—was irresponsible but the Chinese government is wise enough to realise the Australia–China relationship is far greater than the racist ambitions of insignificant politics leaders such as Morrison and Dutton during an election campaign. Morrison was also warning that

China had "crossed the red line"—a reference to the security agreement China has signed with the Solomon Islands—without elaborating what 'crossing the red line' means or what he would do now that China had crossed this red line, claiming he couldn't release any details due to national security issues. This seemed to be an extension of not commenting on 'on water manners' when Morrison was minister for immigration but when political leaders are trying to wage a war with China, it's both foolish and counterproductive, and does little to improve security and international relationships in the Pacific region.

One of Australia's strengths as an international middle power is as a leader in the Pacific Islands, where Australia can provide a positive difference, not only to the smaller nations such as Fiji, Solomon Islands and Papua–New Guinea, but as a stabilising influence for larger near neighbours such as Indonesia. The Coalition has let this influence diminish over the past nine years, without realising that this influence is also beneficial to Australia in better trade deals and leverage with other countries. The new relationship between China and Solomon Islands is a consequence of this neglect and could create diplomatic problems for Australia in the future.

Morrison didn't seem to understand the importance of geopolitical influence in the Pacific region, remembering that he was with former prime minister Tony Abbott and Dutton in 2015, when they joked about water lapping on the doorstep of Australia's Pacific neighbours and rising sea levels. The Coalition has never taken the climate change concerns of the Pacific region seriously; they've cut back foreign aid to the region; they've reduced soft diplomacy measures such as Australian international and shortwave radio broadcasts to the region. It's obvious that the Coalition government has done as much as possible to signal to the region that Australia doesn't wish to hold this sphere of influence anymore, so it's no surprise that China saw an opportunity to fill in this gap, not just in the Solomon Islands, but with infrastructure and financial support to Papua–New Guinea through their Belt and Road Initiative.

The Morrison government did try to prevent the signing of the China–Solomon Islands deal by sending a junior minister to intervene—Senator Zed Seselja—but it was too little, too late: the deal was signed two days later, and a major diplomatic embarrassment to Australia could not be avoided.

RUNNING OUT OF TIME

There were two new opinion polls released during the week and, in what was becoming a recurring theme, there was no discernable change. The Ipsos poll showed a two-party preferred rating of 55 per cent for Labor, and 45 per cent for the Liberal–National Coalition. Newspoll was also released: 53 per cent to Labor; 47 per cent to the Coalition.

There was one slight change, however, with Anthony Albanese now rated as the preferred prime minister—40 per cent in the Ipsos poll; 38 per cent for Morrison—not too bad for someone the media keeps saying is unknown to the electorate.

The election date of 21 May is now just three weeks, the prepolling period commences in just over a week and it's difficult to see what can change during this period, with the absence of a signature issue that can galvanise the community in the final part of the campaign. Of course, Morrison will keep searching for that signature issue—China; a fictitious carbon tax; transgender issues; men in women's sports—but it's becoming more apparent that it's too late to make a significant pitch to the electorate that will change matters for the Coalition.

There's not much that the Morrison government can discuss with the electorate: there is little achievement of note, there have been too many scandals, too much corruption and, to top this off, their economic management has been poor. There is also an expectation that the reserve bank is going to raise official interest rates by 0.25 basis points, which will further damage the Coalition's economic credibility.

While the Coalition's electoral problems are banking up, it must be remembered that it's still the middle of an election campaign: political parties cannot just give up—they must persevere and believe that there's still enough time to turn sentiments around. Morrison is now doing his best to cloud the issues and use the classic conservative tactics to navigate the debate to the issues that aren't important, but act as a distraction to the more serious issues, such as the state of the economy.

Labor has commenced with the narrative that Morrison goes missing whenever there are problems that need to be resolved. Labor hasn't yet made a direct reference to Morrison going on an overseas holiday to Hawaii during Australia's worst bushfire season in 2019/20, although according to focus group testing, this is still Morrison's biggest negative factor within the election: perhaps Labor decided it was too early to push this message, at a time when their own leader was absent from the campaign, although for legitimate COVID-related reasons.

Inflation figures were released during the week and the 5.1 per cent consumer price index for the March 2022 quarter was the highest figure since 1990. This, coupled with speculation the reserve bank will raise interest rates next week, is the galvanising issue that Morrison would be looking for, but the problem is, that it will be an issue that works *against* him, not *for*. With an average trailing gap in the opinion polls between 6 per cent and 10 per cent, if interest rates do go up for the first time in an election campaign since 2007, it's safe to assume that it's the end of the Morrison government and it's a point of no return.

***

MAY

WEEK 4: ALBANESE AT THE KITCHEN TABLE

6 May 2022

The Labor Party has launched its election campaign and it was the first time a major political party had held its launch in Perth. Much fuss was made about this decision, and there were suggestions the location was chosen because Labor needs to win seats in Western Australia to secure an election victory.

It doesn't really matter where a party's election launch is held: it's only available to invited travelling media, party branch members and members of parliament, and it's mainly a televisual event—but it does signal that Labor wants to get away from that New South Wales–Victoria nexus which has dominated federal politics for far too long. Launches have been held much later in the campaign over the past two decades or so, with Labor bucking this trend and launching three weeks before the date of the election but it seemed to be a sensible idea, considering the prepoll period commences on 9 May.

In the 2019 federal election, the prepoll numbers were large: around 30 per cent in New South Wales; over 40 per cent in Northern Territory and 37 per cent in Victoria. One of the advantages Australia has over voting systems in other parts of the world is that election day is held on Saturday, rather a Tuesday or a Thursday in the United States and British systems. With more people now working on Saturdays, extending the voting period makes sense and it's a credit to the Australian Electoral Commission to facilitate this. Of course, it makes elections more difficult to predict if the electorate is voting over a fortnight period, rather than simply on the one day, but in a system that is based on compulsory voting, it's essential to give electors as many options as possible prior to the official day of the election.

In recent elections, political parties have held their launches late—quite often in the final week of the campaign—primarily because they can continue to claim public funding up until the time the campaign is formally launched. But the increasing numbers of prepolling suggests that Labor's campaign is based around the concept of 'election fortnight' rather than 'election day' on 21 May. In the 2019 federal election, Labor narrowly won the vote on election day, but in the preceding three-week prepoll period, it lost quite dramatically: 54 per cent voted for the Coalition in two-party preferred voting, compared to 46 per cent for Labor. One of the recommendations from the Labor Party review from the 2019 election suggested the party focused too much on the election day, instead of the entire prepolling period, and an early launch in 2022 suggests a change in strategy.

The launch adopted a standard approach, based on "A Better Future" and five key themes: medicine; manufacturing; gender pay; equity issues; electric vehicles and housing. The travelling media pack had complained about a lack of policy from the Labor Party, but it seemed to be complaints based on not having anything from Labor to attack and misrepresent, which they were so keen to do during the 2019 election: Albanese wised up to this and restricted announcements on detailed policy—this made political sense: why repeat the same mistakes from the past?

Scott Morrison proceeded to dismiss and ridicule every idea that was presented by Albanese at the Labor launch, especially the shared government equity home ownership scheme, where he suggested that not only would households have bank managers joining them at their kitchen tables, but Albanese as well. Of course, this suggestion was amplified through social media—the choice at the kitchen table—Albanese, who could provide conversations about deejaying, music and comparing Spotify lists; or Morrison, who was likely to talk about himself all night long and bring out a poorly-tuned ukulele?

The 'Anthony-Albanese-at-your-kitchen-table' tactic is standard retail politics to deflect from the merits of the policy, but it seemed to backfire on Morrison. Labor's home ownership plan was modest: it only applied to up to 10,000 loans, with government providing up to 40 per cent equity in a home purchase for people with a taxable income under $90,000 for single people, and $120,000 for couples.

It didn't seem to be available to too many people in the electorate but, conversely, it was not large enough to create wholesale changes to supply and push house prices up, which would defeat the purpose of the policy. While Morrison was quick to deride Labor's policy, he failed to mention that the Liberal Party released a similar policy proposal for the 2022 election, and going back further to 2010, the party had the same policy as Albanese's, where Morrison spoke quite favourably about shared equity schemes:

> Scott Morrison (in 2010): It's the biggest challenge facing those who have mortgages—you got to keep your job to keep your home, and yesterday we suggested that the government take out of that $8 billion they put aside for residential mortgage-backed securities, they take 500 million of that that is already out there and put that into shared equity mortgages, because shared equity mortgages are a really good opportunity.
> If you do get into mortgage stress, you can reconsolidate your mortgage. And you can go into [a] situation where you can have

a portion of the bank take effectively a portion of equity in your in your property. And that way you can reduce your payments.

Australia's incredibly high housing prices across the capital cities and major regional towns is an intractable problem, and misguided government housing policies across state and federal governments over the past thirty years have contributed to this. It's difficult to assess the precise solution at this stage: high housing prices in Australia is a complex problem which needs a wide range of complex solutions, but the solutions need to commence somewhere.

If high housing prices was an easy problem to fix, governments would have fixed the issue some time ago. While the economic policy settings can be easily found, the solutions are almost politically impossible. There are massive negative gearing tax advantages for multiple property ownership in Australia but any attempts to reform this—as Labor found out in the 2019 election—can be amplified and misrepresented, even though Bill Shorten's policy attempted to minimise the detrimental effects of negative gearing, rather than remove it entirely.

Reform in this area needs greater co-operation between federal and state/territory governments. For example, in some states, there are housing and rental shortages, yet there is a substantial number of properties that remain vacant: surely a vacant residence tax could be implemented to boost rental accommodation and ease other pressures within the property market. Other measures could be introduced, but the issue at present is a lack of co-ordination between policy settings from federal governments, and state and territory administrations which are working in a different direction.

Another area that relates to housing prices—interest rates—entered the election campaign and didn't provide much joy for the federal government. The official cash rate increased from 0.1

per cent to 0.35 per cent and fed directly into the cost of living issues that have been discussed for most of the election campaign. True to form, a journalist asked Albanese what the official cash rate is and, on this occasion—much to the disappointment of the journalist—he revealed the correct figure. Morrison's immediate response was to say that an interest rate rise didn't have anything to do with him; holders of mortgages have already factored in rate rises into their household budgets, and the discussions of interest rate rises shouldn't become a political issue:

> Scott Morrison: It's not about politics: what happens tomorrow deals with what people pay on their mortgages, that's what I'm concerned about.
> It's not about what it means for politics, I mean, sometimes you guys always see things through a totally political lens. I don't.

Albanese's response was quick and precise:

> Anthony Albanese: For this guy to say that anything is not political—this is a guy who gets up in the morning and what he has for breakfast is political. This is a guy who when he was in the Lodge with quarantining, didn't take his economic policy adviser; he didn't take his national security advisor; he took his photographer—*he took his photographer!*—everything that this guy does is political.
> This guy, for everything is an opportunity to play politics.

Interest rate increases and decreases will affect different people in different ways. For those in the electorate who haven't got a mortgage, or if they're a renter, they probably don't have too much to worry about. For those who have cash in bank accounts collecting interest, there will be some good news for them. Changes in interest rates seem to affect Morrison in different ways as well: when interest rates go down, Morrison is quick to take ownership and let everyone know it's due to the superior economic management of the Liberal Party. However, when interest rates increase, it's not his fault: Morrison was quick to blame events in other countries, or the war in Ukraine; external pressures; the COVID pandemic. This is typical political behaviour, but good political leaders should be able to take responsibility for the good and the bad, not just pick and choose whatever favours their own political agenda at the time.

The Westminster system of democracy expects that ministers take responsibility for the actions that emanate from their respective departments—the public service does the work to shape the policy into practical outcomes, but the minister takes the credit or the blame for these outcomes. As prime minister, Morrison's responsibilities are different: he can't be expected to take the blame for ministerial blunders, but he can act to sack the minister—if it comes to that—and be responsible for that process.

Interest rates play out in a different way: Morrison can't be responsible for an interest rate increase—that's the responsibility of the reserve bank—but taking credit for rates drops and blaming everyone else when the rates rise plays itself out politically in the public forum. Blaming others for an interest rate rise tends to fit into Labor's narrative that Morrison takes little responsibility for the events that require leadership: no responsibility taken during the bushfires of 2019/20; or for securing COVID vaccines; hotel quarantine; aged care. And no responsibility for creating a national anti-corruption commission, even though it was promised well over three years ago.

Facing criticisms that he failed to create the anti-corruption commission, Morrison ramped up his attacks on a proposed commission, claiming it would a "kangaroo court" and become a "powerful autocracy" that would curtail the activities of government. Essentially, this final point is behind the expectations of the electorate: the public wants a mechanism that curtails the activities of government which, increasingly, have resembled corrupt behaviours not normally expected of government.

The more Morrison protested against the creation of an anti-corruption commission, the more he played into the perceptions that he leads a corrupt government: surely a prime minister that rails so strongly against an anti-corruption commission must have issues to hide from the public? In general, politicians are reluctant to have anti-corruption measures, because most of government actions and activities sail close to the legal wind, and some procurement actions can sometimes be misconstrued as corrupt behaviour, even though there might be valid reasons for a lack of disclosure, especially when it applies to issues of national security.

When he first became Labor leader in June 2019, Albanese was initially lukewarm about an anti-corruption commission, ridiculed for claiming he'd never actually seen any corruption in Canberra during the long time that he'd been in politics. Bill Shorten was half-hearted when discussing an anti-corruption commission in the lead-up to the 2016 federal election: in hindsight, a close election loss might have been swayed towards a victory if he had been more forthright in his support. Albanese has been more strident in his support for a federal anti-corruption commission since that time—possibly because of the undeniably strong support within the electorate—and has promised a commission within six months if Labor is able to form government at this next election.

Conversely, Morrison is not supportive of the commission at all, and it's easy to see why: based on his performances over the past three years, as well as the behaviours of many Coalition politicians such as Barnaby Joyce, Peter Dutton, Christian Porter, Angus Taylor, Bridget McKenzie, Stuart Robert, Alex Hawke,

Mitch Fifield, Josh Frydenberg, George Christensen, Mathias Cormann and Gladys Liu, it's possible that Morrison might end up being one of the first people to appear at the national anti-corruption commission; it has the potential to destroy the federal Liberal and National parties and keep the Coalition out of federal office for the next twenty years or so. Despite these factors, it's essential for the creation of the anti-corruption commission: different versions exist in every state and territory jurisdiction and the absence of one at a federal level is an obvious exclusion that needs to be resolved.

THE COST OF LIVING

It's easy to forget that a political party is made up of other people, aside from the leader: there's a wide range of other members of parliament in different key positions who are also critical in an election campaign. During the week, there was a televised debate at the National Press Club between the treasurer Josh Frydenberg, and the person who wants to take his job, shadow treasurer Jim Chalmers: the focus of this debate was 'cost of living pressure'. 'Cost of living' is an abstract concept—it will mean different things to different people, and the electorate can define what it means according to their own experiences, which means it's the perfect message to use in an election campaign.

There are many economic issues that can come into play: interest rates; national debt; budget management; electricity prices. The economy is always the focus of any political campaign and Labor's key talking points are 'a trillion dollars of government national debt with nothing to show for it' and spreading the benefits of the economy more equitably. For the Liberal Party, the key talking points are the 'tough times' experienced by the community over the past few years due to the COVID pandemic and questioning the wisdom of changing a government at this point of time, because 'there's so much more work that needs to be done'.

This is an extension of the 'don't-change-horses-midstream' rhetoric that was first used by United States president Abraham Lincoln during his campaigns in the nineteenth century, but it's a rhetoric that can be cleverly dismissed: what if the horse is lame, or not fit enough, to get to the other side of the river? The sensible person secures a new horse, that's how. This 'don't-change-horses-midstream' message has been used over many years, and is usually a message to mask poor performances: the New South Wales Labor Party campaign slogan in 2007 was "more to do but heading in the right direction", a tired slogan which reflected a tired government in office for the preceding twelve years. Of course, the rhetoric resulted in election victories for Lincoln in the United States and New South Wales Labor in 2007, but it's questionable whether it will be successful for the Liberal Party in 2022.

Frydenberg is facing an uphill battle to retain the seat of Kooyong and as it is a seat held by Robert Menzies, one of the key founders of the Liberal Party, it holds great significance. Since the creation of the seat in 1901, it has always been held by conservative parties—never by the Labor Party—and held by the Liberal Party since the party was formed in 1944. In a recent opinion poll, the independent candidate, Monique Ryan, was leading 59 per cent to 41 per cent in two-party preferred voting. There has also been a perception that as a safe seat, it's been neglected by Frydenberg—as many safe seats are—and primarily using it to achieve his personal political ambitions, rather than promoting the ambitions of the people in the seat of Kooyong.

Kooyong has never been a marginal seat; logically, this means Frydenberg doesn't have marginal seat campaign experience and there are too many obvious signs of a campaign of desperation. In the suburbs of Kew, Hawthorn and Camberwell—taking up the main parts of Kooyong—many prominent advertising spaces are taken up with massive Frydenberg billboards, none of them include the Liberal Party logo, and most are simply a close up of Frydenberg's face, with "Keep Josh" superimposed in large lettering over his face. *1984*'s Emmanuel Goldstein would be proud of such overpowering imagery imposed upon the public. It appeared to be a scatter-gun approach, throwing money into advertising as if that was the only strategy that needed to be used to win an election, and ignoring the fact that it's the performance of a parliamentarian during the entire three years of the parliamentary term, not just in the final three weeks of an election campaign, that an electorate considers when casting their vote. It was also a significant indication that the Liberal Party understood that it was likely to lose the prized seat of Kooyong to Ryan.

There was also the irony of many of Frydenberg's massive posters which contained the words "stronger economy", pasted onto empty buildings which were previously occupied by bank branches and shops, reflecting the experiences of many small businesses across Australia. The Liberal Party needed to hold onto Kooyong, so that at the least, it could provide a leadership candidate in the event of a likely federal election loss, but it seemed that what the party was providing on the ground was too little, and too late. Frydenberg's leadership ambitions—either as prime minister or the leader of the opposition—appeared to be rapidly slipping away.

There was also the never-ending wrangling between the headquarters of both parties about leaders' debates. The first debate was screened on Sky News, the second one has been scheduled for the fifth week of the campaign on Seven West Media—screening after *Big Brother* concludes at 9pm—and there was speculation that Morrison would not agree to a third debate on the ABC—or even agree to having third debate at all—because he was not a natural debater and didn't want to provide opportunities for Albanese to appear on an even platform, or provide him with more exposure than he needed to.

Of course, this wrangling could be avoided by adopting a set formula for leaders' debates during the campaign—or enacting legislation—like the system used in the United States: two national debates at the National Press Club in Canberra, one debate with one moderator, and then another debate with an expert panel asking the questions, perhaps during weeks one, three and five of the campaign. That would save everyone time, and end the mindless debate about debates, and return the focus to the needs of the electorate and the public interest.

THE FLATLINING POLLS CONTINUE

Once again, published opinion polls revealed no change in public sentiments or how the electorate was going to vote in the election: if anything, the polls were becoming more dire for the Liberal–National Coalition. The Resolve poll showed a two-party preferred vote of 54 per cent for Labor, and 46 per cent for the Coalition. There was no change in the Newspoll result: 53 per cent for Labor; 47 per cent for the Coalition. The Morgan poll slipped down again for the Coalition—55.5 per cent for Labor; 44.5 per cent for the Coalition. The final poll released during the week was the Essential poll at 52.5 per cent for Labor and 47.5 per cent for the Coalition, although their methodology is an extrapolation that excludes genuinely undecided voters.

After four weeks of campaigning, there was no discernable shift in the opinion polls, but it must be remembered that the Labor Party was ahead in over 100 consecutive polls in the lead up to the 2019 election and they ended up losing that election. In this parliamentary term, the Labor Party hasn't been behind in any of the previous 104 major opinion polls, going all the way back to January 2021.

This is a simplistic proposition, but even if the current opinion polls are as incorrect as they were at the 2019 federal election, Labor is still in an election winning position. From this point onwards in the campaign, everything has to go right for Morrison but nothing is flowing in his favour, still adopting the same photo opportunity tactics he adopted in the 2019 campaign: cooking the Saturday night curry; shooting balls on the pool table; scaring the electorate; signposting that idea of 'vote for us, we are not Labor', which is surely one of weakest reasons to vote for a political party, essentially a 'vote-us-because-we-are-not-them' strategy. Morrison also inserted some new pop culture references by suggesting "you can't run the economy like Harry Potter": while he received some laughs from the travelling media pack, it fell flat in the electorate.

In the 2019 election campaign, Morrison had most issues and events move in his favour, and his high watermark electorally, resulted in a bare three-seat majority, an election victory, nevertheless. In 2022, Morrison needs to improve his high watermark—due to electoral redistributions, the Coalition needs to win additional seats just to remain in the same numerical position—and most issues are currently running against him. It's hard to see how or where this will change in the final two weeks of the election campaign.

***

WEEK 5: DEBATE CLUB

13 May 2022

The prepoll period commenced earlier in the week, and postal votes also started flowing into voting booths hosted by the Australian Electoral Commission—real votes are now being cast in the 2022 federal election.

The second televised leaders' debate on Nine Media ended in a tie between Scott Morrison and Anthony Albanese but in a general consensus, the debate was abysmal and, after commencing well with the direct answering of questions and presentation of key messages, it descended into an event best describe as halfway between mud wrestling and a rugby scrum. The questions from journalists Chris Uhlmann, David Crowe and Deborah Knight—all from Nine Media—were incredibly poor, and the moderator Sarah Abo was weak and allowed the two leaders to talk over the top of each other; Morrison kept on interrupting, Albanese's answers were generally cut short, and towards the end, it was a difficult debate to follow. Nine Media wanted this to be a ratings success, and they might have got what they wanted. But as far as a spectacle was concerned, it was abysmal: while Nine Media might have won the ratings battle, and Albanese and Morrison tied, the big loser was the electorate and the democratic process.

Chaotic, fiery clashes and conflict make for better television and, generally, keep audiences engaged and keep the television ratings up. But while it might be good for ratings, it's a question of how this improves the electorate's understanding of the issues that matter, or their understanding of who would perform better as a prime minister.

The Nine Media debate had around 30 per cent of the audience poll undecided in their choice, which suggests the debate was a confusing mess and didn't really offer viewers a chance to gauge the merits of both leaders. The moderator—also a Nine Media journalist—was out of her depth, and a more experienced moderator such as the ABC's Laura Tingle would have provided better contexts, better reasoning, and a far more balanced style of questioning.

It was obvious that Nine Media set the stage for provocation, and asking the question, "what is a women?"—after Morrison had been courting the extremist vote in the electorate, attacking the transgender community and asking "why should men be playing in women's sport"—was loaded, with no right or wrong answer, and seemed to be an attempt to trip up Albanese with a narrative from the conservatives' ongoing culture wars. Perhaps Nine Media was trying to channel a more angry and combative debate but if audiences want to watch something resembling a rugby game or a football match, they could easily switch over to the sports channel: at least that would be more engaging.

The final leaders' debate on Seven West Media appeared to be a more constructive and civilised event, and it confirms that according to studio audiences, Albanese is not performing as badly as the media suggests: whatever mistakes have been made in the past by Albanese—and his cash rates and unemployment rate mistake on the first day of the campaign was still being dragged up by the media—the electorate has moved on and didn't care too much anymore.

This debate was more definitive for Albanese—the audience rated Albanese 50 per cent, and 34 per cent to Morrison—but it was less of a case of Albanese performing brilliantly, and more a case of the electorate just having seen enough of Morrison and wanting to end his time as prime minister. It was also notable during the week that the media had dropped its 'no-one-knows-who-Albanese-is' rhetoric, because the public could see that it was no longer true—it was evident that Albanese wasn't as unknown as the media kept suggesting, and even if he was, how could a supposedly unknown leader be the preferred prime minister in opinion polls and, if he's such a terrible leader, why are studio audiences preferring him over Morrison in the leaders' debates?

Legacy media favours Morrison and the Liberal Party because they're useful to their wide range of vested interests: Albanese isn't as useful. That's the primary reason why the misconceptions and the beliefs are pushed by the media, as if a socialist utopia will suddenly arrive in Australia if Albanese is elected Prime Minister, and it would be the end of the world and the sun would possibly not even rise in the morning. It's also the reason why Labor is presented as the party of 'tax and spend', even though statistics suggest the highest taxing governments, as a percentage of gross domestic product, have all been Coalition—the Howard, Abbott and Morrison governments.

The Labor Party is usually in a battle with the mainstream media but if the attacks on the leader of the opposition are not working, it's time to start attacking local candidates, and in an election where there are 151 different seats, there are so many to choose from. The Labor candidate in the Perth seat of Swan is Zaneta Mascarenhas, and she had her name plastered on the front page of *The West Australian*, with the headline: "Star Labor candidate linked to carbon tax"—Mascarenhas was a part of a local climate action group that advocates for a price on emissions and was very likely to win the marginal seat of Swan, currently held by the Liberal Party. At the same time, *The West Australian* published a highly favourable profile piece on the Liberal Party member, Celia Hammond, who is struggling against an independent candidate—Kate Chaney—in the seat of Curtin.

It's a clear example: in the same edition of *The West Australian*, one article attacks a Labor Party candidate for spurious links to the dreaded 'carbon tax', yet another article highlights the credentials of a Liberal Party candidate. Readers of *The West Australian* would be interested to know that the owner of the newspaper, Kerry Stokes, is the owner of many mineral resource and petrochemical assets—of even greater value than his media assets—and his business interests are heavily favoured by the absence of a carbon tax.

This is a factor that plays out all around Australia: the "Keep Josh" campaign in Victoria; the anti-Labor media messaging in New South Wales and Queensland as well. The mainstream media cannot give up on this Coalition government, even when it seems like it might be far too late for them. But they will keep trying, even though it appears the high level of media support for the government isn't going to make too much difference to the election outcome.

The other issue which has been downplayed in the media is the complete disarray of the New South Wales branch of the Liberal Party: there is a Supreme Court battle between the state branch and party members over preselection issues. There are large battles for inner Melbourne seats—Josh Frydenberg in the seat of Kooyong, challenged by the independent candidate Monique Ryan; Tim Wilson in the seat of Goldstein, challenged by the independent candidate Zoe Daniel—and issues related to the takeover of Liberal Party branches by extremist Pentecostal and conservative Christians, who wish to remove the more moderate candidates who don't fit into their world views. The Liberal Party is not a happy place, with a wide range of internal civil wars brewing in New South Wales and Victoria, and it's not clear to see how these can be stopped.

In contrast to these internal wars in the Liberal Party, the key messaging from Albanese this week has been that if he won the election, he would partner up with the state premiers to develop more cohesive solutions to national issues. It seemed that Albanese had picked up on these ongoing Liberal Party issues in New South Wales and Victoria and presented himself as a 'safe pair of hands' and a unifier, but also to offer a key point of difference to the divisiveness of the prime minister, who attacked Labor premiers in Western Australia, Victoria and in Queensland during most of the pandemic, while lauding the achievements of the Liberal state premiers.

Frydenberg also engaged in these attacks on the Victoria government during the pandemic—and he's now discovering the merits of adopting this strategy, with an uphill battle to hold onto the seat of Kooyong. The key message that senior Liberal Party members have ignored is that the electorate remembers these kinds of attacks on their own populations—why Frydenberg felt attacking the people in his own state would be a good idea is unknown—and the public, generally, doesn't like this type of behaviour from politicians.

During the week, Morrison also doubled down on transgender issues, amplifying divisive and offensive commentary presented by the Liberal candidate in the seat of Warringah, Katherine Deves. While it was obvious that Morrison was magnifying these comments to win seats in other areas in Sydney's western suburbs and possibly other parts of Australia—Warringah was too far out of reach for the Liberal Party—even that part of the equation wasn't clear: at a time when the electorate is looking for constructive solutions and less division, Morrison's focus on transgender issues seemed to be based around personal beliefs and bigotry, rather than any solid research that could suggest that such an esoteric issue, as well as beating up on an already marginalised group of people, could win two or three seats for the Liberal Party.

This is also a high-risk strategy to magnify an issue the electorate doesn't really care too much about. In the unlikely event that attacking transgender people might make a different in some marginal regional seats, it could swing marginal seats away from the Liberal Party in inner city areas, and result in a net zero change. Australia is a far more diverse community than the Liberal Party could ever hope to understand: it is a far more inclusive community than any of the destructive and divisive rhetoric and narrative coming from Morrison and the senior leadership of the Liberal Party.

The racist, homophobic anti-transgender, anti-difference, anti-*other*, conformist monocultural Australia, doesn't exist in the same way anymore: Australia has moved on, despite the attempts by the Liberal–National Coalition to keep pulling back the community to the Australia of yesteryear.

Many commentators are still suggesting Morrison is a "formidable campaigner"—and after he won the 2019 federal election, this is a fair comment—but that was the previous election, and every election campaign is different. In 2022, it's a case of 'all bark and no bite': Morrison keeps pushing the culture war issues that don't resonate with enough people in the electorate to make a difference; he's attacking transgenderism; he's ramping up the need for religious discrimination laws, even though this is third consecutive election campaign that the issue has been revealed, yet still remains unresolved—suggesting Morrison is only highlighting 'religious discrimination' to send a message to a small group within the community—and he's even channeling the mindset of Donald Trump, and started attacking barristers and lawyers:

WEEK 5: DEBATE CLUB

> Scott Morrison: I have serious criticisms of the New South Wales ICAC model, I've never been a fan of how it's conducted itself. And I don't care if barristers and lawyers and others up there in Macquarie Street, sitting around in the barristers' chambers, disagree with me—they agree with disagree with me all the time. I've never had much truck with them over the course of my entire political career, I'll leave them to their jabots and all the rest of it.

It was unwise for Morrison to attack the judiciary in this way, especially in consideration that he'll be depending on lawyers and barristers if he is to ever front up to a federal anti-corruption body in the future, but it was just an extension of Morrison's 'everyman' approach to the election campaign: thumbing his nose at the elite members of society, even though he is one of those elites. The election campaign was beginning to meander, with a belief forming that Morrison had unnecessarily made the campaign too long: it was apparent why he decided on a six-week campaign—he needed at long as possible to turn around a likely defeat into an improbably victory—but the more the public saw of Morrison, they were less likely to vote for him.

Albanese hasn't had a brilliant campaign—he make mistakes on the first day of the campaign, and he was away from the campaign for one week due to COVID isolation—but it could also be one of those elections where the campaign itself is irrelevant: the electorate made their judgements on Morrison some time ago, even before the campaign commenced, and were just waiting for the election day to formalise their judgement on the ballot paper. In any case, a brilliant campaign is one that wins the election, and Albanese might have just done enough to secure a victory.

Morrison's attacks on the New South Wales Independent Commission Against Corruption also suggested that he's either lost for ideas or lacks the understanding of how important the introduction of a federal anti-corruption commission body is to the electorate. Public bodies should be open to scrutiny, and no public figure is above fair and open criticism, whether that be police forces, the Australian Taxation Office, the Australian Electoral Commission, or any other body. But Morrison's attacks made himself look dishonest, unethical and lacking in integrity—why would a prime minister attack an anti-corruption commission if he didn't have something to hide—and the attempt to undermine the justice system in Australia is extraordinary.

The attempts by the media to disengage the audience—with the commentary that the 'election is boring', 'no one knows who Anthony Albanese is', and 'both sides are all the same, so it doesn't matter who gets into office'—seems to have failed, and even still, Morrison's appeal to the disengaged voter has almost evaporated. The disengaged voter seemed to have enough awareness of Morrison to be less inclined to vote for him and this would be a great worry for Liberal Party headquarters. It was becoming more obvious that 'both sides' were not the same, and Albanese was presenting to the public as a far more palatable personality than the divisive Morrison, even to the people who take little interest in politics.

A 5.1 per cent pay rise for low-income workers was another issue that started bubbling under the surface—and in the context of a recent annual 5.1 per cent inflation rate increase, pushing for a wage rise during an election campaign would seem to be a reasonable idea. Labor latched onto the idea first—and representing low-income workers and attempting to boost their wages is one of the key reasons for Labor's existence—but Morrison was quick to deride this wage increase and suggested that it would be difficult for the economy to sustain such an increase.

Of course, Morrison's outcry is feeding into the low-wages narrative the business community keeps pushing, but it's also

WEEK 5: DEBATE CLUB

counterintuitive: if the economy is as good as Morrison keeps suggesting it is, the economy should be able to support a wage rise for the most lowly-paid people in the community. Perhaps after realising the contradiction of this narrative—and the fact that many people within the community were supportive of the wage rise—Morrison quickly shifted to personal abuse, calling Albanese a "loose unit" and suggesting that there were mental stability issues which might make him unfit to be a national leader. This, of course, brought up other problems for Morrison: focusing on Albanese's mental health suggested that Morrison was becoming more desperate and resorting to playground-style abuse because he nothing else to offer.

While many events and moments accumulate during a campaign, this might be the point where the election fate for Morrison was sealed: a campaign that went on for far too long; arguing against a reasonable wage rise for low-income workers; resorting to name calling and abuse—and questioning the mental health of his opponent—also suggested that Morrison's scatter-gun approach of a gambler just hadn't worked. When a leader resorts to childish tactics and abuse, it's obvious that the election is lost to them.

A FURTHER DESCENT INTO THE MAELSTROM

The opinion polls have started going into freefall for the Coalition: every single poll shows them in a losing position and a prospective loss of between fifteen to twenty seats, with many of these likely to fall to the teal independent candidates in Melbourne and Sydney. And with a week before the election day on 21 May, it's not looking very good for Morrison and the Liberal–National Coalition.

No government has ever been able to win from this position in the electoral cycle: that's not to suggest that it can't be done, but it's looking very unlikely, with everything needing to flow in favour of the Coalition for them to win the election, at a time when everything seems to cracking at the edges and falling apart. To highlight this factor, the minister for environment, Sussan Ley, was asked what would happen to Regional Development Australia after the election, only to respond by suggesting she was only focused on what happens in the final week of the campaign and "not painting a picture" of what the government might do after the election. Of course, Ley's painting skills might not be required after the election, because what's likely to happy on election day is not a very pretty picture at all.

The latest Newspoll–YouGov poll suggests Labor winning 80 seats—not a commanding majority but more than enough to form government. The Liberal Party continued with its strategy based on holding on and gaining several marginal seats to offset the likely losses in the safe seats of Kooyong, North Sydney, Goldstein and Dickson. There are still several possible permutations in this election: the most likely outcome is a Labor majority; followed by a Labor minority government—and both scenarios would also see a large crossbench of around thirteen or fourteen seats. Both options of a Liberal–National majority or minority government seem highly unlikely, but even within a minority position, the independents could command that they'll only support a Liberal–National government if Morrison is removed as leader, a likely scenario considered most of the independents—if they are successful—will be elected on a platform diametrically opposite to that of Morrison's. Unless Morrison gains an outright victory, his tenure is effectively over.

At this stage of the campaign, all opinion polls are either static or moving away from the Coalition, at a time when they need to be moving towards the Coalition. To be sure, the polls were wrong in previous election, when they all predicted a solid victory for the Labor Party, but least there was a movement towards the

Coalition several months prior to the election day in May 2019. In 2022, there is no evidence of a similar type of movement toward the Coalition.

The government appeared to be in an oblivious state—aware that something disastrous was going on in the campaign, but unable to pinpoint the issue and certainly unaware about what do to arrest the decline. The mismanagement of sporting funds through the 'sportsrorts' affair in the lead up to the 2019 election was getting some airing, with government ministers appearing to be unconcerned about the allegations of pork barreling and defining the spending in their own way:

> Michael Rowland (ABC news presenter): I can bring you back to the question: I wasn't asking about the Labor Party, this is Steven Charles, a highly respected former judge. He says 'pork barreling', colour-coded spreadsheets, the works—is political corruption. What do you say?
> Senator Bridget McKenzie: When you're talking about what you would see as 'pork barreling', is what in the National Party, we say is delivering for our electorates.

The electorate is expecting their political leaders to implement anti-corruption measures, and the government seems to be not listening to that message. While the Labor Party has campaigned strongly on anti-corruption measures in politics, the teal independents in Sydney and Melbourne are likely to be the beneficiaries. If the current opinions polls prove to be correct on election day, in the post-election stage, the Coalition will have a three-fold set of problems they will need to deal with: a Labor majority government, a loss of many seats—primarily to independents—and dealing with a large buffer zone created by the crossbench, a large barrier between the Coalition and the line where they can return to government in future elections:

once independent candidates win a seat, history has shown they become embedded and very difficult to remove in subsequent elections: Tony Windsor, Ted Mack, Cathy McGowan, Andrew Wilkie and Peter Andren, all secured victories as independent candidates, and served more than one term. And it's no coincidence that independents are surging in popularity: electorates have been ignored by major party members for far too long; this is an inevitable outcome of those electorates being left behind.

Over 300,000 people have voted every day since the prepoll period commenced, and more than one million votes have been cast at this stage of the campaign: at this rate, close to 50 per cent of the electorate will have voted before election day. Many commentators have been claiming there "isn't a mood for change" in the electorate but this is the usual narrative that is promoted by the media that either wants to keep pushing for conservative governments to remain in office or make unrealistic comparisons with Gough Whitlam's 'It's Time' election campaign from 1972—which wasn't the euphoric 'change' campaign many old-timers might like to point out. Whitlam's platform for change occurred in the 1969 election, where the swing towards Labor was 7.1 per cent—not enough to win the election—but enough to create a better opportunity in the following election. While the 1972 federal election ushered in great social and political change, the campaign itself was a relatively sedate affair.

In 2022, there is more of a feeling of the electorate's desire to remove an incompetent government, rather than the "mood for change" but, essentially, it's the same effect: Labor is likely to replace the Liberal–National Coalition in government. If anything, 2022 is reflective of the 1996 federal election: the leader of the opposition, John Howard, wasn't respected or loved by the electorate, but they were keen to remove Paul Keating as prime minister and the Labor Party from office. Howard ran a safe campaign and easily won the election in a landslide victory. Albanese is also running a safe campaign—albeit with some errors and an enforced one-week period of COVID isolation—and there are similar prevailing circumstances in 2022.

Morrison made promises that he ultimately couldn't deliver and couldn't effectively deliver on the issues that should have been delivered. The performances of the Morrison government have been compared with the incompetence of the McMahon government between 1971–72, which was also an appendage to a long period in office for the Coalition—twenty-three years. The Liberal–National Coalition of 2022 is too closely tied to big business, incapable of making wise decisions and, if not corrupt, certainly providing enough material for a future anti-corruption commission to investigate.

The National Party's Barnaby Joyce provided an address to the National Press Club in Canberra, and rather than appearing as a senior government member and deputy prime minister relishing the chance to win another election, he seemed flummoxed, he even stopped half-way through the speech for a very long pause, as if he didn't know what else to say, and not quite even sure why he was there. The junior partner within the Coalition, the National Party always seems to be inoculated from the problems that are created by the Liberal Party: even when Coalition governments are removed from office, the National Party usually holds its seats, and in some cases picks up an extra seat or two. But Joyce cannot be seen as the future of the National Party. He has been one of the dominant figures in national politics over the past decade, but every politician's career comes to an end. Nothing to say and not sure why he's there: it seemed to be indicative of the Coalition at this final stage of the election campaign.

***

WEEK 6: JUDGEMENT DAY

21 May 2022

The election campaign is slowly reaching its final point: all sides of politics have put out their policy ideas over the past six weeks and tried to inform the public about what they plan to do in the future, if they can form government after the election. However, there's only one winner, and the loser will have to go away and prepare themselves for another election in three years' time.

It's not necessarily the case where a great campaign results in an election win but the adage that rings true the most is that a winning campaign—irrespective of how that win is achieved—is always the best campaign.

Neither campaign from the Coalition or from the Labor Party has been astounding but it's fair to say Scott Morrison's campaign has been abysmal and is a striking contrast to the perceptions that he is the "formidable campaigner" that many of his supporters wanted to promote.

Elections are a combination of a referendum of a government's past performances and what all sides of politics are presenting for the future, but Morrison has been found wanting in both areas. This may not have mattered anyway, as it seemed that the electorate made its judgement on the Morrison government some time ago and the events during the election campaign weren't going to change this sentiment.

WEEK 6: JUDGEMENT DAY

While there has been some disappointment about the Labor campaign, their strategy was based more about highlighting the failures of the Morrison government than offering wholesale changes, with Anthony Albanese promising "renewal, not revolution"—a message not directed to the Labor base, who would prefer to see a 'Whitlam-esque' transition in government, but those in the electorate who were ready to see the end of Morrison as prime minister, and see that Labor was the 'safe pair of hands' before voting for them.

The character of each leader is always highlighted during a campaign, but it was Morrison who tended to have the large dissatisfaction rating from the electorate, and Labor's main efforts have been to keep returning to the lack of national leadership provided during the bushfires season of 2019/20, failures during the vaccination rollout, and the tardy response from government during the recent floods in New South Wales and Queensland.

There was a concern from within Labor that these character issues hadn't been highlighted enough by the campaign team, but sometimes these campaign messages appear without effort, and there's little need to interfere when an opponent is making all the mistakes by themselves, especially when those mistakes are highlighted by others:

> Tracey Grimshaw (Nine Media journalist, A Current Affair): Prime minister, you said at your launch on Sunday, "I saved the country". You don't hold a hose; you weren't in your tinny plucking people off rooftops; you weren't doing sixteen-hour days in PPE on COVID wards; you didn't get enough vaccines soon enough; you didn't get enough RATs so that we could finally have a holiday interstate for Christmas; and China has set up base in the Solomons. Do you think maybe you slightly over egged the part about "I saved the country"?

Scott Morrison: [a long pause]... Well, that's quite a long list you've been able to pull together. But let me say this...

The Liberal Party has been pushing the message the Albanese isn't experienced enough to become prime minister, even though he's been in parliament since 1996. Morrison was also pushing the idea that he hasn't had an economic portfolio before; that he's a 'loose unit'—although that can be positive or negative, depending on which demographic is being targeted; and on top this barrage, the peculiar idea that it's not possible for a politician to become the prime minister, if they'd never been in the position. Again, an inherent paradox created by Morrison: he wasn't a prime minister before he became the prime minister, so how did he come to this position?

In the final few days of the campaign, the focus returned to cost of living pressures, inflation and stagnant wages. Morrison and Peter Dutton also returned to their favoured pastime—China—with Dutton raising a scare campaign about a 'secret' Chinese spy vessel 400 kilometres north from the coast of Perth. So secretive and dangerous was the presence of this Chinese spy vessel, that it was subsequently docked at Garden Island—considered a part of metropolitan Perth—while it being repaired. It was a clear attempt by the government to engage with its usual dog-whistling tactics and anti-China racism, which then dovetailed into Dutton's message that Albanese would never be able to 'stand up' to China. Ironically, it was the Liberal Party—and Dutton—who failed to 'stand up' to China, enabling the lease of the Darwin and Newcastle ports to Chinese business interests, and ceding Australian diplomatic interests in the Solomon Islands to the Chinese Communist Party.

While it's easy for Dutton to fill the last days of this election campaign with a few cheap racist pot-shots at China, he seems to have forgotten that the anti-Asian stance of John Howard in the late 1980s almost ended his political career. It might be politically advantageous for Dutton to add to the worsening Australia–China relationships but it's a sign of weakness to allow this situation to deteriorate so dramatically and damage Australia's interests with China.

The Liberal Party held their official campaign launch on the final Sunday before election day—primarily so they could use public funds until they launched their campaign, and then use party funds after that—and the highlight of their launch was the policy of first home buyers accessing 40 per cent of their superannuation funds to purchase a dwelling.

Most government subsidies in areas such as healthcare rebates, childcare subsidies, private schools support—and this applies to governments of all persuasions—simply pushes up the cost of those services for the consumer, and it's likely that this will be the result with this policy as well.

Every affordable housing measure that has been introduced over the past thirty years has resulted in pushing up housing prices, making them even more unaffordable. This has produced the ultimate political conundrum: politicians need to make promises to 'fix housing affordability' but the most politically saleable policies that seem like a good idea to the electorate, are the most destructive policies and do very little to resolve housing affordability issues.

The more obvious solution would be to work with state and territory governments to increase the supply of land and housing, improve housing density in capital cities and rework capital gains tax issues for property investors: these issues would be far more effective than promising an instant hit of cash into the hands of borrowers, which then pushes up housing prices. But better solutions are more complex and difficult to explain: Labor presented a suite of sensible policies to address some of these issues in the 2019 election campaign, but these were mispresented and weaponised into the 'retiree tax' by the Liberal Party and the media, and the Labor Party lost that election. It's obvious that housing affordability will remain as one of those issues which constantly has the wrong solutions applied to it.

The policy also gave the Liberal Party an opportunity to diminish compulsory superannuation and attack industry superannuation funds, two areas which the party is ideologically opposed to. The Liberal Party member for Goldstein, Tim Wilson—who was facing an uphill struggle to win his seat against the independent candidate, Zoe Daniel—used this policy to highlight his populist campaign against superannuation funds, arguing that it would be better to use these funds to purchase property, while ignoring the economic impact the policy would have on housing prices in the short term, and the impact on superannuation funds in the long term.

It was also a policy to hold up the Liberal Party campaign launch—otherwise, what else would they have been able to talk about?—but it brought the unintended discussion that if the policy was so good, why did the Liberal Party do nothing about the issue during their nine years in office, and wait for the final week of an election campaign to make the announcement?

It became evident that is was just another political launch that followed on from previous launches, because this is the schedule that is always applied during a campaign: a bored media looking to catch a leader off-guard with the 'gotcha' questions; getting a 'gaffe' on the first day of the campaign, and running with the narrative that Labor has already lost the election; expecting that a leader away from the campaign for a week—as Albanese was when he contracted COVID—also loses the election (it didn't). Future election campaigns will follow a different direction, because the old style of campaigning isn't as effective as it used to be, and new methods will be required: whether the media can

WEEK 6: JUDGEMENT DAY

adapt to this and reinvent their own role in election campaigns will be an interesting dynamic to explore.

Even in the final days of the campaign, the media was still searching for other mistakes created by Albanese and, as every other tactic had failed to make an impression, seeing if there was any way of diminishing his performances in the eye of the public. Morrison, on the other hand, was still someone who could do nothing wrong, even when he did do something wrong. While campaigning in the Tasmania seat of Braddon, Morrison involved himself with yet another photo opportunity: this time, deciding to engage in a quick game of football with the Devonport Strikers under-8s team.

In his haste to obtain the media exposure, Morrison ran into seven-year-old, Luca Fauvette, crash tackled him onto the ground, and narrowly avoided seriously injuring the boy. The media ran with the story, but promoted it an unfortunate and harmless incident, suggesting the boy was standing in the wrong position on the field, with some news outlets comparing Morrison's soccer skills with those of a "Manchester United midfielder", and suggesting he was "better than Ronaldo", instead of asking why would a large muscley and aggressive 110 kilogram 54-year-old man, decide to join a group of seven-year-old children, lay a tackle in a game where tackling is disallowed, and almost seriously injure a boy.

This incident epitomised Morrison's entire campaign: a relentless pursuit of the media image; putting every else's safety at risk, even a seven-year-old boy; going into places where he's not needed or wanted; and whatever he did, he had helpers in the media who would put a positive spin on the event. It's not hard to imagine how the media would have reacted if Albanese was the one who applied the tackle on Luca Fauvette, rather than Morrison.

Morrison has always played the high-stakes game in politics, and while it's not suggested that this event was premeditated, at least it kept Albanese away from the news headlines, even if was for the wrong reasons. Morrison's risks have usually paid off for him in the past, but in this campaign, his luck has deserted him: this was yet another example.

***

This election campaign has introduced the 'teal independent' into the political lexicon; although the media prefers to use the term 'so-called teal independents', a terminology which raises some doubts about who they are and feeds directly into the Liberal Party's narrative that these candidates are Labor stooges, not independent at all, trying to misrepresent who they are and mislead the electorate.

The teal independents are a loose alliance of independent candidates with a common goal of mitigating climate change by reducing carbon emissions, and introducing anti-corruption measures into federal politics, and appeared either through various 'Voices Of' campaigns around Australia, or through financial and material support from the Climate 200 group. It's difficult to imagine teal candidates such as Allegra Spender (Wentworth), Kylea Tink (North Sydney), Zoe Daniel (Goldstein), Monique Ryan (Kooyong), Kate Chaney (Curtin) or Sophie Scamps (Mackellar) masquerading as Labor stooges—although Ryan was once a member of the Labor Party between 2007–10—but they were targeting seats held by the Liberal Party, and in election campaigns, it seems that any form of abuse is tolerated, especially when it's been delivered by conservatives.

The Liberal Party members who have occupied these seats have been uneventful or promoted to a level higher than their skillsets would suggest. Certainly, Josh Frydenberg has achieved the position of treasurer, but their other members were overly ambitious and the fact that they are struggling to retain their seats, suggests that their respective electorates are not overly impressed with their performances.

While there might a substantial number of losers from the Liberal Party on election day, the other big loser from the campaign is the mainstream media, especially in the manner they have tried to insert and impose themselves upon the campaign and direct the political narrative that suits the vested interests of their proprietors, rather than reporting on the events of the day in a professional and balanced manner. If Labor does win the election on Saturday—and there's many pieces which need to fall into place to achieve the results they're after—it will provide further evidence of the diminishing role of the mainstream media within political affairs.

For most of the six-week campaign, they've amplified government talking points, attacked Labor and magnified errors created by Albanese, and attempted to create a clearer pathway for a return of the Morrison government. It hasn't worked: most of the mainstream media—Nine Media, Seven West Media, News Corporation, the ABC—have reported abysmally and they've been seriously exposed as reliable news services.

There have been some honourable exceptions: the ABC's Laura Tingle has been diligent, fair, objective and professional. Tracy Grimshaw's interrogation of Morrison was exceptional, not so much that it was a deserved exposé of a politician who had seriously underperformed, but it was notable exception in the generally low level of scrutiny that has been applied to a prime minister who must rank as one of Australia's worst and least effective to ever occupy the position.

Post-election—depending on which party wins and has the motivation to do this—there needs to be a reform of the media landscape: media ownership levels which, under current legislation, only encourage concentration, rather than diversity;

truth in journalism and reporting; truth in political advertising, like existing legislation in Canada and New Zealand.

The business model of journalism is based on conflict and sensationalism and with diminishing sales, advertising revenue and subscribers, behaviours have become even more egregious and outrageously sensational. It's not in the public interest to continue with this behaviour and it diminishes the body politic. There are many journalists who need to rethink their careers: certainly, for many, journalism is just like any other job, and they'll be a gun for hire, according to whoever pays the bills. But if the media wants to avoid becoming the biggest loser in future elections, it needs to become more professional, less partisan, more informative, and correctly identify the issues that are relevant to the electorate, not pushing the values that benefit conservative politics and the vested interests of their owners.

THE ISSUES THAT DIDN'T MATTER

The major campaign issues have been based around the cost of living, employment, interest rates and housing but there's also many other issues which haven't featured prominently during the campaign at all. Labor has provided some focus on Indigenous affairs, with Anthony Albanese offering his strong support for the Indigenous Voice to Parliament—and the Makarrata—and has promised a referendum in the next parliament. Morrison hasn't mentioned anything at all, just offering a dismissive attitude to the issue about appearing on National Indigenous TV in an election forum.

> Shuba Krishnan (NITV): Prime minister, why won't anyone from the Coalition appear on the national Indigenous broadcasters' election program? We're in Lingiari, it has the highest population of Indigenous Australians. Are these issues not important to you?

> Scott Morrison: We're investing $30 million in supporting connectivity, particularly for Indigenous communities right across the country. That's how you close the gap, the connectivity for Indigenous Australians.
> Krishnan: Will anyone from your government appear on the national Indigenous broadcaster's election program?… [Morrison gets into the prime minister's car and slams the door].

Indigenous issues have been overlooked during this campaign—at least Labor has announced some policy—but there are other areas which have been overlooked by the government as well. Labor released its arts and cultural industries policy during the week: no announcement from the Coalition. After the focus on women's rights throughout 2021, the March4Justice campaign and the release of the *Set the Standard* report by the Sex Discrimination Commissioner Kate Jenkins, women's issues also haven't featured prominently during the campaign, although given the make-up of the senior leadership of the Liberal, National and Labor parties—all male—this is not surprising. These are important issues but there just hasn't been enough emphasis on them during the campaign.

Women make up over 50 per cent of the population: Labor is offering more substance and policy offerings for women's safety, gender equity and programs to reduce domestic violence, but the Coalition has largely steered clear. To ignore over half of the electorate is foolish but with a low percentage of women members and Senators within the Coalition ranks—only 21 per cent are women, compared to Labor's 43 per cent—it's obvious why there is a lack of awareness of women's issues within the Liberal and National parties.

The arts and the cultural industries are another area where the Coalition is lacking in policy output. While arts and entertainment are sectors that are relevant to every age group, gender and cultural setting all around Australia, the government has decided that the producers of cultural output—musicians, artists, filmmakers, authors and writers—traditionally vote for progressive parties and trying to harness their votes is not worth the effort.

Labor did formally launch its arts policy in the final week of the campaign and, in keeping with the Coalition's general disdain for the arts, the minister of the arts, Paul Fletcher, indicated that there was a document on the Liberal Party website outlining all their offerings, although failing to announce what they were. It appeared that for the Coalition, even announcing their arts policies might be detrimental to their political interests: best to keep it as quiet as possible.

The arts and creative industries sector—along with the university sector—were the hardest hit areas during the pandemic but didn't receive any support through the government's JobKeeper program, and the support that was offered was through a loan support system which they then had to repay. This compares unfavourably to the $21 billion of JobKeeper support to companies which didn't need the support—in some cases, retail outlets such as Harvey Norman received $21 million, even though their profits rose during the pandemic. It was a continuation of a theme which essentially commenced in 1996 when the Howard government was first elected: despise the arts and use everything possible to attack the people who work in these industries; claim that they're the elites and overprivileged, even though many people who work in the arts are some of the lowest paid people in the community. These are attitudes which epitomise the modern Liberal Party's lack of depth, lack of substance, and their own lack of significance in many critical parts of Australian culture and economy.

This defies the Liberal Party's history and previous role in the promotion of the arts, women's issues and Indigenous affairs.

Former prime minister Malcolm Fraser was provided with a smoking ceremony at his funeral—a rare honour. The first Indigenous Senator in Australia, Neville Bonner, was appointed by the Liberal Party. The 1967 referendum to include Indigenous people within the Australian census, and the amendment to *Commonwealth Electoral Act* in 1962 to allow Indigenous people to vote in elections, all occurred under Coalition governments.

The Liberal Party also had the first woman in the House of Representatives and Cabinet minister—Dame Enid Lyon—elected in 1943 and appointed to Cabinet in 1949 as a junior minister. They also had the first full federal Cabinet minister with Margaret Guilfoyle when she was appointed minister for education in 1975. The Australian Council for the Arts was created under a Coalition government in 1968. This is not to suggest that the Coalition was a bastion for Indigenous activism, feminist revolution or radical arts practices, but these examples show how far removed the Liberal Party of 2022 is from the founding principles of Robert Menzies and subsequent Liberal leadership of the 1960s and 1970s.

One other oversight of the election campaign is the coronavirus pandemic: the Labor Party has made a few references to the failures in the vaccination rollout and featured Morrison prominently in their advertising, where he says that "it wasn't a race", when it clearly was. After the resurgence of COVID at the beginning of 2022, this appeared to be the worst stage of the pandemic and neither side of politics was keen to talk about the issue. In the final week of the election campaign, there was a seven-day average of 65 daily deaths from COVID across Australia; 53,000 new infections every day; 3,000 people in hospital; 130 people in intensive care units.

It was clear the pandemic was not over, despite the ignorance of the issue during the campaign, and will continue to be an issue that will require further national management after the election.

Although the two-dose rate of the COVID vaccines across Australia is around 95 per cent, the three-dose rate in only 69 per cent and, at any given time, around 400,000 people are in isolation with COVID illnesses, creating workforce shortages and problems with supply chains across the country. The pandemic is far from over but both sides of politics are behaving as though it is. While COVID hasn't features strongly in the campaign, it will still have to managed after the election, irrespective of which party wins.

THE FINAL POLLS: IS IT 2019 ALL OVER AGAIN?

The final batch of opinion polls were released and offered a confusing picture. Some of the polls remained unmoved, while others suggested the gap was narrowing, the narrative the media always likes to see in the final days of a campaign. There was a wide range in the reported gap between Labor and the Coalition—between 2 per cent and 8 per cent in two-party preferred voting—but irrespective of whether there was slight movement towards the Coalition in some polls, none of them showed the Coalition to be ahead, suggesting an outright Labor victory or a Labor-minority government.

Of course, this is a similar situation to the final week of the 2019 election campaign, only for the Coalition to receive 51.5 per cent of the two-party preferred vote to Labor's 48.5 per cent—opposite to the result predicted by opinion polls—and go on to win a close election with a three-seat majority. It's difficult to accept that the opinion polls will be incorrect for two consecutive federal elections—it's not in the financial interests of pollsters to be constantly wrong—but with such a wide variation in the margins they are predicting, a few polling companies will get it right, the others are going to be wrong and will need to change their methodologies again. But surely, it's not possible they can *all* be wrong again.

In federal elections, there usually is a tightening of opinion polls but, quite often, it's not enough to provide a different result to what opinion polls predicted: certainly, there will be differences in the final two-party preferred vote, and the numbers of seats won or lost, but essentially, if the polls suggest the government will be returned, or the opposition will win, these predictions are usually correct. The opinion poll predictions for 2019 federal election were completely incorrect, as they were for the 1993 federal election, but two incorrect calls out of ten elections is not such a bad result for the pollsters. Despite these factors, everything is still pointing to a Labor victory.

Eight million votes have already been lodged through prepolling and postal votes and, of course, these electors cannot be influenced any further by the respective leaders' campaigns. This represents almost 45 per cent of all votes and makes it difficult to make definitive election predictions. There are the key areas of inner Melbourne and Sydney which are highly likely to be won by teal independents—seats in affluent areas which are never going to be held by the Labor Party—which means that Labor is hoping that seats will be picked in Western Australia and New South Wales, as well as its electorate graveyard site of Queensland, were it currently holds only six of the thirty seats in that state.

As is usually the case in the final week of an election campaign, the machismo references started becoming more frequent, a reflection of the 'blokesworld' of the media and federal politics: most events in politics are "a bruising encounter"; "a tough tussle"; or it's a case of each leader looking for the "knockout blow". And of course, no campaign is complete without the football references, to further emphasise American media academic Jay Rosen's point about the contest of politics and "horse-race journalism", with some media outlets suggesting Morrison was akin to the coach of the AFL team which is four goals down, five minutes into the final quarter of the grand final, kicking into the wind. Aficionados of AFL were quick to point out that no team has ever been able to achieve this in the history of the league which commenced in 1897, but it highlighted how ridiculous these sporting analogies are in the field of politics.

To extend this sporting analogy, no political party has come from this far behind in the political cycle—literally days before election day—and gone on to win a federal election. Aside from opinion polling, it's also the wide range of qualitative perceptions of the Morrison government. There are perceptions of corruption; there are perceptions of incompetence; division, and an underlying element of racism is a constant factor. Morrison appears to be a pathological liar and ignores issues until they become problems and then goes on to claim the problems have been fixed, even if they haven't. It appears to be a government intent on holding onto power without a purpose, primarily to keep Labor out of office.

This is never a valid enough reason to remain in government and, generally, the Morrison era has been a period of ineptitude and incompetence, verging on corruption. Albanese might not be the best leader of the opposition presented by the Labor Party, but he does offer a more positive outlook for Australia and after the nine years of the ineffective Abbott, Turnbull and Morrison governments, it might not be a case of whether Labor deserves to win the election, but whether the Coalition deserves to remain in office.

Elections are important and, despite the narrative emanating from the mainstream media, this has been a very worthwhile campaign. Some elections are more important than others and the 2022 election is one of those. It's evident that the Coalition government needs to be removed: Australia is at crossroads, unsure of which direction to go, but it can ill-afford a government like Morrison's heading into the future. They've achieved little in office; they've damaged the country, with the damage so great that it may take least two terms of an alternative government to repair this damage.

It's been a waste of nine years: incompetent ministers such as Senator Richard Colbeck going off to watch a test cricket match, instead of fronting up to a Senate estimates committee to explain all the disasters from his aged care portfolio. Endless corruption and misuse of Commonwealth funds; with no one held to account or answerable to anyone for their misbehaviours. It's unacceptable but, essentially, it's still up to the electorate to decide whether it's good enough for a government to continue in this mode.

There are too many moving parts for the Liberal–National Coalition that need to fall into place for them to achieve an unlikely victory: of course, many moving parts need to fall into place for Labor to claim victory, but just not as many. One stubborn issue which may play out during the election count on Saturday evening is that because of the way that the votes landed in the 2019 federal election, Labor could achieve 52.5 per cent of the two-party preferred vote and not win the election. This is unlikely, but it's not implausible—in the 2014 South Australia election, the Liberal Party reached 53.0 per cent of the two-party preferred vote, yet failed to win the election.

In 2022, this is an election Labor should win, either a narrow outright victory, or hold a minority government with the support of a large crossbench of Australian Greens and independent candidates. It's not possible to see how the Liberal–National Coalition can achieve any sort of victory. However, if the Coalition does manage to win this election, despite all the incompetence, mismanagement, division and corruption, it might be time to hand over the keys of democracy to them and cancel all future elections. If Labor cannot achieve an election victory in these circumstances that are so highly favourable to them, they will need to do some serious soul-searching about how they will ever be able to return to office. That's how important the 2022 election is to the future of Australia.

***

EVERYTHING MUST CHANGE

22 May 2022

The 2022 federal election has resulted in a narrow victory for the Labor Party—winning 77 seats—but this narrow result is deceptive. The Liberal Party has lost seats in its heartland areas in Sydney and Melbourne—not to the Labor Party, but the teal independents—and the Liberal–National Coalition has won a total of only 58 seats, losing seventeen seats it held before the election, as well as its hold on government.

As a result, Anthony Albanese will be Australia's thirty-first Prime Minister and Labor's thirteenth. It was a staggered pathway to victory for Labor after some concerns in the early stages of counting, where it seemed Scott Morrison was possibly going to reprise his surprise victory from the 2019 election but as the evening rolled out—although the voting figures coming in from the Australian Election Commission painted a confusing picture—once the figures started to stabilise and clearer patterns began to form, it was evident that the Coalition was in for an electoral thrashing, and Labor was the only party that would be able to form government, either in its own right, or in coalition with a patchwork of the new members on the crossbench.

The Australian Greens surprised in picking up two additional seats in Brisbane and the crossbench expanded to the largest ever in federal history—increasing from seven seats to sixteen. While it wasn't a crushing victory for Labor, it was a terrible night for the Liberal Party: a loss of seventeen seats, a new buffer zone created by a large crossbench—primarily through the new force in Australian politics, the teal independents—and the prospects of a long stint in opposition.

In politics, anything is possible, of course, but the magnitude of this loss will dampen expectations of a quick recovery for the Liberal Party. In federal politics, a first-term government is usually rewarded with a second term, as though it's the wish of the electorate to verify its choice from the preceding election, and even during the chaos that afflicted national governments from late 2009 onwards, the Labor Party achieved a second term in 2010 after it removed Kevin Rudd as its leader. The Coalition also recorded a second term in 2016—and a subsequent third term in 2019—even though there was a chaotic transition between the Abbott and Turnbull governments. Indeed, the last federal government to be removed at the end of its first term was the Scullin Labor government in 1931, over 90 years ago.

The primary vote for the both the Liberal and Labor parties went down—a drop of 5.7 per cent to 35.7 per cent for the Liberal Party, and a drop of 0.8 per cent to 32.6 per cent for Labor—but it's the two-party preferred vote that matters the most in Australia, and Labor was well ahead on that number. The erosion of the primary vote for major parties meant that the vote for the Australian Greens and independents increased, and it's difficult to see how the major parties will be able to reclaim these lost votes.

There are many strong independents coming through: in this election, the seats of Curtin, Goldstein, Kooyong, Mackellar, North Sydney and Wentworth moved from the Liberal Party ledger, over to the crossbench. As can be seen with independent members such as Andrew Wilkie, Zali Steggall and Helen Haines, once independents take hold—provided they perform adequately in the eyes of their electorates—they are difficult to remove. Other members aligned to smaller political parties—Adam Bandt, Bob Katter and Rebekha Sharkie—have also managed to win several consecutive terms.

This reduction in the primary vote for the major political parties continues a trend that commenced in the 1970s and it is surprising that it has taken this long for independent candidates to gain a stronghold in the House of Representatives, especially in the context of a far more diverse community and changes in so many other areas of consumer tastes and interests.

This election result should be the first step in the realignment of politics in Australia for political parties on the centre-right, who will need to reflect upon the offerings they are making to the electorate and work towards making themselves more electable. As it stands, this is an excellent win for progressive politics—a narrow victory for the Labor Party, a large collection of independents who want to make positive changes in politics, including introducing anti-corruption measures, action on climate change and renewable energy, and improvements in women's safety and gender equity, while the political parties which occupied the government benches for nine years and opposed most of those measures, have been removed from office and unlikely to return in a hurry.

While the result might seem like an endorsement of the Labor Party and Albanese, it was more a repudiation of the Liberal Party and values that it holds. And, of course, the biggest loser was Morrison, who appeared to be a large drag on the Coalition vote. There was also some commentary that the election result also signaled the end of neoliberalism as an economic philosophy, but the end of an era is never so clearly defined by a specific date: if changes do arise in economic thinking, it takes many years for this to become apparent. Economic changes, when they do occur, also affect different parts of the country in different ways and it was apparent that there is still some economic uncertainty in Queensland, where the Liberal Party only lost two seats, and still holds twenty-one of the thirty seats in that state.

Tasmania also swung towards the Liberal Party, where they managed to hold onto seats they were expected to lose. That's where the relatively good news for the Liberal Party ended: in Victoria, they lost four seats and had a 1.7 swing against them; in New South Wales, a loss of six seats and a 3.2 per cent swing against; South Australia, a further one seat lost and a 3.3 per cent swing against.

But the lowlight for the Liberal Party was the massive losses in Western Australia, which validated Labor's unusual decision to launch their election campaign in Perth for the first time ever. In a reflection of the massive landslide victory Labor achieved in the Western Australia election in 2021 under premier Mark McGowan, federal Labor picked up an extra four seats, while the Liberal Party lost six seats and had a massive 10.5 per cent swing against it. Western Australia is parochial state, an issue Morrison failed to recognise when he constantly attacked the Western Australia Labor government during the early parts of the COVID pandemic and the long periods of border closures in that state, and then going on to admonish the Western Australian public, when he said that it was time to "get out from under the doona" and made comparisons with the cavemen from *The Croods*, a description which was peculiar, insulting and politically insensitive. It may have taken a while, but Morrison found the hard way in taking on this approach with the Western Australian electorate.

After all the opinion polling problems that arose from the 2019 federal election, pollsters predicted the correct outcome. While there a difference in the final two-party preferred predictions, every pollster predicted either a narrow Labor victory, or a Labor-controlled minority government but, importantly, none predicted a Coalition victory of any kind. The result ultimately presented a swing of 3.7 per cent to Labor, for a two-party preferred vote of 52.1 per cent, and 47.9 per cent to the Coalition—while it was a terrible loss for the Coalition in terms of seats lost, the party should at least be heartened that the two-party preferred vote wasn't as severe as it could have been.

In the Liberal Party heartland areas of Sydney and Melbourne, the swings against the party were large: Kooyong had a swing of 8.3 per cent against Josh Frydenberg; Goldstein, a 10.7 per cent swing against Tim Wilson; Mackellar, 15.7 per cent against Jason Falinski; North Sydney, a swing of 12.2 per cent against Trent Zimmerman—these were reflective of the anti-Liberal Party swings in the New South Wales state by-elections that were held in February. The seat of Wentworth also had a swing of 5.5 per cent against Dave Sharma: while these seats fell to independents, Labor also managed to pick up the seat of Bennelong, with a swing of 7.9 per cent against the Liberal Party candidate; Higgins, a seat once held by former treasurer Peter Costello, also fell to the Labor Party, with a swing of 4.7 per cent. Seats, once they are lost, are difficult to regain in future elections. The fact that these seat losses occurred in areas that have been long held by the Liberal Party should be a great area of concern in any post-election review performed by the party.

After the result became clear on election night, there was conjecture whether Morrison would continue as the leader of the Liberal Party and whether he would leave parliament altogether. Bob Hawke, Paul Keating, Julia Gillard, Kevin Rudd and Malcolm Turnbull all retired after they lost the prime ministership—John Howard and Tony Abbott were voted out of their respective electorates—and it was expected that Morrison would follow suit. At least one part of question was answered by Morrison:

> Scott Morrison: I, as leader, take responsibility for the wins and the losses. That is the burden and that is the responsibility of leadership. And as a result, I will be handing over the leadership at the next party room meeting to ensure that the party can be taken forward under new leadership, which is the appropriate thing to do.
> I've had the great privilege to lead this great party and to lead this great nation.

It wasn't a surprise that Morrison stood down as the leader—the previous prime minister to continue as the leader after an election loss was Gough Whitlam in 1975—but the decision to remain in parliament was as surprise. Politics is a fired-up cesspit of ambition and after achieving the post of prime minister, the pinnacle of the political system in Australia, there's not much else to be achieved: it was unclear why Morrison wanted to remain as the member for Cook, unless it he considered to be a deserved political sabbatical at taxpayer's expense.

There were election surprises in other parts of the country, as there usually are on election night. The Australian Greens won two seats in Queensland—one from the Labor Party in the seat of Griffith, and one from the Liberal Party in the seat of Brisbane. There was an expectation that the teal independents were going win seats, but not so many—Kooyong, Goldstein, North Sydney, Mackellar, Curtin, Wentworth and Warringah, as well as a Senate position in the Australian Capital Territory, won David Pocock.

The results for the newly-formed New Liberals—forced to campaign under the acronym 'TNL' after a decision by the Australian Electoral Commission which ruled their name was too similar to the Liberal Party—was also surprising. Their leader, Victor Kline only received 0.9 per cent of the primary vote in the seat of North Sydney and 6,331 primary votes across the eight seats they contested. The highest primary vote achieved by any TNL candidate was the 1.6 per cent result in the seat of Hawke. Clearly there's more work to do, either with their political marketing or policy development: TNL is a nondescript name that is hardly going to inspire confidence, but all political parties need to start somewhere and learn the lessons when they do make mistakes.

There was also a surprise for the Labor Party. Kristina Keneally was the Labor candidate in the seat of Fowler in western Sydney and was defeated by independent candidate Dai Le. Keneally had been parachuted into the seat after Labor member Chris Hayes retired, and was expected to win the seat but the lack of local knowledge and the adverse publicity created when her candidacy was announced—Keneally lives on Scotland Island in the affluent northern parts of Sydney, whereas the seat of Fowler is a migrant working-class area in the south-west—contributed to the 15.6 per swing against the Labor Party on election night. Keneally's preselection was primarily to resolve a factional issue within the Labor Party, after she was allocated an unwinnable position on Labor's New South Wales Senate ticket.

Why the Labor Party placed a former New South Wales premier and well-performing Senator into an unwinnable position is anybody's guess, but the internal politics of the party are sometimes inexplicable to outside observers. The strong message was: political parties shouldn't install a candidate without local branch support, although Labor did install Andrew Charlton—who resides in Sydney's eastern suburbs—into the multicultural western Sydney seat of Parramatta, and he managed a swing towards him; perhaps there were many other issues in play in the seat of Fowler.

Every election night includes victory and concession speeches—unless there's no clear winner on the night, as occurred during the 2010 election—but concession speeches have a place in history for a departing prime minister, and need to provide hope for their political party for future elections, irrespective of how disastrous the loss has been:

> Scott Morrison: It's a difficult night for Liberals and Nationals around the country, as nights like this always are. They are humbling, but so is victory: victory is also humbling and always should be. Tonight, I've spoken to the leader of the opposition and the incoming prime minister Anthony Albanese, and I've congratulated him on his election victory this evening.
> In this country at a time like this, when we look around the world, and particularly when we see those in the Ukraine, fighting for their very freedom and liberty, I think on a night like tonight, we can reflect on the greatness of our democracy. This has been a time of great upheaval over these past few years, and it has imposed a heavy price on our country and on all Australians. And I think all Australians have felt that deeply.
> And we've seen in our own politics, a great deal of disruption, as the way people have voted today, with major parties having one of the lowest primary votes that we've ever seen. That says a lot, I think about the upheaval that is taking place in our nation. And I think it is important for our nation to heal, and to move forward. But at the same time, three years ago, I stood before you, and I said I believed in miracles. I still believe in miracles, as I always have. There's another great miracle which I want to give thanks for tonight, and that is the miracle of the Australian people. What Australians have endured over these past few years has shown a tremendous depth of character and resilience and strength.
> And each and every day, I've had the great privilege to lead this nation over the last more than three and a half years. And the one thing I've always counted on has been the strength and resilience and character of the Australian people. It has been the Australian people under the strong support of a strong

government that has enabled all of us to come through to where we are today. And I think that's something that all Australians can give thanks for.

As we move forward, we hand over this country as a government in a stronger position than we inherited it when we came to government, those years ago under Tony Abbott. We leave government having secured our borders many years ago, and we leave government having restored our nation's defences. I've always believed that the purpose of a strong economy is not an end in itself, but to ensure a stronger nation that can provide the services that its people depend upon.

But tonight, it's a night of disappointment for the Liberals and Nationals. But it's also a time for Coalition members and supporters all across the country to hold their heads high.

We have been a strong government, we have been a good government. Australia is stronger as a result of our efforts over these last three terms and, over the next three years, I have no doubt under strong leadership of our Coalition, three years from now, I am looking forward to the return of a Coalition government.

Election night speeches are quite different for the winning side. The Labor Party faithful had assembled at the Canterbury–Hurlstone RSL Club on election night, in the heart of Albanese's seat of Grayndler. Labor federal election victories are rare, and this one was a long time coming: while former prime minister Julia Gillard managed to form a minority government seventeen days after the 2010 federal election, the election itself had no winner, with no party achieving the 76 seats needed to govern in its own right. It was fifteen years since Labor's last election night victory, when Kevin Rudd declared that his team was going to have a "strong cup of tea and an Iced VoVo" before getting back to work, and this crowd was certainly going to savour the moment.

Among the sea of red in the massive hall in Sydney's inner west were Labor's key players milling among the crowd: Tony Burke, beaming with a smile as big as the Sydney Harbour Bridge; Wayne Swan, Labor national president and veteran of many campaigns—relieved rather than elated—he'd seen too many false dawns for Labor in the past; Dee Madigan, Labor's successful advertising campaign manager; Labor candidates who failed at the 2016 and 2019 federal elections, but became a critical part of the 2022 campaign; New South Wales Labor members who hadn't tasted victory since their own state election win, also in 2007. These were the people who worked hard to get Labor elected and it was a night to celebrate.

While Rudd's election night speech failed to grasp the magnitude of the 2007 victory, 2022 was not going to disappoint. The Canterbury–Hurlstone RSL Club had the feel of the rock music barns Albanese frequented as a youth: a heaving mass of supporters, with the background noise of the muffled thumping bass rhythms from Gang Gajang's 1985 hit song, 'Sounds of Then (This is Australia)'. The two large format video screens near the front of the stage streamed the election night broadcasts from the ABC and Sky News, and these had already declared that Labor had won the election and would be able to form government in its own right.

There was an air of expectation within the building, with the audience waiting for Albanese to arrive onto the stage to make the historic announcement that Morrison had offered his concession and Labor had won the election. After a long wait, Senator Penny Wong arrived on stage, announced that "Australians had chosen change, hope, and looked to the future, a better future for all" and then invited Albanese to the stage, who appeared with his partner, Jodie Haydon and son Nathan.

Albanese paused on stage for what seemed to be an eternity, fluctuating between the emotions of relief, tears of joy and the realisation that an elusive Labor victory had been achieved and he was now Australia's new prime minister, a scenario that seemed improbable two years early, at the start of the pandemic.

His speech was well considered, reiterated the key points of what a new Labor government hopes to achieve in office, and the poignant message of no one being left behind in the community.

> Anthony Albanese: I begin by acknowledging the traditional owners of the land on which we meet. I pay my respects to their elders past, present and emerging. And on behalf of the Australian Labor Party, I commit to the Uluru Statement from the heart in full. And I say to my fellow Australians, thank you for this extraordinary honour. Tonight, the Australian people have voted for change. I am humbled by this victory and I'm honoured to be given the opportunity to serve as the thirty-first prime minister of Australia. My Labor team will work every day to bring Australians together. And I will lead a government worthy of the people of Australia. A government as courageous and hardworking and caring as the Australian people are themselves.
> My fellow Australians, it says a lot about our great country that a son of a single mum who was a disability pensioner, who grew up in public housing down the road in Camperdown can stand before you tonight as Australia's prime minister.
> Every parent wants more for the next generation than they had. My mother dreamt of a better life for me. And I hope that my journey in life inspires Australians to reach for the stars. I want Australia to continue to be a country that no matter where you live, who you worship, who you love or what your last name is, that places no restrictions on your journey in life. And I hope there are families in public housing watching this tonight. Because I want every parent to be able to tell their child no matter where you live or where you come from, in Australia the doors of opportunity are open to us all.

And like every other Labor government, we'll just widen that door a bit more. Friends, we have made history tonight. And tomorrow, together, we begin the work of building a better future. A better future for all Australians.

It signaled a clear transition in Australian politics and, as to be expected in these situations, Albanese's speech had the enthusiasm of a winning leader; Morrison's had the damp feeling of a celebration gone wrong—words had to be delivered to commemorate not only his government, but the Coalition governments of the past nine years—but it was clear that wanted to get off the podium as soon as he could. Like his counterpart in the United States, Donald Trump, Morrison only wants to be seen as the winner who can never lose, but he was magnanimous and, unlike Trump, he didn't reject the outcome of the election result and discredit his opponent.

After the election, Morrison spent much of the day blaming everyone else for the loss, as though he was an external commentator providing analysis on an event that he was not a part of. It was a peculiar end to his time as prime minister, but the electorate is rarely sympathetic to the leader they have just voted out. Politics is brutal and it's also a field that must move on to the next phase as quickly as possible: it's the end of one part of Australia's political history and the sun still rose on the day after the election, despite the torrential rain that hit Sydney that evening. But this time around, it felt that it would take some time to repair the damage caused by nine years of an aimless and drifting Coalition government.

A CHANGE ELECTION

Every federal election night is covered by the mainstream media through free-to-air television, but their coverage on the night was almost as poor as their coverage and analysis of the six-week election campaign. Once it became evident that the Coalition was going to lose the election and had no chance of forming government, the coverage from all television channels was funereal, and suggested it was also a bad result for Labor—it's not often to see an election victory, especially a party's first win in nine years, painted as a loss and for all the negatives to come through, but that's exactly what occurred:

> Leigh Sales (ABC): Let me bring in Tanya Plibersek here... because when you look at the Coalition's result, that should be a landslide, basically, for Labor. But it's not, because there's so many others and Greens. So, I guess the question for you is, what has Labor done wrong, that it hasn't been a landslide for you?
> Tanya Plibersek: [bemused] I don't know that you can draw conclusions about what we've done wrong, when we are obviously the party that is most likely to be able to form government...
> Sales: ...but it's not decisive...
> Plibersek: ...and a win is a win is a win.
> Senator Simon Birmingham: ...on 31.7 per cent at present Tanya... less than a third of Australians have voted for you.
> Plibersek: ...particularly in this environment where around the world, people are worried about change. We've been through the pandemic, there's economic insecurity. I think I'm focused on what we've done right, because that's looking very good to me.

Other journalists on the night focused on an undeserving election win for Labor, a poorly run campaign with 'gaffes' and errors—Albanese's absence from the campaign due to COVID, even though he had no option but to isolate—the 'least-worst option', and offering a modest agenda to the electorate. This was the analysis provided on the ABC; other mainstream media outlets were far more scathing of the result, as though Darth Vader, Lex Luther, Voldemort and every other super villain was now going to occupy the government benches at parliament house in Canberra: for them, it was obviously the end of the world, and Australia was going to sucked into a vortex that could only be rescued by the Liberal–National Coalition at some point in the future.

> Rowan Dean (Sky News): We are faced with three years of hardcore left-wing government that will destroy the fabric of this nation. We will see our living standards crushed, our livelihoods damaged, our cultural institutions devastated, our kids' future prosperity decimated, because despite every warning we gave you, Scott Morrison and the bedwetters betrayed their conservative base, and then they all lost their seats. Talk about instant karma!
> But there is a silver lining to this cloud. Early 2025—Donald Trump will be sworn in as the next US president. And a few weeks later, Peter Dutton and the Liberals will be swept into power in Australia, following three disastrous and incompetent years of a teals-led Labor government, where parliament obsesses over woke identity politics, climate and Indigenous issues, as the economy grinds to a halt under their watch. It's going to be a long three years.

Obviously, Sky News—which is, essentially, the media wing of the Liberal Party—didn't take too kindly to the Labor victory.

And that was one of Rowan Dean's more measured and less hysterical performances. If Australia had a professional media that wanted to discuss election results in a more meaningful manner, the conversations would have focused on a fascinating and unusual election result, the remapping of Australia's political landscape, and how the election result offers some exciting possibilities for politics over the next five-to-ten years. But all they could muster was to mope, as though their favourite football team had unluckily lost a grand final; complain about how undeserving Labor's victory was and show little enthusiasm for a new Labor prime minister. It was churlish, unprofessional and, to extend the sports analogy, it would be akin to watching a grand final of an elite competition—AFL, NRL, Super Rugby or Super Netball—but the post-game coverage focusses on the losing team, outlines how they can improve in the following season, shows disdain for the victorious team, and claims they were cheats and undeserving winners.

For many people engaged with politics, mainstream media provided an unsatisfactory presentation of both the election campaign and the election night: even when no more votes could be influenced and the result was clear, they couldn't stop campaigning for the Coalition and against the Labor Party. But ultimately, it made little difference: legacy media no longer has the influence it once had and the rise of social media has meant that many people—not all—are receiving their news and forming their political views through other avenues.

Of course, it's never as simple as suggesting that all mainstream media is mediocre—there are many notable exceptions and excellent examples of excellent political reporting and journalism; journalists such as Laura Tingle, Paul Bongiorno, Malcolm Farr, Katharine Murphy, Rick Morton, Amy Remeikis, to name a few—but most focus upon the 'gotcha' questions and even when Adam Bandt called out the media with his "Google it, mate!" comment, they failed to heed the lesson, continued to humiliate themselves with inane questioning and, in the end, they failed to deliver the material that should be expected from them in the public interest.

Of course, the behaviour of media has a more complex undercurrent running beneath it, with proprietors such as Rupert Murdoch and Kerry Stokes attempting to use their media assets to support their other substantial vested interests. Journalists shouldn't be cheerleaders for their political party of choice but there are too many in the media who seem to be incurious about politics: one of more amazing results in federal political history has been dismissed with disdain, just because their side of politics lost.

Post-election discussions could have focused on the possibilities that arise from having a sixteen-member crossbench in the House of Representatives; or what the appearance of the teal independents could mean for the body politic and what national affairs will look like into the future. Generally, they were more enthusiastic to focus on the negatives for the Labor Party, and despite the best efforts by the media, to prevent it from happening, Labor won the election.

The seat of Reid on the edge of the inner west of Sydney was regarded as a litmus test for the overall campaign, with the perception that it was a microcosm of Australia: the margin of the seat—held by Fiona Martin from the Liberal Party by 3.2 per cent prior to the election—along with the demographics, geography, location and diverse nature of the seat, suggested that the effort required to win Reid would be reflected in the overall election results: win Reid, win the election.

As it turned out, the Labor candidate, Sally Sitou, achieved an 8.4 per cent swing to her and easily won the seat through a strong, disciplined and persistent campaign. It's no coincidence that Sitou was present at Albanese's first public appearance at a Marrickville café the morning after the election victory. The mantra of 'win Reid, win the election' turned out to be correct.

The ABC usually employs several outside broadcast teams, and a camera crew was present at Sitou's election night function at the Canada Bay Club but, for some reason, there was no live cross for the ABC audience. While this might be considered a minor matter, the seat of Reid has been a critical litmus seat over the past three elections: Malcolm Turnbull launched the Liberal Party campaign in Burwood in 2016; Bill Shorten launched the Labor Party campaign there as well in 2019. There were appearances in Reid by many sitting members from all sides of politics during the prepoll period and on election day. It seemed unusual that the ABC supplied outside broadcasts from the locations of many losing candidates from the Liberal Party, but ignored one the most critical seats in the election campaign in which a Labor candidate won. Again, it highlighted their focus on the losing team, rather than the winners.

Senator Simon Birmingham pointed out many times during the evening that Labor's primary vote of 32.6 per cent was the lowest result since the 1934 federal election, when it recorded just 26.8 per cent of vote. This point then dovetailed into conversations about a lack of legitimacy for the Labor victory because less than a third of the electorate voted for the party, but it was an irrelevant argument. Australia's electorate system is based on two-party preferred voting intentions, and, unlike the British first-past-the-post system, it provides for a fairer electoral result. All parties have benefitted from this system since it was introduced in Australia in 1918.

Of course, this is a narrative to suit the losing Liberal Party which, instead of looking at its failures in terms of its policy and leadership, decided it was better to now attack a system which they had benefitted from in the past, and had been in place for 104 years.

News Corporation didn't handle the defeat of the Coalition very well either. The symbiotic relationship between News Corporation, the Institute of Public Affairs and the Liberal Party has been well documented in the past, but it's increasingly apparent that News Corporation is the media wing of the Liberal Party, the Liberal Party is the political wing of News Corporation, and the Institute of Public Affairs is the glue that binds these players together.

Albanese had barely been sworn in as prime minister and only just started warming the seat when News Corporation published an article suggesting Albanese wouldn't be the prime minister at the next election, berating the public for making the wrong decision on election night, and outlining all the difficulties Labor will have at the 2025 federal election. This might be a fair question, considering Kevin Rudd was ousted before the end of his first term—as was Tony Abbott in 2015—but in the world of News Corporation, a grace period of a few days for a new Labor prime minister can never be granted.

Just like rust, the cancerous influence of News Corporation on the Australian political landscape never sleeps and is always there: Murdoch's political party of choice is no longer in office but the battleground for future election campaigns needs to be prepared from day one. Old habits are hard to break, but at least the influence of mainstream media in being able to sway elections has diminished, and that can only be a benefit for democracy and the public interest in Australia.

***

THE AFTERMATH

Albanese was officially sworn in as Australia's thirty-first prime minister—and Labor's thirteenth—on the Monday after the election, 23 May 2022. It was an interim five-person cabinet—four senior Labor frontbenchers and the prime minister—so Albanese could attend the with the Quadrilateral Security Dialogue meeting on 24 May, with US president Joe Biden, the prime minister of India, Narendra Modi and prime minister of Japan, Fumio Kishida.

Albanese was well received by the group—almost as though there was an arrival of a new-born baby on the scene—and the occasion enabled him to promote Australia's agenda on the international stage. For all the commentary that 'nobody knows who Anthony Albanese is': there'll be more information to be revealed about Albanese over the next three years at least, so the media might just have to get used to it.

Labor is now the national government and whatever issues the party may have with factional issues, internal structures, or policy divisions—and these will always exist in all political parties—election victories will always gloss over these: there are more important matters of state that need be dealt with, and while these issues are usually bubbling under the surface, the period immediately after an election victory is usually the time that they recede to a lower depth, appearing occasionally, before descending back into the deep.

Election losers have a different set of problems, especially after they've had a long sting in government and punished by the electorate with a crushing election defeat. Peter Dutton was appointed as the leader of Liberal Party—unopposed—and, therefore, became the leader of the opposition. While it's becoming apparent the Liberal Party might not have learned the lessons from this election defeat, there was no real option: the only realistic contender for the leadership—Josh Frydenberg—had lost the seat of Kooyong—and other credible leaders such as Simon Birmingham, reside in the Senate. A move to Dutton seemed to be a continuation of the Abbott years of government, which were, in turn, a continuation of the Howard years. At a time when the Liberal Party needed to make a clean break from the past, they decided to make a break from the future instead.

Progressive people around Australia suggested that this was a good outcome for them, because they considered Dutton to be an unelectable leader. But it's never as simple as that: the leader installed immediately after a crushing election loss is rarely the leader at the following election. But their primary purpose is to rebuild the party, instill confidence in the party and seek to develop the policies that can help them win elections in the future. The Liberal Party tends to avoid these processes, basing their return to government on negative political tactics, not offering much alternative, and pouncing on any flaws or mistakes committed by the government. Abbott was an expert of these spoiler tactics as leader of the opposition during 2009–13, managed to return the Liberal–National Coalition to office in 2013 with his highly negative campaigning style, but didn't know what to do in office once he got there, except for implementing his ideological obsessions of cost cutting and continue with the ongoing culture wars.

Dutton might not be the leader the Liberal Party needs now, but they have no one else. Abbott has provided a template for a return to government through a maniacal 'destroy everything' strategy, but destroying everything leaves nothing behind, even if the Liberal Party does return to government, as was the case with Abbott: oppose everything, even the things that the Liberal Party supports. It's a nihilistic form of politics and, ultimately, provides favours for no one, not even the Liberal Party.

While it might be easy to dismiss Dutton as a potential prime minister, politicians can change. One other consideration for Dutton is that since 1931, every newly elected government has secured at least two terms: that's not to suggest that this will occur with this Labor government, but Dutton—or whoever becomes the subsequent leader—would be looking at a likely stint of at least six years in opposition. There's also the sixteen-member crossbench that has created a large buffer that will make it extremely difficult for the Coalition for return to office at the 2025 election.

Since the pandemic commenced in early 2020, political trends across many elections around the world—not all—have swung towards centre-left governments, yet the Liberal Party has chosen a prominent member of its National Right faction. Dutton is the hard man of Australia politics—or, at least, that's an image that he cultivated during his time as minister for immigration, home affairs, and defence—and now he is trying to soften his public image. Politics is all about offering a points of difference to political opponents, but the difference Dutton is trying to present to the electorate might not be the difference they will be seeking in future elections.

On election night, Albanese stood on the stage at the Canterbury–Hurlstone RSL Club in front of the Aboriginal, Torres Strait Islander, and Australian flags, which he also did at his first media conference. It was a long-overdue step, and a simple step, for a prime minister to take. Would Dutton ever take on this approach? The Murugappan family—a Sri Lankan couple who arrived in Australia as boat arrivals during 2012 and 2014, whose children were subsequently born in Australia—had been in various forms of immigration and community detention since that time and were due to be removed from Australia by Border Force in 2018, before legal action stopped the deportations. One of Albanese's first acts as prime minister, was to release this family into the community, provide them with bridging visas, and subsequently, permanent visas. This was an act that Dutton could have performed at any time while he was minister for home affairs but chose not to.

Albanese also committed to the Uluru Statement and promised to work towards a referendum for the Voice to Parliament. The flavour of government has changed and the electorate seems sympathetic to this change; after all, they'd just turned their backs on the years of division presented from Coalition governments. The electorate wants to see the end of division in politics but Dutton, like two of his predecessors, Abbott and Morrison, thrives on division. How can Dutton reconcile this propensity to seek division for political benefit, at a time when the electorate expects a different approach to politics?

It's only the first week of the new government, but everything feels different: in the aftermath of an election, everything slows down after the intense work from all sides of politics during a campaign—everyone needs to rest and regroup. But the aftermath of a 'change election' is different in other ways. In the same way Rudd's national apology to the stolen generations in 2008—after years and obstinance from former Prime Minister, John Howard—was a relatively simple statement to make, Albanese is implementing acts that are simple and don't require too much effort.

Displaying the Aboriginal and Torres Strait Islander flags—both are recognised as national flags—at the new prime minister's media conferences, was a simple act but important symbolic act.

Releasing the Murugappan family was also a simple act and reflected the values of the Australian community. Dutton could have chosen to do one or both of those acts but chose not to. It's a significant indication of who he is as a person and as a political leader.

These are small but significant acts and it's clear Albanese wants to set up clear signposts for the kind of Labor government he wants to lead. But there are other challenges Labor will need to the address and, as is always the case, the economy is going to be one of the major issues that will need to be managed effectively over the next three-to-five years. The new treasurer, Jim Chalmers, has already signaled the difficult circumstances that will need to be addressed:

> Jim Chalmers: The challenges in the economy are pretty clear— we've got high and rising inflation and, therefore, rising interest rates. We've got real wages falling backwards, quite substantially. And we've got a trillion dollars of debt in the budget, which will take generations to pay off but is not currently going to deliver a generational dividend... the challenges that I'm inheriting from my predecessor [are] pretty serious challenges.
> We want to be upfront about that: we've already begun the work of trying to address particularly those three challenges that I mentioned.

Chalmers does have to play the politics of economic management quite forcefully: every incoming government announces that the national finances are far more severe than anticipated, and Chalmers is no different to the preceding treasurers in an incoming government. Managing expectations— and preparing for the worst outcomes but then expecting the best—are the primary issues that the Labor government will need to focus on over the next three years.

Labor tends to arrive in office during times of great economic uncertainty: perhaps it's bad luck, perhaps it's an expectation from the electorate that Labor tends to repair the economy to benefit more people more broadly, and this is one of those times. In 1929, the Scullin government won office at the advent of the Great Depression.

John Curtin inherited a wartime economy in 1943 but learned the lessons of failure between 1929–31, and applied the right levels of stimulus to the economy. Gough Whitlam arrives in 1972, just when the Australian economy is tired and is then hit by the world energy crisis and stock market crashes in 1973–74. Bob Hawke comes into office at a time of high inflation, high unemployment and a recession. Rudd then had to deal with the global financial crisis in 2008, which he manages successfully in Australia and avoids an economic recession. Chalmers comes into office when all these factors arrive at the same time: high inflation, increasing interest rates, an economy still recovering from a pandemic, a massive national government debt, increasing energy prices.

A political party can never choose the most favourable time to enter office. Electoral laws dictate that elections are held every three years and if a party performs well enough as an opposition and goes on to form government, they must deal with issues that confront them, irrespective of who created those issues.

While Labor is facing difficult economic circumstances, they are now the government: this is far better than languishing on the opposition benches, as they have for the past nine years, and for twenty of the past twenty-six years since 1996. Labor arrives into government with a good team: many of their Cabinet were ministers during the Rudd and Gillard governments between 2007–13. Many of the team have been in parliament for some time: Albanese is the most experienced, having first entered parliament in 1996. Although coming from a smaller jurisdiction, minister for finance, Senator Katy Gallagher, was previously the chief minister of the Australian Capital Territory.

No government is perfect but there is an expectation from the electorate that governments need to be less imperfect and act in the public interest. This was sadly lacking for most of the time of the Coalition government, especially during the time of the Morrison era. Whitlam's slogan for the 1972 campaign was 'It's Time', still the most memorable in Australian political history. Fifty years on, Labor toyed with 'Build Back Better'—borrowed from Joe Biden's United States presidential campaign in 2020—and 'Building Back Stronger', before choosing 'A Better Future' as its final election slogan.

It's not as memorable as Whitlam's 'It's Time' but, as in 1972, Australia arrives at crossroads in 2022. Despite the negative narrative from the media, Labor had a well-earned and well-deserved election victory. Despite the noise and static emanating from News Corporation on the sidelines, the electorate 'got it right' on election night, as they always do: that's the essence of democracy. And despite the narrative from the media, the 2022 federal election was exciting, interesting, and offered all sorts of possibilities for the future, including a more diverse government, and a larger crossbench which involved a broader range of political players: this is also the essence of a democracy and produces better political outcomes.

Australia can never afford to have a prime minister such as Morrison ever again, or the calibre of his government, which wasted its time in office and, even to itself, seemed to be unsure about what its purpose was. Albanese seems to have no doubts about the role of government, especially for a Labor government, and especially after the meandering nine years of the Coalition. 'Change elections' offer an opportunity for renewal, reflection, and a chance to reset the direction of the nation. Former prime minister, Paul Keating, said that "when you change the government, you change the country" before losing the 1996 federal election to John Howard, who proceeded to transform the country in a radically different way: more inward-looking, more hostile to outsiders, more conservative and more individually focused communities.

While it can never happen overnight, Albanese has an opportunity to transform the country in a different way, one that is more inclusive, offers opportunities to a broader range of people, politics and institutions that are more reflective of the diverse nature of the Australian community, and work towards a fairer society with, in his words, "no one left behind".

There are difficult times ahead for Australia and the new Labor government is facing many challenges, especially of an economic nature. Despite these many challenges, the 2022 federal election was good election to win; they always are.

***

GOOGLE IT, MATE!

'Turnbull describes vaccine rollout as "worst failure of public administration in Australian history",' ABC, PM, 1 July 2021. https://www.abc.net.au/radio/programs/pm/turnbull-describes-vaccine-rollout-as-worst-failure/13427830

'An Onion headline: Australian leader eats raw onion whole,' *The Washington Post*, Adam Taylor, 13 March 2015. https://www.washingtonpost.com/news/worldviews/wp/2015/03/13/an-onion-headline-australian-leader-eats-raw-onion-whole

'Prime Minister promises millions to help bring koalas back from the brink', ABC News, Jessica Ross, 30 January 2022. https://www.youtube.com/watch?v=xXNJcmWtkIc

'Will a hung parliament lead to 'chaos'? What a Gillard v Morrison comparison reveals', Nick Evershed, *The Guardian*, 5 May 2022. https://www.theguardian.com/news/datablog/2022/may/05/will-a-hung-parliament-lead-to-chaos-what-a-gillard-v-morrison-comparison-reveals

'Damning Legislation', Ian Thorpe, ABC News, 9 February 2022. https://www.abc.net.au/news/2022-02-09/ian-thorpe-religious-discrimination-bill-no-friends/13747118

'The Federal Parliament and the Protection of Human Rights', George Williams, Parliament of Australia, 1999. https://www.aph.gov.au/About_Parliament/Parliamentary_Departments/Parliamentary_Library/pubs/rp/rp9899/99rp20

'Leaked text messages show Gladys Berejiklian did call Scott Morrison 'horrible person' after he denied it on 7.30', Samantha Maiden, News Corporation, 5 April 2022. https://www.news.com.au/national/federal-election/leaked-text-messages-show-gladys-berejiklian-did-call-scott-morrison-horrible-person-after-he-denied-it-on-730/news-story/874ec128d807a339714951be4d894a63

'Making change, making history, making noise: Brittany Higgins and Grace Tame at the National Press Club', Michelle Arrow, *The Conversation*, 9 February 2022. https://theconversation.com/making-change-making-history-making-noise-brittany-higgins-and-grace-tame-at-the-national-press-club-176252

'Gender dysphoria', Kids Health Information, The Royal Children's Hospital Melbourne, September 2020. https://www.rch.org.au/kidsinfo/fact_sheets/Gender_dysphoria

'You love them unconditionally: The story behind MP's moving speech on religious discrimination bill', Rachel Clun, *Sydney Morning Herald*, 10 February 2022. https://www.smh.com.au/politics/federal/you-love-them-unconditionally-the-story-behind-mp-s-moving-speech-on-religious-discrimination-bill-20220209-p59v39.html

'My nephew was beautiful and courageous. The love and acceptance of his family was not enough', Stephen Jones, *The Guardian*, 8 February 2022. https://www.theguardian.com/commentisfree/2022/feb/08/my-nephew-was-beautiful-and-courageous-the-love-and-acceptance-of-his-family-was-not-enough

'Be Like Gough: 75 Radical Ideas To Transform Australia', John Roskam, Chris Berg & James Paterson, Institute of Public Affairs, 5 August 2012. https://ipa.org.au/ipa-review-articles/be-like-gough-75-radical-ideas-to-transform-australia

'Grace Tame & Brittany Higgins address National Press Club', Madeline Hislop, *Women's Agenda*, 9 February 2022. https://womensagenda.com.au/latest/grace-tame-brittany-higgins-address-national-press-club/

'Jenny Morrison is drafted in as the PM's 'secret weapon' in election fightback as they give Karl Stefanovic a cosy home tour', Olivia Day, *Daily Mail Australia*, 10 February 2022. https://www.dailymail.co.uk/news/article-10493817/Scott-Morrison-enlists-secret-weapon-wife-Jenny-interview-Karl-Stefanovic.html

'Tony Abbott says he is 'the guy with the not bad-looking daughters',' Helen Davidson, *The Guardian*, 4 September 2013. https://www.theguardian.com/world/2013/sep/04/tony-abbott-daughters-not-bad-looking

'Today in TV History: Bill Clinton and His Sax Visit Arsenio', Danny Spiegel, *TV Insider*, 3 June 2015. https://www.tvinsider.com/2979/rerun-bill-clinton-on-arsenio-hall

'Scott Morrison shoe Photoshop fail gives Australian prime minister two left feet', Lisa Martin, *The Guardian*, 9 January 2019. https://www.theguardian.com/australia-news/2019/jan/09/scott-morrisons-shoe-photoshop-fail-gives-pm-two-left-feet

'Why did Scott Morrison get red-carpet treatment on airbase visit when previous prime ministers didn't?', Ellen McCutchan, ABC News, 26 May 2021. https://www.abc.net.au/news/2021-05-17/scott-morrison-red-carpet-raaf-williamtown-visit-fact-check/100139660

Boris Johnson resigned as Prime Minister on 7 July 2022, after a series of Conservative Party resignations and a loss of confidence in his leadership.

'Weak Australian leadership inhibits potential relationship reset with China', Bruce Haigh, *Global Times*, 14 February 2022. https://www.globaltimes.cn/page/202202/1252207.shtml

'Prime Minister accuses Kristina Keneally of wanting to protect violent abusers in extraordinary attack over deportation bill', Brett Worthington and Jake Evans, ABC News, 15 February 2022. https://www.abc.net.au/news/2022-02-15/scott-morrison-accuses-labor-protecting-criminals-deportation/100831402

'Scott Morrison welding video: Australia reacts', News.com.au, 20 February 2022. https://www.news.com.au/finance/work/at-work/prime-minister-scott-morrison-trashed-for-bizarre-welding-error/news-story/18f2fcb7e8a0d2e8f0b505fe99d0546a

'Australia to spend $70 million on ammunition, small missiles to help Ukraine fight against Russia', ABC News, 1 March 2022. https://www.abc.net.au/news/2022-03-01/scott-morrison-russia-ukraine-war-weapons-lethal-aid/100871304

'Liberals celebrate as carbon tax repeal passes lower house', Mark Kenny & Judith Ireland, *Sydney Morning Herald*, 26 June 2014. https://www.smh.com.au/politics/federal/liberals-celebrate-as-carbon-tax-repeal-passes-lower-house-20140626-3awd4.html

'Brisbane company paid $1.4bn to run offshore processing on Nauru despite no arrivals since 2014', Ben Dougherty, *Guardian Australia*, 10 April 2021. https://www.theguardian.com/australia-news/2021/apr/10/brisbane-company-paid-14bn-to-run-offshore-processing-on-nauru-despite-no-arrivals-since-2014

'Home Affairs rebuked over Paladin's $532m contract', Angus Grigg, Lisa Murray and Jonathan Shapiro, *Australian Financial Review*, 28 May 2020. https://www.afr.com/policy/foreign-affairs/home-affairs-rebuked-over-paladin-s-532m-contract-20200528-p54xds

'Bored by the campaign? The parties are prisoners of stereotype', Peter Hartcher, *Sydney Morning Herald*, 16 April 2022. https://www.smh.com.au/national/bored-by-the-campaign-the-parties-are-prisoners-of-stereotype-20220414-p5adib.html

'Peter Dutton says Australia should be prepared for war – but are we?', Daniel Hurst, *The Guardian*, 29 April 2022. https://www.theguardian.com/australia-news/2022/apr/29/peter-dutton-says-australia-should-be-prepared-for-war-but-are-we

'Campaign goes off script as Morrison accidentally tackles little Luca', James Massola, *Sydney Morning Herald*, 18 May 2022. https://www.smh.com.au/politics/federal/campaign-goes-off-script-as-morrison-accidentally-tackles-little-luca-20220518-p5ami4.html

'The election is a race – it's a horse race', Trevor Bell, *Rationale*, 20 April 2022. https://rationalemagazine.com/index.php/2022/04/20/the-election-is-a-race-its-a-horse-race/

'It's hard to know when to come out from under the doona. It'll be soon, but not yet', Becca Schultz, *The Conversation*, 11 May 2020. https://theconversation.com/its-hard-to-know-when-to-come-out-from-under-the-doona-itll-be-soon-but-not-yet-137879

INDEX OF PEOPLE

A

Abbott, Tony 12, 14, 22, 32, 39, 57, 86, 143, 199, 205, 221, 239, 264, 268, 271, 275, 284, 286, 287, 288
Abo, Sarah 237
Albanese, Anthony 2–3, 6, 8, 13–14, 24–25, 28, 31, 46, 48, 50, 54, 60–63, 69, 71–72, 74, 77–80, 82, 92, 99, 121–124, 156, 166, 169–170, 178, 181–185, 187–190, 192, 194, 200, 203–204, 206–214, 216, 222, 225–227, 229, 231, 235, 237–239, 241, 243–245, 249, 251–252, 254–258, 264, 267, 269, 274–278, 280, 282, 284–285, 287–292
Albanese, Nathan 276
Alexander, John 175
Aly, Anne 172
Andren, Peter 248
Andrews, Daniel 7, 46, 78, 141
Asher, Stephanie 219

B

Baillieu, Ted 116, 140
Bandt, Adam 13, 46, 182, 183, 205, 269, 281
Banks, Julia 161
Barnes, Jimmy 207, 208
Barr, Natalie 105, 106
Baudrillard, Jean 60
Beazley, Kim 34, 51
Berejiklian, Gladys 24, 30, 32, 41, 65, 139, 161
Biden, Joe 90, 211, 285, 291
Birmingham, Simon 12, 144, 212, 279, 283, 286
Bishop, Julia 62
Bjelke-Petersen, Joh 112
Bogle, Eric 220
Bongiorno, Paul 173, 193, 281
Bonner, Neville 261
Boyce, Colin 215
Burke, Tony 211, 212, 276
Bush, George H. 58, 74

Bush, George W. 87, 109
Butler, Mark 46

C

Canavan, Matt 215, 216
Carlson, Tucker 89, 90
Cash, Michaelia 12, 37, 190, 212
Cassidy, Barrie 193
Chalmers, Jim 206, 211, 232, 289, 290
Chaney, Kate 205, 240, 256
Charles, Steven 247
Charlton, Andrew 158, 159, 273
Chifley, Ben 11
Christensen, George 54, 232
Churchill, Winston 220
Clare, Jason 211, 212, 214
Clinton, Bill 57, 58
Colbeck, Richard 38, 265
Coombes, Sharn 46
Cormann, Mathias 149, 232
Costello, Peter 10, 60, 271
Crowe, David 237
Curtin, John 9, 11, 12, 205, 240, 256, 268, 272, 290
Cusack, Catherine 164, 176

D

Daniel, Zoe 133, 240, 254, 256
Dean, Rowan 280, 281
Derrida, Jacques 60
Deves, Katherine 201, 202, 216, 241
Dibb, Jihad 172
Downer, Alexander 12
Downer, Georgina 12
Drury, Ray 165
Dutton, Peter 3, 12, 61, 63, 70, 71, 72, 75, 96, 97, 104, 105, 111, 112, 113, 114, 126, 127, 128, 143, 144, 146, 149, 206, 211, 212, 216, 219, 220, 221, 231, 252, 253, 280, 286, 287, 288, 289

INDEX OF PEOPLE

E
Easton, Penny 144
Elliot, David 79
Entsch, Warren 46

F
Falinski, Jason 271
Farr, Malcolm 173, 281
Fauvette, Luca 255
Fierravanti-Wells, Concetta 159, 160, 161, 163, 169, 171
Fifield, Mitch 232
Fisher, Andrew 220
Fletcher, Paul 196, 260
Flint, Nicolle 138
Forrest, Andrew 198
France, Ali 113, 127
Fraser, Malcolm 60, 155, 195, 261
Frydenberg, Josh 12, 52, 62, 73, 110, 126, 127, 128, 144, 149, 151, 152, 153, 155, 161, 162, 164, 205, 206, 212, 232, 233, 234, 240, 241, 256, 271, 286

G
Gallagher, Katy 144, 184, 185, 291
Garrett, Peter 159
Gerrard, John 20
Gillard, Julia 11, 33, 34, 39, 60, 116, 204, 205, 271, 275, 290
Goldstein, Emmanuel 234
Goldwater, Barry 91
Green, Antony 7
Grimshaw, Tracey 251, 257
Guilfoyle, Margaret 261

H
Haines, Helen 9, 205, 268
Hall, Arsenio 58
Hammond, Celia 240
Hawke, Alex 132, 160, 231
Hawke, Bob 11, 14, 60, 64, 78, 117, 124, 184, 271, 290
Haydon, Jodie 276
Hewson, John 167, 209
Higgins, Brittany 41, 45, 46, 48, 161
Hockey, Joe 143, 199
Houston, Brian 11

Howard, John 11, 34, 38, 39, 61, 71, 75, 76, 79, 87, 93, 117, 118, 123, 124, 129, 143, 148, 167, 177, 184, 198, 209, 239, 248, 252, 260, 271, 286, 288, 292
Hughes, Billy 10
Hunt, Greg 96
Hurley, David 127
Husic, Ed 172

I
Ibrahim, Fauziah 217, 218

J
James, Tim 65
Jenkins, Kate 259
Johnson, Boris 59
Jones, Stephen 42
Joyce, Barnaby 45, 46, 94, 102, 105, 106, 157, 161, 212, 231, 249

K
Katter, Bob 205, 269
Keane, Bernard 193
Keating, Paul 11, 34, 60, 80, 81, 85, 118, 138, 155, 166, 167, 168, 184, 248, 271, 291
Keenan, Michael 161, 202
Keneally, Kristina 63, 144, 159, 175, 211, 273
Kennedy, John F. 209
Kerrin, John 184
Kishida, Fumio 285
Kissinger, Henry 91
Kitching, Kimberley 130, 131, 142, 143, 144, 163, 170
Klan, Anthony 173
Kline, Victor 272
Knight, Deborah 237
Koch, David 104, 106
Krishnan, Shuba 258, 259
Kubrick, Stanley 112

L
Latham, John 128
Latham, Mark 167, 209
Lawrence, Carmen 144
Le, Dai 273

Ley, Sussan 12, 35, 132, 175, 191, 212, 246
Lincoln, Abraham 233
Liu, Gladys 62, 232
Lyons, Enid 56
Lyons, Joe 10, 56

M
Mack, Ted 248
Madigan, Dee 276
Maiden, Samantha 144
Malinauskas, Peter 67, 137
Marles, Richard 46, 211
Marshall, Steven 61, 66, 67, 115, 116, 117, 139, 140
Martin, Fiona 175, 282
Mascarenhas, Zaneta 239
McDiven, Christine 174
McGowan, Cathy 12, 248
McGowan, Mark 46, 116, 117, 248, 270
McIntosh, Melissa 193
McKenzie, Bridget 97, 98, 99, 191, 231, 247
McLuhan, Marshall 61
McMahon, Billy 249
Menzies, Robert 14, 87, 128, 167, 233, 261
Miller, Rachelle 190, 191, 207
Minchin, Nick 143
Mirabella, Sophie 12
Modi, Narendra 285
Molan, Jim 160
Morrison, Jenny 55, 56, 59
Morrison, Scott 3, 6–8, 11–13, 17–31, 33–42, 44–50, 52–63, 65–81, 84–87, 92–93, 95–96, 98, 103, 108–116, 118–132, 134–136, 138–141, 143–149, 152, 155, 157–158, 160–179, 181–187, 189–192, 194, 197–202, 206, 208–212, 215–217, 219–223, 226–232, 234, 236–239, 241–246, 249–252, 255–259, 261, 263–267, 269–272, 274, 276, 278, 280, 288, 291
Morton, Rick 281
Murdoch, Rupert 60, 78, 89, 90, 91, 168, 200, 282, 284

Murphy, Katharine 173, 281
Murray, Paul 124
Murugappan family 287, 289

N
Napthine, Denis 116, 140
Newberry, James 179
Newman, Campbell 116
Nixon, Richard 91, 209

O
O'Dwyer, Kelly 96
O'Keefe, Chris 125
Öztürk, Serkan 173

P
Palaszczuk, Annastacia 97, 116, 117
Palmer, Clive 7
Payne, Marise 24
Peacock, Andrew 128, 143, 177
Perrottet, Dominic 17, 23, 32, 33, 96, 97, 131, 174
Plibersek, Tanya 144, 206, 211, 212, 279
Porter, Christian 231
Price, Melissa 212
Probyn, Andrew 193
Putin, Vladimir 87, 88, 89, 90, 91, 174
Pyne, Christopher 96, 179

R
Randall, Don 131
Reagan, Ronald 73, 128, 155
Reith, Peter 71, 79
Remeikis, Amy 173, 281
Rinehart, Gina 198
Robb, Andrew 62
Robert, Stuart 231
Ross, Jessica 35
Rowland, Michael 247
Rudd, Kevin 14, 33, 34, 39, 57, 60, 61, 116, 155, 158, 178, 204, 268, 271, 275, 276, 284, 288, 290
Ruston, Anne 196
Ryan, Monique 52, 112, 126, 128, 155, 233, 234, 240, 256

INDEX OF PEOPLE

S
Sales, Leigh 279
Scamps, Sophie 256
Scullin, James 10, 81, 268, 290
Seselja, Zed 222
Shanks-Markovina, Jordan 113, 173, 179
Sharkie, Rebekha 9, 12, 205, 269
Sharma, Dave 52, 162, 271
Shaw, Ryan 112
Sheridan, Greg 110, 111
Shorten, Bill 14, 31, 82, 123, 166, 167, 197, 206, 212, 228, 231, 283
Sinatra, Frank 72
Singh, Lisa 160
Sitou, Sally 282, 283
Spender, Allegra 51, 256
Stefanovic, Karl 55, 121, 124, 125
Steggall, Zali 9, 12, 32, 200, 205, 268
Stokes, Kerry 10, 60, 240, 282
Stone, Shane 102
Sukkar, Michael 133, 134, 135
Swan, Wayne 276

T
Tame, Grace 41, 46, 47
Taylor, Angus 231
Tehan, Dan 12
Thatcher, Margaret 71, 73, 78, 128, 155
Thorpe, Ian 40
Tingle, Laura 25, 26, 29, 173, 238, 257, 281
Tink, Kylea 256
Towke, Michael 161, 166, 171, 172
Trump, Donald 59, 89, 90, 91, 139, 242, 278, 280
Tudge, Alan 190, 191
Turnbull, Malcolm 20, 39, 73, 127, 142, 143, 149, 159, 264, 268, 271, 283

U
Uhlmann, Chris 237

V
van Onselen, Peter 24
Vanstone, Amanda 115
von Bismarck, Otto 142

W
Warne, Shane 131
Whitlam, Gough 14, 74, 155, 167, 168, 195, 248, 251, 272, 290, 291
Wilde, Oscar 148
Wilkie, Andrew 9, 205, 248, 268
Willesee, Mike 209
Wilson, Greg 131
Wilson, James 94
Wilson, Tim 62, 131, 133, 134, 135, 179, 240, 254, 271
Windsor, Tony 248
Wong, Penny 144, 211, 276
Wright, Adisen 186

Z
Zelenskyy, Volodymyr 86, 91
Zimmerman, Trent 132, 271

www.ingramcontent.com/pod-product-compliance
Lightning Source LLC
Chambersburg PA
CBHW050305010526
44107CB00055B/2115